William the Conqueror

ABOUT THE AUTHOR

Peter Rex was Head of History at Princethorpe College for twenty years. His other books include *1066: A New History of the Norman Conquest*, *The English Resistance: The Underground War Against the Normans*, *The Last English King: The Life of Harold II*, *Edgar: King of the English*, *King & Saint: The Life of Edward the Confessor*, and *Hereward: The Last Englishman*. He sadly passed away in 2012.

PRAISE FOR PETER REX

The English Resistance

'An invaluable rehabilitation of an ignored resistance movement' *THE SUNDAY TIMES*

Harold II

'Rex's powerful defense of Harold is refreshing' *THE DAILY MAIL*

'A learned new biography' *THE FINANCIAL TIMES*

Hereward

'Like oakum from a knotted rope of legend, Rex picks out the facts of his life' *THE TIMES*

'Rescues Hereward, a genuine folk hero, from the oblivion into which he has fallen' *FRANK MCLYNN*

William the Conqueror

The Bastard of Normandy

PETER REX

AMBERLEY

First published 2011
This edition published 2016

Amberley Publishing
The Hill, Stroud
Gloucestershire, GL5 4EP

www.amberley-books.com

British Library Cataloguing in Publication Data.
A catalogue record for this book is available from the British Library.

ISBN 978-1-4456-6017-2 (paperback)
ISBN 978-1-4456-1006-1 (ebook)

Typesetting and Origination by Amberley Publishing.
Printed in Great Britain.

CONTENTS

INTRODUCTION

Previous biographies of William of Normandy have been of two kinds. F. M. Stenton and Hilaire Belloc wrote quite short monographs outlining the main features of his career and reign and commenting on his character. In 1964 Professor David Douglas (to whose inspiring teaching I owe my own fascination with Anglo-Norman History) wrote his magisterial *William the Conqueror. The Norman Impact Upon England*. It is not simply a biography and contains a compelling analysis of the nature of William's achievements and of his reign as Duke and King. David Bates wrote his version, focusing on an attempt to make sense of William's career and on his formidable personality. The principal French biographies are those of Michel de Boüard, *Guillaume le Conquérant* (1966 and 1984) and Paul Zumthor (2003).

All these modern historians have been, hardly surprisingly, persuaded by the consistency of Norman claims to accept, to a greater or lesser extent, the main thrust of those claims and the Norman justification for the Conquest of England. More recently a more sceptical note has been sounded, especially about the legal basis of Duke William's claims.

Increasingly dissatisfied with the readiness with which some accept William's actions at face value, I have attempted to produce a portrait of the man and his achievements, which takes account of the effects on his character of his birth in bastardy and the manner in which he was deprived of close contact with his mother and deserted by his father. An attempt is made to allow for the realities of Norman politics and the extent to which recourse was made by some Norman writers, they can hardly be described as historians, to the invention of suitable stories and anecdotes in support of what are often quite incredible claims.

The sources are very incomplete and much that it would be useful to know has been lost or was never written down. The writing of the history of the eleventh century requires the historian to attempt to provide motives and explanations for events that are only sketchily described at best. This biography of William of Normandy is only one possible version based as far as possible on the latest research by a large number of scholars to whose work I am greatly indebted. The interpretations offered and the portrait of William that I hope emerges are my own responsibility, as are any errors. I am also greatly indebted to my son Richard for his valuable criticism of the first draft of this work.

Peter Rex
Ely. 2010

I

NORMANDY IN THE EARLY ELEVENTH CENTURY

William of Normandy, of Franco-Scandinavian descent through his father, Duke Robert I, 'the Magnificent', was born into the violent and turbulent society that was Normandy at the end of the third decade of the eleventh century.

The duchy occupied an area of Northern France, in Carolingian times once known as Neustria. As what has been cogently called 'an expression of history rather than of geography', Normandy had no natural frontiers. The province was almost identical with the Archdiocese of Rouen and its six dependent bishoprics of Bayeux, Avranches, Coutances, Évreux, Lisieux and Sées. Neustria had once been a province of the Roman Empire and under the Carolingians had been ruled by a count based at Rouen. The Dukes of Normandy, descendants of the Viking leader they called Rollo (that is, the Norseman Rolf the Ganger), derived the few legal powers they had from their status as Counts of Rouen, because the Frankish Kings had regarded Normandy as a march land ruled by a count.

When William became Duke after the death of his father Duke Robert on pilgrimage to Jerusalem, he found himself surrounded by members of the powerful comital families. All without exception were Richardides, descendants of Dukes Richard I and Richard II and so inextricably linked to the ducal house itself. Duke Richard I had created the first lord to be styled 'Count', Rodulf of Ivry, his half-brother. After that the male Richardides all had the right to the title of 'Count' while remaining subject to the authority of the reigning duke. At first it was only a title and not linked to a specific territory. Then Richard I's sons were given the Comtés of Évreux, Brionne and Eu, so defending a particular area of the border. After that each of the Richardides had to be given territory. The first of the next generation, William, son of Richard II, became Count of Arques, in the Pays de Talou.

Below that level came the vicomtes, ducal officers rather than deputies of the counts. They also were members of the nobility, though of lower rank, soon building up their power and wealth and seeking to intermarry with the comital families. Some of these men also became castellans, holding castles on behalf of the Duke. Such castellans who came to rule over the area surrounding the castle and all of its inhabitants, even those who were not actually their vassals, achieved economic, military and judicial rights within an area around the castle, which later came in England to be called a 'castlery'. They could collect a tax, the 'taille', (in practice, effectively protection money) and had control over mills, ovens and tolls on roads and bridges.

On the fringes of the aristocracy came the 'milites' or warriors. By the eleventh century these men, who fought for a lord, were mounted soldiers, cavalry, who in addition to fighting for a lord acted as his escorts during excursions and at councils. Many simply lived at the lord's expense in his household, but some were given landed estates, which came to be termed 'fiefs', though they rendered no specific dues or rents for their fiefs (which they held and had the use of but did not own). They were expected, as 'fideles' or faithful men, to give the lord their support and perform military service when the need arose. They swore an oath of fidelity or 'fealty' and were expected to do their lord no harm but to render him aid, physically and by good counsel. They were not yet members of the nobility (they really only became so during the twelfth and thirteenth centuries), but members of the nobility who undertook training as mounted warriors fought alongside them, so blurring the distinction between noble and non-noble milites. These milites became, in English usage, 'knights'.

In AD 911 Rollo and his Viking followers had acquired the land they ruled from the Frankish King, Charles the Simple. These Vikings, a mixture it seems of Danes and Norsemen, then became the lords of the territory, occupying positions of power and forming a new aristocracy, although they could only ever have been a minority of the population, which was predominantly Frankish. At the time of William's birth, the former Vikings had become thoroughly French in speech, manners, behaviour and religion.

William's father, Robert, second son of Duke Richard II and his wife Judith of Brittany[1], held the position of Count of the Hiémois, a district lying between the rivers Orne and Dives governed from the bourg and castle of Falaise. Shortly after the death of Duke Richard II, 23 August 1026, with Count Robert's elder brother, Richard III, as reigning Duke, Robert caught his first glimpse of William's mother, the daughter of a local tanner or embalmer of Falaise. Robert was immediately struck by her beauty and took her as his mistress. Of that union was born William the Bastard.

Within a year of his accession, Richard III died unexpectedly and Robert was able to make himself Duke. The brothers had never been on good terms and Robert was jealous of his brother, proving recalcitrant and unwilling to accept Richard's accession. He attracted around him a circle of unruly supporters. Although he had been made Count, he had been refused control of the castle of Falaise and the surrounding bourg. Robert openly rebelled against his brother and seized control of Falaise for himself, occupying the castle. At first, Duke Richard had accepted the situation, allowing an accommodation with Count Robert to be reached by which the Count was allowed to retain control of Falaise. But Robert remained troublesome; Richard lost his patience and, in the spring of 1027, appeared in arms before the walls of Falaise with the knights of his household.

Robert closed the castle against the Duke. Unable to take the castle by storm, since it stood on a rocky eminence above the River Ante, a tributary of the Dives, Richard decided on a siege. He first summoned the aid of William Talvas, Lord of Bellême, (to whom he had granted the castles of Alençon and Domfront) and set about besieging the castle, attacking it with mangonels and ballistae. But the keep withstood all assaults for several months until Count Robert was forced to surrender.

In August, on the 5th, Richard, who had shown no previous signs of ill health, after dining, perhaps too well, fell sick and died on either the 5th or the 6th. There were immediate suspicions of poisoning and the finger was pointed at Count Robert. But the conditions under which the Duke was conducting his siege, given the general lack of hygiene, would have become obscenely insanitary, and death from some virulent viral or bacterial infection is more than probable.

Count Robert naturally fell under suspicion, largely perhaps because he now moved swiftly to secure his installation as Duke, consigning Richard's illegitimate son Nicholas to the ducal abbey of Fécamp where he became a monk.[2] Robert no doubt had the support of powerful nobles who were tired of the disorder of Richard's reign and hoped for better things from Robert.

Duke Robert I was a young man, thought to be between the ages of seventeen and twenty, and still very impulsive.[3] He was extravagant in his habits, given to conspicuous expenditure, hence his name of 'the Magnificent'.[4]

He began his reign with a violent quarrel with his uncle, Archbishop Robert of Rouen, possibly because the Archbishop sought to restrain his impulsiveness. This cleric might well have thought himself entitled to some sort of regency. The Archbishop certainly challenged Robert's authority. Accordingly, the Duke besieged his uncle in his castle of Évreux, possibly justifying his assault by pointing out that the Archbishop was also Count of Évreux and that he was attacking him in that capacity.

Robert succeeded in driving out his uncle, who fled into exile at the French court. From there, on the advice of the canon lawyer Fulbert of Chartres, he placed Normandy under Interdict[5] and excommunicated the Duke. The chronicle of Hugh of Flavigny records the widespread fear and alarm this caused, which resulted in Normandy being 'debauched with anarchy' as the ducal power was weakened by the Interdict.

Much of the trouble was the work of the Richardides, a number of whom had deserted the Duke and gone over to Archbishop Robert. But if, as seems likely, the Richardides had hoped to seize power at the moment when Richard III died, then the struggle that followed had been much more intense than the Chroniclers admit. Hugh of Ivry, Bishop of Bayeux, for example, remembering how his father, Ralph of Ivry (half-brother of Duke Richard I), had held power during the minority of Richard II, might have hoped to play the same role for Robert.

So Hugh of Bayeux, who was simultaneously Bishop of Bayeux and Count of Ivry, fortified his castle and defied the Duke. Hugh appealed for and received an offer of reinforcements from the French royal lands just over the border, but unfortunately for the Bishop, they did not arrive in time. Duke Robert seized the castle and the Bishop fled into exile. William Talvas of Bellême, who held fiefs over which the Duke had no authority,[6] also defied Duke Robert from his castle of Domfront, where he too was besieged until he surrendered. He was then forced to attend the Duke, crawling on all fours and saddled like a horse, and required to do homage. In a show of magnanimity the Duke then returned the forfeited lands to Talvas, to be held on terms of abject vassalage, possibly even requiring military service.

The four sons of William Talvas were violent and troublesome. During the ongoing power struggle between the Duke and the Archbishop, the eldest, Guerin, murdered his own cousin during a 'friendly' visit, and William of Poitiers comments that Guerin was later seized and 'strangled by Satan'. The other three, Fulk, Robert and William, took up arms against Duke Robert, raiding the ducal demesne. They were easily crushed by local loyal forces. Fulk was killed in the forest of Blazon, Robert was injured in a secret attack, and only William escaped. He was reported to have fled back to his father, who, enraged, promptly died of apoplexy. The Duke was demonstrating his ability to put down rebellions. Later, when he campaigned in Flanders, Duke Robert acted with such ferocity that he earned a reputation for cruelty, which resulted in his being confused in men's minds with a purely fictional character, 'Robert the Devil'.

Robert punished the Church for the Archbishop's opposition to his rule by seizing some of its property. He took over possession of the lands of a number of abbeys, notably Fécamp, Argences, Heudbouville and Maromne. He licensed Roger I of Montgomery to destroy the market at Vimoutiers belonging to the abbey of Jumièges. He also seized the lands of the bishoprics of Rouen and Bayeux. By such actions, Duke Robert gradually sought to re-establish ducal authority, though the very brevity of his reign prevented his 'successes' from bringing a permanent renewal of his power.

During all this, Count Alan III of Brittany, seeking to profit from the disorder in Normandy, chose to refuse to perform the homage to Duke Robert that he owed to the Dukes of Normandy, who had been his guardians during his minority. Count Alan occupied debatable lands on the border with the duchy. The Duke promptly drove out the Bretons, occupied the castles of Charnes and Pontorson, giving custody of them to Nigel of Saint-Sauveur, Vicomte of the Cotentin, and a certain Avrais le Géant. This was also the occasion when he reinforced his attack on Brittany by means of a naval attack near Mont-Saint-Michel made by a fleet dispatched from near Fécamp.[7]

The conflict between the Duke and Archbishop Robert soon reached a stalemate, and the two men, possibly at the urging of magnates on both sides, were brought to realise that a compromise had to be reached if disorder were to be ended. The Archbishop was recalled to Normandy and restored to office, receiving back his property, and in return promised loyalty to the Duke thereafter. Charters list the possessions that were restored. Robert seems to have become convinced of the need to be reconciled with the Church, perhaps influenced by the example of other great lords who were making significant gifts to the Church and restoring monasteries as a penance for their sinful behaviour. Finally, Count Alan of Brittany was required to become Robert's vassal, so strengthening Normandy's dominance over Brittany.

It was to appear later that the Duke had in fact 'got religion'. He had, after all, been excommunicated, a very serious matter in the eleventh century, and Duke Robert would have been influenced by the religious impulses of the age. The Vicomte of Arques, Gisselin, for example, had founded La Trinité-du-Mont in 1030; the Duke had confirmed his gifts to the Church and exempted the monastery from various ducal obligations. He himself made grants to, among others, Fécamp, Saint Ouen in Rouen, Saint Wandrille, Jumièges and Mont-Saint-Michel. These actions cast some light on the Duke's decision in 1035 to leave his duchy and go on pilgrimage to Jerusalem. Some argue that this decision might also explain why he never married, but this is unconvincing. The more usual motive for a pilgrimage was to fulfil the conditions of an imposed penance. It is possible that this was imposed upon him as a condition for the lifting of his excommunication, and that he now felt secure enough to leave his duchy in the capable hands of Archbishop Robert.

In the early 1030s Robert had, seemingly, also turned his attention to England, because Normandy was host to the exiled Aethelings, Edward and Alfred. There was reason for such interest since they were half-Norman, sons of King Æthelred and Emma, daughter of Richard I. Although Richard II had allowed the exiles to remain at his court, he had done nothing more for them, and they lived in obscurity during his reign. Robert, however, possibly at the time when he took control of the Vexin, had arranged a marriage for their sister, Goda, to Drogo, Count of the Vexin, after he had accepted the change of lordship. They were to have three children, Walter (who was to become, briefly, Count of Maine), Ralph, known as the Timid, Earl of Hereford, and Fulk, later Bishop of Amiens. Drogo and Robert had also become firm friends.

Norman writers make much of Duke Robert's alleged affection and support for the Aethelings, based mainly on their presence in his entourage. They are found in his company at Fécamp, witnessing his charters. The Norman sources talk enthusiastically of Robert's negotiations with Cnut the Great on their behalf (which came to nothing) and his alleged plan to invade England in order to restore them to power.

William Calculus or Cailloux, a monk of Jumièges, in his work *The Deeds of the Norman Dukes*,[8] says that Robert assembled a vast fleet at Fécamp, which set off into the Channel but unfortunately encountered a storm which blew it off course.[9] The fleet ended up at Jersey, so Robert changed his mind and used it to support his invasion of Brittany, which was going on at the same time.

There is no mention in any other source of any intention to invade England. The explanation for the change of mind is provided by William of Jumièges, who concluded that the invasion failed because God had decided that the Aetheling Edward should be restored to his kingdom peacefully rather than by force of arms. A more realistic explanation is that Robert had intended all along to invade Brittany by sea and had allowed men to think he intended an attack on England in order to conceal his intentions from the Bretons.

That the fleet had been intended to go to England and only arrived in Jersey because of the storm looks highly improbable. Fécamp is in Upper Normandy, on the coast about 5 or 6 miles from Cap d'Antifer, 75 miles by sea from the Cherbourg Peninsula; the Channel Islands are right round on the western side of the peninsula, nicely positioned for an attack on Mont-Saint-Michel, at its base. That the Duke really had intended to attack Brittany all along looks more likely. That there was ever any intention on Robert's part to invade the England of Cnut the Great is absurd.

But William of Jumièges seized upon this to demonstrate how the Duke had shown favour to Edward, so providing a motive for Edward's alleged gratitude for the support he had been given in Normandy. That was in turn then used to explain why Edward had chosen William of Normandy to be his successor.

The source explains that Duke Robert, after his fleet reached Jersey, ordered that part of it which had survived the storm, under the command of a man called Rabel, to go to Brittany and lay it waste by sword and fire. That attack had its effect. It forced Count Alan III to negotiate peace. It says that when Alan told him of the terrible destruction in Brittany and of the ruthlessness of the Duke's campaign, Archbishop Robert agreed to negotiate between them.[10] He arranged a meeting between the two princes with the assistance of the abbot of Mont-Saint-Michel at which he implored the Duke to be merciful and so 'with Christ's help, softened the bitterness of their hearts so that the dissension was resolved ... and he could unite them in peaceful harmony'. It was agreed that the River Couesnon was to be the frontier between the two states, and according to Norman sources, Count Alan renewed his homage. Duke Robert then created the County of Mortain and gave it to his cousin William Warlenc, another Richardide. Archbishop Robert had now established himself as a powerful force in the affairs of the duchy with increasing influence in domestic affairs.

Duke Robert was now a force to be reckoned with and perhaps had sufficiently intimidated his immediate neighbours to be satisfied that Normandy would not be attacked in the near future. The mystery of his real intentions towards England remained unresolved. Now he threw everything into disarray by announcing his intention to go on pilgrimage to Jerusalem. The reasons for his decision remain obscure.

On one level, one can argue that this was typical of the religious impulses that frequently governed men's actions in the eleventh century. Certainly he made it plain that he was going to Jerusalem for the benefit of his immortal soul. He was not content, as English earls were, just to go to Rome. Others had gone to Jerusalem at the end of the tenth century and the beginning of the eleventh. There was a spirit of ecclesiastical reform brewing in the Church, which caused many princes and nobles to found and endow monasteries, retire to them themselves or to go on pilgrimage.

But there is another, more prosaic, explanation. Duke Robert had found it impossible to prevent men from leaving Normandy to seek their fortunes elsewhere, in Spain, in Italy or in Sicily. The Duke was obliged to consent to this, suggesting that he had no means of insisting on their remaining in Normandy. Had they been obliged to perform regular military service, he could have insisted on them remaining to fulfil their obligations. The continuous private warfare that was ongoing also suggests that military service could not be regularly exacted.

Some argue that Duke Robert had begun to recognise his fundamental lack of power and that Archbishop Robert and his supporters were becoming increasingly influential. Certainly it is true that after the Duke's death became known, the Archbishop was to assume a de facto position as regent to the young prince William, though he is never accorded the title. It had been the Archbishop's influence that enabled the Duke to obtain the consent of the magnates to his departure and to the nomination of his son William as the heir and successor. The Archbishop also made sure of the acceptance of William's succession after his father died. But the religious motive looks much more credible if it is accepted that Duke Robert was acting from a position of strength and felt secure enough to leave the duchy, expecting his own safe return.

Duke Robert, having made what arrangements he could for the continuation of the government of Normandy during his absence, and accompanied by his friend Count Drogo of the Vexin, set off on his journey. They travelled by way of Rome, then through Greece to Byzantium, where Duke Robert made a great impression on the Emperor, Michael IV, the Paphlagonian, by his conspicuous display of wealth, and then they reached their destination. On the way Duke Robert's health had begun to fail, and he resorted to being carried on a litter, as he could no longer ride. Meeting a returning Norman, who inquired as to his state of health and asked what news of him he should take home, Robert told him, 'Tell them you saw me being carried to Paradise by devils', a reference to the tribesmen recruited to carry him. Reaching Nicaea on the return journey, his illness brought about his death, 3 July 1035. News of the death reached Normandy when a faithful supporter, Toustain, returned home. Count Drogo also died on that journey. William was now Duke of Normandy.

2

BIRTH & UPBRINGING OF THE BASTARD

At some time before he became Duke, probably during 1026 when he took up residence at Falaise in defiance of his brother Richard, Count Robert, Count of the Hiémois, looked out from a window in the keep at Falaise. The keep stood on the site of the present castle ruins on a rocky height over the River Ante, a tributary of the Dives.[1]

He looked down, so it was said, into the valley of the River Ante and saw a young woman of the town wading in the river in order to wash her clothes, and was struck by her beauty. Another version of the tale says she was with a group of young women and they were performing a country dance. Most likely both versions could be true and Robert had observed her more than once.[2]

William of Malmesbury accepted the dancing story version and says that Robert 'could not refrain from sleeping with her' and embroiders this by asserting that 'he kept her for some time in the position of a lawful wife' and 'hence forward loved her above all others'.[3]

Robert ordered that the young woman be brought to him, as he wished to spend the night with her. The storytellers embroider the tale, alleging that at the moment of giving herself to the young Count, the girl tore her chemise from top to bottom and discarded it. The astonished Count asked why she had done so and she replied that it was not fitting for the hem of her garment, which had touched her feet, to be turned towards his face.[4]

It is likely that her parents were persuaded to accept the situation. But there is no immediately contemporary record of the object of Robert's infatuation being called 'frilla' (that is, a concubine 'married' in the Danish manner rather than Christian matrimony)[5] and she is not even named. William of Malmesbury distinctly refers to her as a concubine.[6] She is first named in a charter of 1082 with more details about her emerging in the twelfth century.[7] In Latin she was called Herleva and, more simply, she was known as 'Arlette' (a familiar diminutive). Wace, in the *Roman de Rou*, spells her name, rather unfortunately perhaps, as 'Arlot', one of several other curious variations on it.

Despite later assertions that Robert fell passionately in love with Herleva, the affair was in reality only a passing one. Once she had given birth to a son, William, and he had survived the perils of infancy, she was quickly married off to a suitable nobleman, and until after Duke Robert's death she remained firmly in the background.

The tales that survive about William's early years relate only to omens of his future greatness. William spent his earliest years with his mother, possibly even in her family home in the suburb of Falaise called Guibray. But as soon as it was safe to do so, the child was removed from Herleva's care and taken to the castle of Falaise where he was recognised as Robert's son.

Furthermore, there is evidence that Duke Robert had a daughter later by a different, unnamed, concubine. William certainly had a half-sister, called Adelaide, who could well have been the offspring of another concubine, as attributed to Duke Robert by Robert of Torigny.[8] The idea that Herleva was Robert's great love is the result of the statements recorded in later authors such as Orderic Vitalis and William of Malmesbury and appears to have little factual basis.

Orderic Vitalis says that her father was called 'Foubert' (usually taken to be 'Fulbert'), a commoner of Falaise, an artisan engaged in the leather trade. He is variously described as a 'polinctor', 'parmentier' or 'pautonier', all of which can mean 'tanner' but also, a less likely idea, 'embalmer'. He was certainly regarded as of low class and socially almost an outcast. The trade of tanner was despised not least because of the offensive odours involved in the tanning process, which made plentiful use of human or animal urine. Tanners also often ran a side line as brewers and were suspected of giving 'body' and strength to their brew by adding animal matter to it. So they were often unpopular, regarded with jealousy and ostracised.[9]

Herleva's parents would doubtless have preferred that she marry within her own class rather than become a concubine, but she was probably flattered to be chosen by the Count. Later the family profited from the connection. Fulbert became a Ducal Chamberlain (*cubicularius*) and Herleva's brothers, Walter and Osbern, had places at Court as 'Uncles of the Duke'. The elder, Walter, was one of those who kept watch over the young Duke during his minority. Walter married well and had children, Clara, who became a nun, and Matilda, who married Ralph Tesson, Lord of Thury. But these appointments at court came only after William became Duke; there is no sign of them in Duke Robert's entourage. They benefited from William's affection for his mother. In bringing them to Court, William was providing himself with the family, a grandfather and uncles, he had previously lacked. He later brought to Court his half-brothers, Odo and Robert, sons of Herleva by Herluin de Conteville.

In 1027, Richard III had died unexpectedly and Robert had become Duke. William was born towards the end of 1028. No record exists of his day of birth. Infancy in the eleventh century was a perilous time and many babies died before they were two years old, so their existence was barely noticed until it was clear that they would survive. Even allowing for that, the sources still remain vague about William's exact age.

His father's liaison with Herleva obviously caused something of a scandal, though stories about the affair were not written down until the twelfth century. The birth of a bastard became a convenient excuse for criticising the new Duke Robert, who had many enemies among the Richardides. (Orderic Vitalis later recorded how, during the revolt of William of Arques, 'all the men of Talou abandoned the Duke [William] because he was a bastard'.)[10]

In this period of the eleventh century, with a movement for reform brewing throughout the Church, clergy were becoming more insistent on expecting men to reject concubinage and to marry with the approval and blessing of the Church in the sacrament of Matrimony. It is probable that the liaison with Herleva was one cause of friction between Robert and his uncle, the Archbishop of Rouen.

The sources first speak of William's age in discussing the decision of his father to desert his duchy to go on pilgrimage and his nomination of William as his successor. Orderic Vitalis and William of Malmesbury both claim that the boy was at least seven years of age in the year his father died. That death was on 2 or 3 July 1035. Orderic actually says 'puer utpote octo annorum', in his eighth year. This can mean that he was seven years old and in his eighth year or that he had reached the age of eight. Malmesbury says the Duke 'had at that time a seven-year-old son, the child of a concubine'.[11]

Orderic, however, adds to the confusion by claiming that William was aged sixty-four when he died in September 1087, which is impossible; it would require his birth to have been in 1023! The best clue is in the anonymous document, *De Obitu Willelmi*, which states that when he died (9 September 1087) he was in his fifty-ninth year. Taken at face value that puts his birth as between September 1028 and September 1029. Allowing for the evidence of Orderic, a birth in the autumn or winter of 1028 becomes likely, so William of Malmesbury would be right to say that he was seven when his father died. But there can be no certainty.

Of William's early years little is known beyond the usual myths which surround accounts of the birth of famous men. Such myths predict marvels but are of course based on hindsight. Thus, Herleva is said to have had a dream in which she saw a tree spring from her body and mount up to heaven. It became so vast that it overshadowed the whole of Normandy. The twelfth-century writer, Benoît of Sainte-Maure, embellished this by claiming that it overshadowed England as well!

Another tale records that the midwife placed the new born child on a straw mattress while she turned to do something else. The child, it was said, immediately grasped the mattress with both hands and pulled it over himself. The midwife, returning, saw this and exclaimed, 'Ah! My Lord, what a man you will be! How you will conquer and seize possessions for you have learned so early, and of your own accord, how to fill your hands and arms!' William of Malmesbury's version has the child grasp the rushes on the floor.

A story of particular interest, though this too may well have been 'improved' in the telling, concerns dreaded William Talvas of Bellême (a powerful baron from the border between Normandy and Anjou renowned for his cruelty).[12] He is said to have been passing through Falaise one day when a malicious bystander persuaded him that he ought to see the Duke's baby son. 'My lord,' he cried, 'enter this house here and see the son of your Seigneur; such a visit would be well regarded and give proof of your loyalty!'

Talvas entered the house and the child was brought to him. Wace says, 'I do not know whether the infant laughed or cried, but when Talvas came close and looked at him, he cried out thrice, "Shame on you! For through you and your family mine will be gravely abased and through you and your line my heirs will be gravely injured."' Talvas possibly did see the child in this manner and no doubt made some cutting remark which has been embellished by hindsight.

Sources such as William of Jumièges conclude, as one would expect, that William grew and developed well, as they say that he flourished under the protection of God, who loved him and brought him good fortune. Another example of the benefits of hindsight! They add that his father, Robert, never loved him the less because he was not born in lawful wedlock. Once the dangerous period of infancy was past, William was taken to his father and continued to receive his education at Falaise. It is likely that this included stories about his father's exploits, from which William learned something of the arts of politics and diplomacy and the use of military force to obtain one's ends.

William of Jumièges says that he was taught good conduct, discipline, respect (for superiors), Church practices and even perhaps some serious study, though his reading and writing remained rudimentary at best.

But at some time between 1030 and 1035 (the sources are contradictory), Herleva ceased to be Robert's concubine and was married off to a minor noble, Herluin de Conteville. She had three legitimate children by him, Odo, Robert and Muriel. Orderic Vitalis thought she married after Robert's death but that might only be his own opinion. Her marriage is unlikely to have been delayed because her eldest son, Odo, was made Bishop of Bayeux in succession to Bishop Hugh, probably in 1049 or a little later when he would have been about eighteen years of age and able to conduct the secular affairs of his bishopric. Had Odo been extremely young, his critics would not have missed the chance to point it out, so a birth much later than 1031 is unlikely.

William of Malmesbury contradicts Orderic, asserting that Herleva married Herluin before Robert's death. If Odo was eighteen in about 1049, then his mother could well have been married as early as 1030, possibly even as part of the settlement between the Duke and Archbishop Robert. The latter probably insisted that Duke Robert put away his concubine as a condition of their agreement.

William's removal from the care of his mother when he was still only a very young child, two or three years old, has to have had an effect on his character. To that must be added another psychologically damaging loss. In 1035 his father, too, of whom he saw little enough anyway because he was frequently away on campaign, deserted him, leaving him, aged seven, in the hands of various relatives. William was, in a real sense, the product of a dysfunctional family. His father was not lawfully married to his mother so many regarded him as a bastard, and by the age of seven he had lost both parents.

As against that, of course, he retained contact with his grandfather and his maternal uncles after he became Duke. But the death of his father, followed quite soon afterwards by the bloody events of his minority, must suggest that he was a deeply maladjusted personality, able to adopt a stern and ruthless persona that enabled him to dominate his contemporaries.

In support of this, one can adduce his imprisonment of his half-brother Odo in 1082 and his frequent and damaging quarrels with his eldest son Robert Curthose, resulting in the latter's consequent absence from his father's deathbed. William had been adamant that he could not surrender control over Normandy to Robert, despite repeatedly saying he would do so when the time was ripe. It never was. William perhaps saw retention of control over Normandy as essential to his control over England, a sign of deep-seated insecurity.

William indeed was to display characteristics of ruthlessness and even sadism. Although his propagandists praise him for the fact that he did not make use of capital punishment (except in the case of Earl Waltheof), he had a preference for perpetual imprisonment as the punishment for noblemen. Moreover, he frequently inflicted savage penalties on those who defied him, condemning men to be mutilated by the loss of nose, hands and feet and to be blinded. They were then left to suffer until they died, a penalty far worse than execution. To that one can add the savagery of the infamous harrying of the North. One edict has survived that sums up William's judicial policy: 'I forbid that any man be executed or hanged for any offence, but let his eyes be gouged out and his testicles cut off.'[13]

The sources describe him as stern, unbending and ruthless, avaricious and even superstitious. Tales about William suggest that he was prone to the kind of religious awe which is perilously close to superstition. In adult life he was direct and plain spoken in manner, physically hardy, a powerful and sturdy man, but capable of great aggression and outbursts of rage.

Yet despite these possible character flaws, it remains the case that he displayed great leadership, commanding his men decisively and successfully, always managing to keep within the limits of what was possible, though it is true that the invasion of England was a tremendous gamble. He paid minute attention to detail, especially in military and financial matters, maintaining strict discipline over his men. Perhaps because of the treachery on the part of the Richardides he encountered in his youth, he had a tremendous sense of the importance of loyalty and fidelity, which enabled him to acquire a hard core of loyal supporters who were devoted to him. He became well-schooled in all forms of warfare, especially in the conduct of sieges, and acquired a great reputation as a commander. He never hesitated to resort to drastic methods and his campaigns were characterised by pillage, robbery and devastation.

His early reign saw the growth and development of knightly power, which spread violence, intimidation and horrifying brutality throughout both the duchy and, in due course, the Kingdom of England. But William was able to develop measures designed to disperse, control and direct it. Then, in 1066, he exported knightly violence to England.

His personal conduct was in many ways exemplary. It is claimed by William of Jumièges that Duke William knew the Scriptures and possessed robust Christian faith. He attended church morning and evening and displayed 'eucharistic piety' in combating the heresy of Berengar of Tours. Quite early in his reign Lanfranc of Pavia became his confessor and retained a great influence over him for the rest of his life.

William's first recorded public act came shortly before 1035. Humphrey of Pont Audemar undertook the foundation of the abbey of Préaux and Duke Robert attended the foundation ceremonies. A charter was issued on that occasion, and tradition records that it was placed on the altar by William, who had accompanied his father.[14]

Then Duke Robert announced his intention of going to Jerusalem. There was much consternation among the prelates and magnates of Normandy, and pressure was immediately brought on the Duke in an effort to change his mind, but to no avail; Robert was adamant. An assembly of bishops and magnates was summoned to Fécamp early in 1035, on 13 January, where Duke Robert made a formal announcement of his intentions and set about making arrangements for the continuation of the government of his duchy in his absence.

No one had expected this, for the Duke was still only a young man, not yet thirty. His decision must have rendered the bishops and magnates speechless with indignation. It does seem to have been a remarkably irresponsible act even if undertaken in response to the religious impulses of the age.

But the Duke, supported by the wily Archbishop, overcame all objections to his decision and then proceeded to demand recognition of his seven-year-old son as his successor. He is said to have brought William before the assembly and said, 'This is my son. I will not leave you without a lord. He is small but he will, God willing, grow!' The barons and bishops were compelled to swear the customary oaths of fealty and obedience to the young William. No doubt they hoped the situation would be only temporary and that Robert would return in due course from his pilgrimage. As an added precaution, William was sent with a delegation, including the Archbishop, to perform homage to his overlord, Henry I of France, so that his position was recognised and he was assured, in theory at least, of the protection of his feudal superior.

After Robert's departure in 1035, Gilbert of Brionne, Count of Évreux, a grandson of Duke Richard I, was given powers to supervise William's continued upbringing and to arrange his tutoring. He also oversaw the tutoring of the children of the recently deceased Lord of Montreuil-l'Argillé and Échauffour, that is William of Giroie, a Breton adventurer who had come to power in the Ouche. He had built two castles and married a daughter of the Lord of Montfort-sur-Risle, by whom he had seven sons and four daughters; these were the 'fitz-Gérés'. Gilbert's involvement with this family was to lead to his murder in about 1040.

It is noticeable that Herleva, despite her marriage, was not permitted to be one of William's guardians, just as earlier Duke William Longsword had excluded his mistress, Sprota, from the guardianship of his son Richard I. Duke Robert in fact appointed as leading guardian Alan III of Brittany, though this can never have been more than a formality. It was really most useful in effectively nullifying any claim Alan himself had to the duchy as a descendant of Richard I.

Among others who assisted the young Duke William were Archbishop Robert, who in practice dominated the others, Mauger (a son of Richard II, who succeeded Archbishop Robert as Archbishop of Rouen), the brother of Count William of Arques, Thorold (called Turquetil by the Normans) who was William's tutor or governor,[15] Osbern the Seneschal, Fulbert, now Chamberlain, Osbern's son William, who was about the same age as the young Duke, and Walter, brother of Herleva. It also seems that Count Baldwin IV of Flanders was asked to be a guardian but he might well have declined. For his own safety William was placed in the castle of Vaudreuil.

Charter evidence reveals the structure of his household. At the head of the signatures came Archbishop Robert, usually followed by those of several bishops and abbots, then came members of the ducal family such as Count Gilbert, William of Arques and Mauger of Corbeil, then lesser vassals such as Humphrey de Vieilles, Waleran de Meulan, Osbern the Seneschal and his brother Robert, Turold the Constable and Rabel (who had commanded Duke Robert's fleet), and finally vicomtes and lesser advisers. The style differs little from that of Duke Robert's charters and suggests a good deal of continuity of administration of the duchy.

There were many Richardides, some with claims to the dukedom, but at first none had much support. Then, just as Robert's accession had frustrated the ambitions of the Richardides, so now did that of William.[16] While Archbishop Robert lived and dominated the circle around the young Duke, no serious efforts were made to displace him. An indication of the Archbishop's dominance is shown by the fact that he was able to add parts of the dowry of Duchess Judith of Brittany (first wife of Duke Richard II) to the estates of his cathedral.

The situation that arose during Duke Robert's absence was both precarious and dangerous, but until the Duke's death was known, Archbishop Robert retained firm control and this continued until his own death in 1037. None of those who later rebelled dared to challenge the status quo. There is no record of conditions in Normandy at the time, but the Cartulary of Bayeux[17] refers to lands lost by the bishopric 'after the death of Duke Robert'. Bishop Hugh of Bayeux was determined to recover his losses, some of which had occurred under Duke Robert, and brought a suit for recovery before a court held, significantly, by Archbishop Robert, Eudo the Count (of Penthièvre) and Nigel the Vicomte (of the Cotentin), which found in his favour. William is not even mentioned, let alone consulted. Decisions were being taken without reference to the wishes of so young a child, though it seems likely that he was required to be present when actions were taken in his name, so giving them legitimacy.

But fierce rivalries were soon to make themselves felt as those eager to share power jostled and manoeuvred for positions of influence, though the situation remained stable until Archbishop Robert died. William was to have good reason to be grateful to his uncle, Walter, and maintained close relations in due course with his half-brothers Odo and Robert, who were both to profit from their relationship to the Duke. Perhaps in the early years there was some mutual affection between them and a similarity of temperament.

But coming events cast their shadows before them. Shortly after Duke Robert's death, Roger de Tosny, who had been absent in Spain fighting the Moors when the Duke went on pilgrimage, returned to Normandy.[18] On being informed of the accession of the young Duke, he refused point blank to acknowledge William as his lord saying that he would never accept as prince an illegitimate child.[19]

He did nothing which directly threatened the Duke himself and made no attempt to depose him. Instead, he withdrew to his own castle from where he proceeded to wage private war against his neighbours, defying ducal power as guardian and guarantor of peace. He ravaged the lands of Humphrey de Vieilles and was, in due course, assassinated by Humphrey's son Roger 'of Beaumont' in 1040. Roger de Tosny had voiced the unspoken opinion of many Norman lords who found it hard to accept a bastard as Duke, even though most had sworn to recognise William.

3

MINORITY

Only after the announcement of his imminent departure on pilgrimage in 1035 had Duke Robert presented his young son William to the magnates as their new lord. He then entrusted him 'to his tutors and guardians who would wisely look after him until his majority'. The Archbishop took the leading role, but Count Gilbert, Alan III of Brittany and Osbern the Steward were also named as guardians since they were Duke Robert's chief supporters, and it is possible that Count Baldwin IV of Flanders was asked to act, though he seems in practice to have declined.

When news broke of the Duke's death, it would have looked as though the regime would be plunged immediately into chaos. The problem was that when a ruler died his government died with him and all authority entrusted to others became void. But Archbishop Robert's authority seems to have been so complete and unquestioned that he was able to refuse to surrender that authority. He simply acted as though he was now regent (though the title was never used) and asserted his right to carry out the Duke's wishes by remaining in power. He could have claimed the succession for himself but did not do so, but he was uniquely placed to dominate the situation arising from Duke Robert's death.

No one else was powerful or influential enough to challenge the cleric's assumption of this power, especially as he had control of the young Duke's person. He had arranged the approach to King Henry I of France to whom the young William was sent shortly before or after Robert's departure, to do homage. Other pretenders to the ducal throne had no support. It was only after the Archbishop's death in 1037 that discontent began to surface, taking the form of murder, mayhem and assassination rather than open rebellion. Then for some twelve years the chief feudal families competed with each other for control of lands and power. They were compelled by the decline in ducal authority to protect their own estates and tempted to enlarge them. The Richardides especially began to contemplate disputing William's right to be Duke, but they did not seek to destroy the authority which derived from a duke's position as 'Count of Rouen'.

So, after the death of Archbishop Robert, the nature of the controlling faction around the young Duke changed. The situation soon became unstable, lacking the steadying hand of the Archbishop. It is likely that, after the death of Count Alan of Brittany in 1039/40, Gilbert of Brionne, Count of Eu, had become the leading figure among those appointed by Duke Robert as guardians and tutors. These men naturally continued to administer the duchy in the name of the young Duke. They had been chosen from among those mentioned by William of Jumièges as having been summoned by Duke Robert, namely 'Archbishop Robert of Rouen and the magnates of his duchy'. Only the Archbishop was named – an acknowledgement of his greater importance.

By the time Count Gilbert found himself in the leading role, personal tutors had been found for the young Duke, specifically a certain Turold and then, possibly somewhat later, Ralph Moine or 'the Monk' and a 'Master William'.[1] William of Jumièges adds that William, 'deprived of his father during his childhood, was educated to develop his natural qualities by the wisdom of his prudent guardians' but goes on to reveal the shadow of developing strife, saying that many Normans 'built earthworks in many places and erected fortified strongholds for their own purposes' and then says they 'immediately hatched plots and rebellions and fierce fires were lit all over the country'.

The first sign of real trouble came with the outbreak of private warfare between Hugh I de Montfort (son of Thurstan of Bastembourg, the Vicomte) and a certain Walkelin of Ferrières. It was a much more serious matter than at first appears, since Roger of Tosny and Ralph of Gacé (son of Archbishop Robert) were both involved. In the resulting struggle Hugh and Walkelin both fell in battle and many others were slain. Again William of Jumièges is the informant. He describes this as a period when 'in this state of disturbance the madness of certain persons belched forth in greater strength', though he is careful not to name them.[2] In the event a compromise was reached from which Ralph of Gacé emerged as a leading guardian, though the new Archbishop, Mauger, had improved his position in the government and had assumed control.

The Archbishop did what he could to curb the violence, calling a Church Council in 1042 which attempted to promote the Peace of God movement, but to little avail. But his action was to prove to be a useful precedent in 1047 for similar action by Duke William.

So there was a disastrous and rapid descent into violence as lords with little to lose strove to protect their own interests in the absence of the hand of a strong duke at the helm. The Richardides were now only too ready to dispute the right of his guardians to exercise jurisdiction, and some wanted to gain control of the young Duke for themselves and rule in his name. This resulted in moves to remove those currently in control by resort to assassination, which produced shocking mayhem. Almost all of those closest to the young Duke perished by violence and four of his guardians were assassinated.

It was probably in 1039 or 1040 that Count Alan III of Brittany, taking advantage of the disorder, crossed the Couesnon and attempted to enforce his rights as guardian, claiming that Duke Robert had entrusted William to his care. He advanced as far as Vimoutiers and besieged it, only to die some time before October 1040.[3] He was, as a Richardide, buried at Fécamp, the ducal monastery.[4] He left a young son, Conan, as his heir, but Alan's brother, Eon de Penthièvre, seized control, claiming to be Conan's guardian and driving out his mother Bertha, Alan's widow. She took refuge at the Court of the Count of Maine, who then married her.

Count Gilbert's assassination, which occurred shortly afterwards, was the result of a carefully planned attack. One morning, while out riding (as he was accustomed to do) accompanied by his brother-in-law Fulk fitz Géré and Walkelin of Pont-Échaufroi, he was ambushed by a certain Odo the Fat and another fitz Géré brother, Robert. Rightly or wrongly, Robert appears to have thought he had been betrayed by the Count. Gilbert and Walkelin were slain and only Fulk escaped. It is not impossible that Fulk was in on the plot, as that would explain his survival.[5]

The 'prime suspect' in the assassination was the man who stood to benefit most from Gilbert's death. That was Ralph of Gacé, second son, out of wedlock, of Archbishop Robert. He was the instigator of the plot; as Orderic Vitalis states,[6] Odo and Fulk only carried it out. To cover his tracks, Ralph set his own men onto the sons of Giroie (that is, fitz Géré) and for a time drove them into exile, while he manipulated events to secure his own position as guardian of the young Duke.

Gilbert's murder opened the floodgates. Duke William's personal tutor, Turold, was next to be assassinated 'by traitors faithless to the country', who again remain unnamed. But worse was to come. Shortly before April 1042 William was residing in the castle of Vaudreuil. Precautions had been taken for his safety and one or other of his tutors slept in the same room. But William, a son of Roger I of Montgomery, crept secretly into the castle and found his way to the young Duke's chamber, seeking out his real victim, Osbern the Steward.

He found him, sleeping beside the young Duke. Mercilessly he slit Osbern's throat. It is likely that William, roused by the commotion, actually witnessed Osbern's death throes. He certainly must have found the body and raised the alarm. He would have been about fourteen years old and this was probably the first violent death he had witnessed. Whatever the overall psychological effects of these horrors, William emerged hardened by his experiences.

It was not the only occasion when death threatened William closely, and in the period immediately after the murders, his maternal uncle, Walter, assumed a protective role. Like Osbern, he mostly slept in William's bedchamber, and more than once, warned or aware of danger, he smuggled the young man out of the castle and hid him in the homes of loyal villagers until the danger had passed.

William of Jumièges is circumspect about the identity of the assassins; one of them at least, William of Montgomery, was a benefactor of his abbey! In a most interesting passage, the writer, ostensibly referring to those involved in the efforts of King Henry I of France to profit from the troubles in Normandy, tells his readers that he cannot name those guilty 'of shamelessly inciting' the King 'to bring ruin upon the country', and informs them that 'I should have mentioned them by name had I not wished to avoid their burning hatred. But yet I whisper to all of you, my friends, surrounding me, that these are the very men who now claim to be the most faithful and have received so many honours from the duke.' Superficially he is referring to those involved in the French King's activities, but the passage follows directly after his summary of the murders from which he has contrived to omit the names of the perpetrators. This passage could well, therefore, be referring to those responsible for the assassinations.

In the immediate aftermath of those assassinations, it was the Richardides, Archbishop Mauger of Rouen and his brother William,

Count of Arques, who became the leading figures in the cabal around the Duke. Count William had received his Comté as a benefice to be held of the dukes by service to them, and it was likely that the obligation to serve a minor was now becoming irksome to him. Both of these men were William's uncles.

It is charter[7] evidence which reveals that these two had become prominent. The Archbishop's name heads the list of witnesses and his name is followed by that of the bastard; 'William, Count of the Normans'.[8] After that 'William the Count's master' (his personal tutor) signs and, in fourth place, 'William, Count of Arques'.[9] This was not a complete list of those in a position of influence and Count Gilbert was not yet dead.

But among those rising in influence, and soon to dominate the Duke's counsellors, was Raoul or Ralph Gacé, known apparently as 'Tête de l'Ane' or Ass's Head, the instigator of the murder of Count Gilbert.[10] He, like the Archbishop and the Count of Arques, was a member of the rising generation of nobles. Among his associates he numbered Guy of Burgundy (a grandson of Richard II) who had been given charge of the castle of Brionne after the murder of Count Gilbert.

So, despite the formation of a new governing clique, or even because of it, the duchy continued its descent into endemic feuding, described as one of the darkest periods in Norman history. Crime after crime led to more and more bloodshed. Bjarni of Glos-la-Ferrière, a vassal of the Steward, avenged the murder of his lord Osbern. He found his way into Montgomery's dwelling, with a band of followers, and killed William (the murderer of Osbern the Steward) and all his associates they found there. Roger of Tosny continued to ravage the lands of Humphrey of Vieilles until he was himself assassinated by Humphrey's son, Roger of Beaumont.

Elsewhere, the sons of Giroie of Échauffour fought the sons of William Talvas of Bellême and the castle of Alençon fell into the latter's hands. Hugh, Bishop of Sées and Count of Ivry, fortified his castle in defiance of ducal authority, and a certain Thurstan Goz, Vicomte of Exmes, took control of the castle of Tillières.

The attitude of the Richardides and their supporters arose from their sense of their own innate superiority over the rest of the population, because of their Scandinavian ancestry. Roger of Montgomery, for example, claimed to be 'Normand entre tous les Normands', that is, the most Norman of all Normans. Their vassals were bound to their lords by personal rather than territorial ties, as the holding of estates by knight service was not yet fully established. They were subjected to their lords by commendation rather than by knight service. Although it was common to refer to them as 'milites', this did not imply 'knightly' status as opposed to that of being a fighting vassal. It does not yet quite imply the existence of a class of fully trained cavalry warriors. In conflicts between neighbouring lords, the existence of these vassals led to a demand for more territory with which they could be rewarded for their service.

Astonishingly, despite the widespread mayhem, ducal administration never entirely collapsed. This was largely due to the efforts of the fifteen or so vicomtes who remained loyal and continued to collect ducal revenues and enforce the laws. So they discharged their duties and witnessed ducal charters. They seem to have avoided the temptation to join the wave of disorder at least until towards the end of William's minority. Charters reveal that legal processes continued and that sanctions could be applied against offenders. It also seems that the bishops as a body continued to support the young Duke. So the tradition of ducal authority and the administrative machinery survived despite the disorder. This contributed much to the unity of the duchy. Its vital importance is shown by the deadly situation that arose in 1047 when the western vicomtes themselves revolted.

But somehow or other Ralph of Gacé became the dominant figure, securing for himself control over the young Duke and the office of 'Princeps Militie Normannorum' with command over the Norman Militia, a body of knights that he was able to put to good use to enforce his commands. As a son of Archbishop Robert he was, though illegitimate, a cousin of Duke Robert and so, once removed, of William.

Nonetheless, internecine warfare continued, conditions in many places deteriorated, and even the peasantry was driven to organise associations for their own defence.

A graphic example of the type of disorder that was rampant and the reaction to it is provided by the case of the 'Sons of Soreng' who terrorised the district around Sées. This gang of brigands, led by Richard, Robert and Avesgot, the sons of a baron named William Soreng, went out pillaging and ravaging until one day they came to Sées. There they occupied the cathedral and made it their headquarters, using it to store their ill-gotten gains. They brought their horses into the building together with bedding for them and turned it into a stable.

The Bishop, Ivo of Bellême, seeing his church desecrated and being used as 'a cave full of brigands and the haunt of prostitutes', called on the aid of the Vicomte of the Hiémois, Hugh de Grandmesnil. With his support, the Bishop took the church by assault, driving out the Sons of Soreng, but instead of retreating, the three sons took refuge in the Clock Tower from which they showered arrows down upon their attackers.

Frustrated, the Bishop decided to burn them out. Faggots of wood were brought by the inhabitants of the town and heaped around the tower. But when they were fired, a gust of wind blew the flames towards the cathedral, which also caught fire, rapidly became an inferno, and burned to the ground.[11] In the confusion the Sons of Soreng escaped, covering their retreat with a hail of arrows and dispersing in different directions.

The eldest, Richard, took refuge in a cabin near a pond where he was surprised while asleep by Richard of Sainte-Scolasse whose land he had pillaged. He tried to escape but a peasant whom he had robbed and hung in chains went after him and killed him with an axe. His brother Robert managed to reach Écoudré but was pursued, captured and beaten to death by a band of irate peasants. The third brother, Avesgot, was hit by an arrow while being attacked by the inhabitants of Chambois.

But worst of all of these disorderly barons were the family of Bellême. In Duke Robert's time, William Talvas of Bellême, who had managed to recover the family lands, got possession of the castle of Alençon with the aid of William fitz Giroie. He showed no gratitude for the aid he had been given. He and his wife, Heudebourg, quarrelled bitterly, she reproaching him for his cruelty and deceit, so he had her strangled. Having disposed of his first wife, mother of Arnoul and Mabel, William successfully demanded the hand in marriage of the daughter of Roger of Beaumont. He then invited to the wedding that same William fitz Giroie along with his brother, a monk of Marmoutier known as 'Le Clerc', because of his exceptional literary culture.[12]

William's brother tried to dissuade him from attending the wedding, saying he had a bad feeling about it, but was overruled. William preferred to put his trust in his own height and physical strength. So the two went off to Alençon, unarmed but with a suitable escort. William Talvas welcomed his guests effusively, offering his hospitality. Secretly he had told his own vassals that he thought his guest was planning some act of treachery and said that they were not to let him out of their sight even when he went hunting. His familiars understood his real meaning and set upon William of Giroie, driving him out of the house and there, before terrified witnesses, proceeded to put out his eyes, cut off his ears and castrate him. The unfortunate victim survived and became a monk at Le Bec.

Two of his brothers vowed vengeance, ravaging the lands of William Talvas, right up to the gates of the castle where William had taken refuge. In vain they tried to break in while Talvas cowered within. So cowardly was he that even his sons were revolted, and in order perhaps to save themselves and retain control of the castle, the eldest, Arnoul, compelled his father to leave his fortified refuge to perish under the blows of his enemies. Arnoul himself was to die later in curious circumstances.

In the course of his own depredations Arnoul stole a pig belonging to a monk, who followed him, begging for its return. Arnoul and his companions slaughtered the pig and ate it and then fell into a deep sleep. While Arnoul slept, an unknown assailant crept up and strangled him. It was claimed later that it had been his own brother, Olivier, although he had a reputation of being a good knight. In old age Olivier became a monk at Le Bec so perhaps he needed to do penance for fratricide.

So quarrels multiplied and murders became everyday events. Despite this, it is worth noting that the writers of the time were prone to exaggerate the evils. They claim, wrongly, that there was a seven-year famine (it only affected one year) during which many houses were ruined and the roads were choked with dead bodies, while men crowded into the churches to beseech the saints for aid.

But it was now about 1042 and churchmen were becoming gravely concerned. There was an attempt to introduce into Normandy the Peace of God in order to reduce the violence. This was an effort by the Church, inspired by Abbot Odilon of Cluny in the tenth century, to restrict private warfare to only a few days a week and to exclude it altogether during penitential periods of the liturgical year such as Advent. It aimed also to protect certain classes of persons from attack: clergy of course, peasants and merchants. An advocate of the Peace movement, Richard of Saint-Vanne, came to Normandy and was received at Rouen where the Archbishop, Mauger, and his clergy paid him close attention. They certainly adopted some of his liturgical practices but in the fevered atmosphere of the time were unsuccessful in securing adoption of the Peace. However, in the cathedral library Richard of Saint-Vanne's book, the *Livre de Richard*, was preserved. Richard, though, died a disappointed man.

So far, William had survived. That he continued to do so could well be the unintended result of the interventions of King Henry I of France. These interventions were largely self-interested, as he sought advantage for himself and the increase of his own prestige. His efforts were never, as the Norman apologists for Duke William like to insist, the result of an agreement between equals. The apologists[13] present these affairs as the result of negotiations between independent sovereign princes, but in fact it was a matter of the relationship between an overlord, King Henry, and his vassal, Duke William.

Henry signalled his intention to act in this way as early as 1035 when he accepted William's homage and again supported the young Duke in 1039, making himself in a sense responsible for his safety. It was even claimed that he personally invested William with the arms of knighthood. If he did so, then it was in virtue of his rights as overlord. The King hoped, of course, to make Normandy a permanent addition to his royal demesne.[14]

Then, amidst all the troubles, King Henry made a real incursion into Norman territory, crossing the border and laying siege to the castle of Tillières-sur-Avis, which he regarded as a threat to French interests. He appears to have had a degree of support in doing so from within Normandy itself. Perhaps he had been claiming that he was acting, as his overlord, to safeguard the young Duke's best interests. Henry had certainly recovered the lands in the Vexin he had ceded to Duke Robert, and the sources insist that in doing so he had claimed to be exercising his rights as William's suzerain. Orderic Vitalis comments that William, who was 'only a weak boy, could not defend his rights'. The Archbishop made no attempt to prevent it either. Henry had also readily received at his Court numerous disaffected and exiled Norman lords, notably Roger of Montgomery.

The castle of Tillières had originally been built by Duke Richard II to protect his southern border against the Comté of Blois. Then Count Odo of Blois ceded the town and territory of Dreux to France and in so doing brought the frontiers of Normandy and France up against each other.

In 1040 Tillières was held by Gilbert Crespin, a member of the ducal court, who had charge of the castle before Ralph of Gacé had become part of the government. When King Henry appeared in force before the castle and demanded entry, as he could rightfully do as William's overlord, Gilbert refused to admit him despite the fact that Ralph of Gacé had given prior consent. Ralph and King Henry had agreed that the castle should be handed over to France on condition that its fortifications were to be destroyed, and Henry had agreed neither to reoccupy the castle nor rebuild it for his own use or that of any of his vassals for at least four years (by which time Duke William would just about have reached the age of majority).

But Gilbert Crespin refused to go along with this diplomatic farce, suspecting that Henry might not keep to his agreement. The King, as one might expect, reacted with violence, breaching the bailey walls and destroying the buildings within it, which were home to the castle garrison; Gilbert was forced to surrender. He was really acting in accordance with his oath of fidelity to Duke Robert. However, he now found a solution to his dilemma by surrendering the castle but not to King Henry. Instead, he surrendered it to the young Duke himself, which allowed Ralph of Gacé to surrender it to the King. This pretty comedy must have amused the French King, who burnt the castle down while watching from a safe distance, laughing his head off.

Henry then went on to Argentan, which he burned down, pillaging and ravaging as he went before returning to Tillières. He then, advancing as a pretext for doing so the resistance offered by Gilbert Crespin, broke his promises, restoring the ramparts in stone and installing his own garrison. So Ralph of Gacé found that his policy of appeasement had failed. Some have speculated that Gilbert had been encouraged in his gesture by hints from the young Duke William, who as he grew older was perhaps beginning to chafe at the restrictions placed on his freedom of action.

Henry's progress through Normandy also provoked action from another quarter. Thurstan Goz, Vicomte of the Hiémois, now also defied Ralph's policy. Thurstan was a man of Scandinavian descent, son of Ansfrid 'le Danois', who had been a favourite of Duke Richard II. Thurstan now fortified his castle of Falaise, following Gilbert's example, and defied Ralph. He installed a stronger garrison, employing mercenary troops, many of whom were French. William of Jumièges even suggests that he put himself at the disposal of the French King. On the other hand he might have been trying to hang on to the castle on William's behalf, so threatening the politics of appeasement followed by Ralph. Exactly what was going on remains unclear, as the situation was becoming more and more confused.

What is clear is Ralph's next move. He gathered together the Norman Militia (Militie Normande) and laid siege to Falaise. It is possible that the young Duke, now about fifteen years old, was himself present, observing siegeworks at first hand. (The year was now almost certainly 1042.) The walls of Falaise were soon breached, but as it was almost night, Ralph postponed the final assault until morning. That allowed Thurstan to escape and flee into exile, taking his French mercenaries with him.

But Thurstan was exiled only temporarily, as he was allowed back a short time later, which gives some support to the idea that he had at least the tacit support of William. The affair provides a neat insight into the effectiveness of Ralph of Gacé's rule. He had been able to make effective use of the Militie Normande to deal with a defiant vicomte. But it could also be a sign of the increasing influence of the young Duke, who might have urged Ralph into action. This could be the moment referred to by William of Jumièges, who records how William as a young man 'shone in the profession of arms as much as in public affairs'. William of Poitiers also, though he gives no indication of the date, suggests that William had at about this time been knighted, and he waxes lyrical about how splendid it was to see William controlling his horse while brandishing his sword and wielding his shield. The Archdeacon might even have witnessed what he describes, and as he had been a soldier himself before becoming a cleric, he was well qualified to make the comment.

From 1042 onwards order seems to have been gradually restored to Normandy as the worst of the outrages died down, though it was by no means fully restored. The policy of Henry I had been to safeguard William's position against those who sought to gain control over him and that had perhaps caused Norman factions to provide the King with support. But there were still many threats and challenges to the young Duke as he strove to establish his own dominance. William was now rising fourteen or fifteen and thus approaching the age of majority. Whether he could now insist on his rights would depend upon his strength of character.

His education and training, as befitted a prospective duke, had continued as circumstances permitted. He had been trained in the company of the sons of Giroie and his closest companion, in age and temperament perhaps, had been William, son of Osbern the Steward. Their association had developed into firm and lasting friendship. Both boys enjoyed an extraordinary degree of physical strength. Orderic Vitalis says that Duke William had acquired toughness of mind and heart and became a man who was grave and thoughtful. He is described as capable of great violence yet master of his emotions and full of authority.

He was to judge his guardians harshly, and it cannot be said that he approved of their policies or methods of government. There could well have been moments of great conflict between William and those who claimed jurisdiction over him though no stories survive to illustrate what they might have been about. He certainly never forgot how his uncle Walter had intervened to save him nor that he had been deprived of his mother's care. He maintained close relations with the members of his mother's family after he assumed control of the duchy, making his maternal grandfather a chamberlain and raising his mother's other sons to high office.

It is likely that during the Minority two contrasting parties had formed, rivals for control over the young Duke, but King Henry's intervention stirred up conflict between them, provoking rebellion and acts of brigandage, especially in Lower (or Western) Normandy. Certainly a movement now developed there which threatened the very basis of ducal authority, aimed at the life of the Duke himself, as a number of lords formed a cabal around a prospective rival candidate. Many of these nobles were men of inordinate pride. William Talou, for example, liked to style himself 'Nutis Superni Regis Comes', Count by inspiration of the King of Kings (i.e. God Almighty!).

The spread of 'adulterine' castles (built without ducal licence) posed a considerable threat to the position of the Duke. Even members of the ducal court resorted to this kind of defiance. William Talou, Count of Arques and brother of Archbishop Mauger, built a formidable 'donjon' or keep at Arques on a promontory overlooking the confluence of the Béthune and the Varenne. The wife of the Count of Bayeux, Auberée, built the castle of Ivry and had the architect beheaded lest he build others like it. One of the largest castles was that of Montfort-sur-Risle, covering 4½ hectares with three lines of entrenchments and a moat 50 metres wide and 9 metres deep.

Normandy itself was threatened on all sides by rivals; Flanders to the east, Anjou to the south and Brittany to the west. But fortunately for the young Duke, the lands remained intact, and many lesser vassals stayed loyal and gave service in the ducal army. In fact the fundamental spirit of Normandy and the very survival of the duchy owed much to the work of many obscure servants, most of whom cannot be identified, who rallied round their young master.

The Chroniclers are discreet. They resort to high-flown vague rhetoric to veil the brutal truth about the means adopted by the Bastard in his assumption of power. The one certainty seems to be that William was able to dismiss and drive out Ralph of Gacé some time between 1044 and 1045, but exactly how this was accomplished remains unknown. William thereafter set about freeing himself from the limitations on his power posed by the Richardides. William of Poitiers, in between passages of mere rhetorical exaggeration, lets slip a few genuine facts. They boil down to the assertion that, upon reaching the age of majority, the Bastard took full possession of his duchy, mainly by force. A number of prominent men were exiled as cowardly (*ignavus*) or destructive (*corrumpus*), and new counsellors were named to replace them. Exactly how and when remains obscure, but William had now attained the age of majority and found that ambitious rivals were now looking not merely to exploit him as their puppet but to displace him completely.

4

THE STRUGGLE FOR SURVIVAL

The year 1042 had been a year of famine. After that, between then and 1045, relative peace, the peace of exhaustion perhaps, was gradually restored so that the young Duke appeared, outwardly at least, to have overcome all opposition. The most violent of the recent rebels and trouble makers had seen their power broken, the worst of these brigands had been punished, and Ralph of Gacé seems to have simply faded into insignificance. Probably, William, some time between 1044 and 1045, had managed to dismiss or drive him out of his guardianship. He certainly disappears from the record, the effect perhaps of the gradual assumption of power by the young Duke after the defeat of the rebellion of Thurstan Goz during 1042. During this time William freed himself from the grip of the Richardides. But that did not happen suddenly, and it looks as though power, with the removal of Ralph of Gacé, was exercised by the arch-Richardides, Archbishop Mauger and William, Count of Arques.

Exactly how William achieved dominance remains something of a mystery since his panegyrists, William of Jumièges and William of Poitiers, were careful to omit all reference to his methods. They merely attribute to him a formidable physical presence behind which lay a mind of great subtlety and cunning and imply that he achieved dominance by sheer force of personality. It might have been so, but this reveals nothing about either the strategy or the tactics used by the young man. Nothing is revealed. No overt moves are described. Only one thing seems certain and that is that by 1045, at the age of about eighteen, William was in command of his duchy, a fact which was to provoke the most dangerous conspiracy against him that had yet been constructed.

There is no record of any actual ceremony marking his assumption of ducal authority, because that would have been largely regarded as having taken place back in 1035 when he was accepted by the barons as the heir of Duke Robert. William of Jumièges records that the Normans had accepted him at that time as their lord and that they had sworn to do military service for him. It may be that there was a solemn public ceremony during which William appeared enthroned and bearing the sword which was the symbol of ducal authority, but there is no record of it.

However, it is known that there was a ceremony, a semi-liturgical rite used by the dukes, akin to the crowning and enthronement of a king, during which the new duke would take solemn possession of a sword. Laudes (that is, a litany) were sung which are later recorded as including the salutation 'To William, Duke of the Normans, health and perpetual peace.'[1] Evidence that a 'Sword of State' figured in public appearances of the Duke is displayed in the Bayeux Tapestry, which repeatedly pictures the Duke enthroned, holding a sword.[2]

The *Carmen de Haestingae Proelio* might have borrowed from this rite, when it claimed that Earl Harold had brought a sword and a ring, by implication gifts of King Edward, as evidence of the Earl's mission. There is, of course, no corroboration available for this episode, and it could be simply the invention of the author. Meanwhile, and quite coincidentally, just as William was progressively assuming sovereign power in Normandy, the end of the Danish dynasty of Cnut the Great was taking place in England. Harold I Harefoot died in 1040, his half-brother Harthacnut in 1042, resulting in the acceptance and coronation of the Aetheling Edward as king in the same year. Despite later Norman claims to the contrary, Duke William played no part in these events. He was, in any case, fully occupied in dealing with the consequences of the baronial disturbances in Normandy.

William had now, by 1045, become the leader of the warrior aristocracy of Normandy, though he had yet to consolidate his grasp on power. His experiences as a child and as a young adult had shaped him into a warrior, with a particular mastery of siege warfare. But the very harshness of his childhood would have created in him a kind of ruthlessness which probably led him to demonstrate piety in his quest for power. The effects, indeed the trauma, of his childhood would also have created in him, behind the public display of conventional piety, a deep-seated reliance on religion, which, as various incidents later in his life show, bordered on the superstitious.

His ruthlessness led him to carry out acts so atrocious that they were to induce in him a fear of damnation which drove him to perform acts of piety aimed at securing his salvation, or so Orderic Vitalis insists. That would explain his various gifts to churches, his foundation of abbeys (notably Battle Abbey) and his demonstration of fear and trembling during the coronation of 1066. Orderic puts into his mouth a long deathbed speech in which the King confesses his various crimes and shows a marked reluctance to pass the crown of England directly to any of his heirs. The passage is, in fact, a remarkable piece of historical reconstruction and analysis of the Conqueror's career but could well have been based in part on what was remembered afterwards by those who were present.

Others have commented, with justification, that William's displays of public piety were carefully crafted to meet the demands of warfare and the needs of politics. William is compared by some to his grandfather, Richard I, who was himself a cruel and ruthless ruler, a consummate politician and master of 'Realpolitik', which he cloaked in a demonstration of piety and obedience to the Church.

To William himself there is attributed a most significant remark: 'I was schooled in war from childhood.' That type of upbringing formed a man of authoritarian character, determined always to exert absolute and effective lordship. One factor, which displays William's unique blend of political acumen and public piety was to come after his defeat of the serious assault on his position that arose in 1046–47. That is his use of the Truce of God as an instrument by which he acquired the exclusive right to use violence to restore order and maintain peace during times of the year when the Truce bound others to abstain from its use.

It does seem that it was shortly after William's first public military involvement, around 1042, at the siege of Tillières, that he was recognised as being now of full age and thus able to govern in person. His Court was established at Valognes.[3] It was then that some began to fear that he would become their master and, as a result, serious revolt was planned. William of Poitiers, in an undated passage, boasts that William, having now reached the age of knighthood, swore 'to uphold the cause of the weak and to impose laws which would not be burdensome'. William of Poitiers adds, before going on to slander the reputation of the Duke's guardian, William, Count of Arques, that William forbade 'slaughter, fire and pillage'. The writer is concerned principally to exonerate Duke William from charges which must have been levelled against him. William of Poitiers insists that 'we are impelled by right reason to place on record that through his virtuous restraint he always avoided slaughter unless the pressure of war or some other grave necessity compelled it'.

It must be said that, although this kind of clemency characterised William's treatment of members of the nobility, he had no compunction about using extreme violence against commoners. William of Poitiers insists that, 'while other princes used capital punishment ... putting prisoners to the sword', Duke William preferred imprisonment or exile. But the record shows a decided readiness on the Duke's part to resort to barbaric methods of mutilation: putting out eyes, cutting off noses, feet and hands, and leaving the victims to survive or die as circumstances dictated. Even the use of imprisonment was seen as worse than execution as instanced when Guibert of Nogent complained about the treatment of his own father, condemned by William 'to perpetual incarceration'.

William was still, despite the support of the Archbishop of Rouen and recognition by the French King, in a precarious position, though overt opposition had so far been postponed. But formidable opposition could be expected from the Richardides. The rebellion that arose in 1046–47 was to be the gravest crisis to arise so far in the conflict between the young Duke and the barons. It was provoked, as far as can be ascertained, by William's emancipation from the tutelage of his guardians and his first assumption of personal authority. The ambitions of the Richardides formed the background to the revolt, its proximate cause being the dynastic ambitions of Guy of Burgundy. But the probable aim of the leading participants was the overthrow of the Bastard.

Guy saw himself as better fitted and entitled to reign, seeing himself as the 'legitimate' duke in more senses than one. He was grandson of Duke Richard II and his wife Judith, through his mother Adelaide (wife of Renaud, Count of Burgundy), and of legitimate birth. He had acquired lands in central Normandy and was backed by a group of irreconcilables from among the western baronage: Haimo le Dentu (the Toothy) of Creully and Torigny (Manche); Nigel II, called Falconhead, the provost or vicomte of the Cotentin; Renouf de Briquessart, vicomte of the Bessin (Calvados); Grimoult du Plessis; and Raoul Tesson, lord of the Cinglais, called Le Blaireau (meaning Badger), whose principal castle was at Thury-Harcourt (Calvados).

As well as these men, and possibly in conjunction with them, the town of Rouen itself, or at least a large group of its citizens, also rebelled, and so the movement against the Duke spread. It is even possible that Archbishop Mauger encouraged this movement. Certainly it spread into the valley of the Seine. The citizens' grievances were economic rather than political, and sources suggest that they wanted to profit from the effects of the baronial revolt, which reduced William's immediate authority, in order to extract from the Duke a grant of commercial privileges, perhaps control over or receipt of the city tolls.

Guy of Burgundy had been brought up in Normandy along with the Bastard by Count Gilbert and, after Gilbert's murder, had been given the castle of Brionne. He had remained in favour at Court and witnessed a charter for Jumièges sometime after 1045. He was adopted as the head of the conspiracy after having attracted the support of this powerful group of magnates who saw him as the most plausible claimant. As the revolt spread, they attracted more support not only from Guy's possessions in central Normandy but from Lower Normandy.

Many of the details of what followed come from the writings of Robert Wace in the twelfth century but his knowledge of the topography of their movements, and of William's flight, allows historians to place their confidence in the accuracy of his account. He was, after all, secretary/archivist of the Abbaye-aux-Hommes at Caen.

The central group planned originally to seize the young Duke while he was out hunting in the forests near Valognes, close to Nigel's castle of Saint-Sauveur-le-Vicomte. They swore an oath of mutual support to strike William wherever they might find him. They had given no advance hint of their treason. There is no sign of a reluctance on their part to perform their duties. Unfortunately for the conspirators, and luckily for William, their plotting and their swearing of an oath was overheard by a jester called Goles. He immediately took horse and rode off to Valognes to warn the Court. Wace's account is vivid. Goles arrived at the castle at night, finding everything shut up. He began banging on the door, crying, 'Open! Open! Or you will all die! Where is William? Why does he sleep? If his enemies find him here he will never leave the Cotentin! Nor live till morning!'

William, roused by the resulting uproar, demanded no further explanation, hastily dressed as best he could in shirt and breeches, throwing a cape over his shoulders, jumped on a horse and rode south, aiming to escape from the Cherbourg Peninsula, lest he be trapped by the conspirators. Rapidly he reached the dangerous ford across the Vire at the Chapel of Saint Clément, near Isigny (where he paused to pray). Turning east and finding that the direct route led through Bayeux (which was Briquessart's administrative centre), he bypassed the town on the seaward side. Sunrise found him at Ryes in Calvados where he encountered the lord, named Hubert, who was astonished to see his overlord 'dressed like a devil', riding an exhausted horse. Pulling himself together, Hubert ordered his sons to help the Bastard reach Falaise by a route avoiding all towns and provided them and William with fresh horses. So William and his three companions rode off through the valley of the River Orne, crossing it near Foupendant, at a place called the Lopsided Beech Tree, near Thury. On they rode to Harcourt and shortly afterwards arrived at Falaise.

Meanwhile, the conspirators had pursued the fleeing Duke. When they, in their turn, arrived at Ryes, Hubert sent them off in the wrong direction. So they had now lost the element of surprise and therefore separated to go each to his own castle as had been agreed.

Wace was writing poetry rather than a coherent account and provides William with all the trappings of a heroic journey.[4] But his topography is accurate and the route of William's ride was long known as 'The Duke's Way'. It seems probable that William did follow an escape route from Valognes to Falaise which was remembered and passed on by word of mouth.

Wace wrote of the wave of emotion which swept through the Norman people when news broke of the failure of the attempt on the Duke's life but provides no details. It remains unknown also how long it was before William reached Falaise and exactly how long it was before he dared to set out to make an appeal to King Henry for help. This was his first overtly political move. The fact that he had to do so is, in itself, an indication that he had not underestimated the strength of his enemies. The move disconcerted the enemies by its very simplicity. William was making use of the hierarchical order that his enemies had sought to evade. The Hiémois and the region around Caen had been lost, as the vassals there had failed to respond to William's summons. His orders had not been passed on. So William made use of his own position as a vassal and appealed to his overlord. It then seems that the King decided, apparently without hesitation, to fulfil his duty as overlord by providing his vassal with the military support he needed, accepting that the Duke had been deprived of the peaceful enjoyment of his fief. No doubt he also saw that the weakening of Norman power would encourage the ambitions of the Count of Blois and Chartres.

So while Guy and his fellow conspirators were busy gathering allies, William left Falaise and went in person to seek out King Henry, at Poisy, then Laon and finally found him at Compiègne. William then returned to Normandy and called on the assistance of knights in Upper and Central Normandy, that is from the Pays de Caux, the Roumois, Evrecin, Lieuvin, Pays d'Auge and Hiémois. The knights there had been angered by such open rebellion and the attempts of Guy of Brionne to exact tribute. They converged on Falaise to rally to the defence of their Duke.

William assured them that although Guy had some sort of claim it came to him in the female line, from his mother, and that he had no means of gaining the aid of his father, the Count of Burgundy. The loyalists assembled on the plain south of Caen where Herleva's family had lands. That implies that the revolt was confined to Lower Normandy, east of the River Orne. Little or nothing is known of how far the revolt had any support among the local population, nor of the attitude of the clergy, though the Abbey of Mont-Saint-Michel does appear to have supported it. A reduction in Norman power would have suited the abbots, who tended to support the Dukes of Brittany.

Sometime, therefore, in 1047, the two sides began gathering their forces. Exactly when remains uncertain, but during the spring, having spent the winter preparing, King Henry advanced from the south-west towards Mézidon and gathered an army on the plain to the west of Caen, not far from the little River Muance. It was now just before Easter. He is said to have heard Mass in the Church of St Brice at Valmeray. On the same day, the Bastard and his men arrived from the north and joined the French contingent. For their part, the rebels gathered near a village called Billy.

The place where the two sides confronted each other was known as Val-ès-Dunes and contained a number of hamlets. Several other places in the area contain a reference to 'Le Val'. It was a lightly undulating plain about 5 km by 3 km. The area is about 12 km from Caen and Wace implies that it was located towards the south and south-west of a river, although this cannot be relied on since it was a commonplace of the Chansons de Geste to locate battles in this manner. However, in this case he might well have been right. The plain around Billy was to the south and south-west of the River Muance.

The numbers involved are equally vague. Ralph Tesson was believed to have had 400 companions yet an assessment made in 1172 gives the Honour of Tesson the service of only forty-five knights and Ralph is unlikely to have had many more in 1047. It is thought that the rebels had in all about 200 knights and 600 footsoldiers, but there is no evidence at all as to the size of the Franco-Norman army. Wace, as was usual at the time, mentions only the part played by the knights, although it is likely that there were archers among the footsoldiers. It was said that the two sides were, when battle commenced, about an arrow's flight apart, near enough to identify their adversaries.

Ralph Tesson, one of the leading rebels, had apparently stationed himself somewhat apart from the rest, causing King Henry to ask whether he was an ally or the enemy. 'William,' he inquired, 'who are these so well-equipped men? Do you know what they intend to do?' 'Sire,' replied the Duke, 'I think they might belong to my side. Their leader is Ralph Tesson who has no reason to be displeased with me.' Some speculate that perhaps William had some prior indication or knowledge that Ralph had parted company with the rest.

In truth, Ralph dithered. He had not expected to find himself confronted by his overlord, sword in hand. Yet he had sworn, at Bayeux, to strike William as soon as he saw him and his knights no doubt urged him to keep his sworn word. He reminded them, 'Whoever takes up arms against his lord by that very fact forfeits his fief.' Having spoken thus, and before battle was joined, and in response to his knights' demands, Ralph spurred his horse into a gallop and headed straight for the Duke, ordering his men not to follow him. Pulling up before him, he struck the Bastard lightly with his glove and cried out, laughingly, 'Thus have I kept my word! I promised to strike you and it is done. I am not foresworn. Take no offence at my gesture.' So saying, he turned and rode back and, with his men, left the field of battle. He remained uninvolved until near the end when victory for William was assured, and then threw the weight of his strength in on William's side.

This comedy by means of which Ralph avoided the fulfilment of his oath was by no means unusual in that age and other examples are easily found. Later versions of the event were embellished. Ralph was said to have cried out, as he approached, 'Toirie!' or 'Turie!', seen by some as an invocation of the Scandinavian god Thor, that is, 'Thor aie!' or Thor aid me! But Ralph had no Scandinavian ancestry.

A more prosaic explanation is that he was using the name of his chief residence, 'Thury!'.

His defection was a bad blow for the rebels but they nonetheless joined battle. Nigel and his men cried 'Saint Sauveur!', the name of the church close to the vicomte's castle. Haimo le Dentu cried 'Saint Amand!' (near Torigny) and Renouf de Briquessart invoked Saint Sever, patron of a monastery near the River Vire. The French naturally rallied to the cries of 'Montjoie!' and 'Saint Denis!' and the Normans as was their custom cried 'Deus Aie!', that is 'God be our aid!'[5]

The struggle lasted only a few hours and Wace records only the bare outlines. Nothing is recorded about tactics used by either side nor about the part played by the infantry except that one of Nigel's infantrymen unhorsed King Henry, who was saved only by the strength of his hauberk, a feat which stuck in men's minds. It provoked the telling rhyme

> From the Cotentin there came the lance
> which then knocked down the King of France.[6]

Henry no doubt would have preferred to have it forgotten.

Haimo le Dentu was killed by a Frenchman and his body was found stretched out on his shield. William himself led his men with reckless bravery. He entered the battle trying to seek out one of his mortal enemies, Renouf de Briquessart, the perjured vicomte. In particular, William encountered a knight from Bayeux, by the name of Hardrez, known among the militia of de Briquessart for his strength and audacity, and struck him such a blow with his sword that he pierced his neck 'between throat and chin'. The Count of St Pol, King Henry's brother, and his French contingent then counter-attacked, killing all those who had dared attack their lord.

In the end the tide of battle turned against the rebels to the advantage of the French and Normans. Fear spread among the rebels and there were more defections. William came across Renouf and he, overcome by panic, fled, throwing away his lance and shield. The more cowardly of his men followed suit, pursued by William and his Normans. Of the leaders of the conspiracy only Nigel remained, fighting on furiously as befitted his cognomen of Falconhead. Had his companions shown the same bravery, the French would have paid dearly for their intervention. The losses of the rebels grew and their adversaries pressed harder and harder. At last Nigel in his turn gave up the struggle. The rebels fled in disorder, hoping to cross the Orne and take refuge in the Bessin region, pursued and harassed by the French and by William's men. There was a good crossing point on the Orne between Fleury-sur-Orne and Saint-Martin-de-Fontenay, the ford of Athis. There the fleeing men pushed and jostled one another and a number of them were drowned, their bodies choking a nearby millrace, that of the mill of Barbeillon.

Wace says nothing of the part played in the battle by Grimoult du Plessis but he afterwards fled south-west, hoping to take refuge in his castle. Local traditions and place names still bear witness to his flight and the pursuit undertaken by his enemies. Near Caumont-sur-Orne, where Grimoult crossed the river, stands the Chapel of Notre Dame de Bonne-Nouvelle so called because the knights cried 'Good News' when told by local peasants that Grimoult had passed that way. He was caught before he reached safety. He was then imprisoned at Rouen, iron chains on his feet, where he shortly afterwards was found dead on the same day that one of the knights, Sall de Lingèvres, was due to attempt to vindicate du Plessis by trial by battle, as he had requested. Of all the defeated rebels Grimoult du Plessis was the only one punished in body. William, in what looks like an act of penance, distributed du Plessis' property to the Church. Nigel of Saint Sauveur lost his fiefs, was banished and took refuge in Brittany. Nothing is known of the immediate fate of the others, especially Renouf de Briquessart, but a few years later they were appending their names to ducal charters, so it seems that they were relatively soon restored to favour. As for the prime mover of the conspiracy, Guy of Brionne, Wace records nothing of his part in the battle. Guy was certainly present, and while most of those who fled went west or south-west, Guy chose to make for his castle of Brionne.

It was he whom William chose to pursue, but Guy, though wounded during the battle, managed to regain his castle without being caught. Brionne stands on the Risle (though the keep which stands there at present was only built in the twelfth century). The fortress was protected by stone walls and situated on an island which divided the two arms of the Risle. William of Poitiers reports that it was considered to be impregnable as neither of the arms of the river could easily be crossed except by boat as there was no ford.

William decided to blockade the castle by constructing siege works upstream, above the island, and downstream on both banks of the

Risle. The siege was long drawn out, perhaps for as much as three years, before Guy was prevailed upon to surrender. The Duke then offered him a pardon on condition that the castle was pulled down, promising to receive his rebel cousin at Court. This magnanimous offer was (as William perhaps expected) contemptuously rejected, Guy probably knowing quite well that he would never really be accepted in Normandy as a member of the ducal entourage. He retired to his native Burgundy.

Remarkably, both contemporary historians of the period, William of Jumièges and William of Poitiers, as well as Wace 120 years later, report the political effects of the victory at Val-ès-Dunes in similar terms. William of Jumièges rejoices: 'Happy was the battle that in one day made so many castles collapse, the haunt of troublemakers and criminals.' He implies that the battle led to the surrender and/or dismantling of the castles of the rebels.

Contemporary accounts record the destruction of castles that had over several decades been built by insubordinate vassals, and the sources unanimously attribute this to the effects of the victory. When William of Jumièges wished to evoke the troubles of 1037–42, he recorded how, while William was still a child, many Normans betrayed their fealty and built fortifications of earth (motte-and-bailey castles), which became secure hideouts. These were unauthorised castles (later called 'adulterine') and were a sign of their builders' desire to free themselves from ducal authority. So the victory at Val-ès-Dunes held back the wave of insubordination of which the building of castles was the insolent symbol as well as a means of military opposition. Nonetheless, barons rushed to renew their oaths of fealty, though some were required to surrender hostages to the Duke.

William now appeared, at least in theory, to have achieved real power over a class of lords who were now too divided to risk further rebellions. But there were troubles still to come though these were not connected to this particular rebellion. William was careful to deal with the merchants at Rouen. He chastised them and reduced their privileges, believing that they had contributed at least a little to the threat against him. The international situation, as one might describe it, was largely favourable to William. Count Baldwin of Flanders was at war with the German Emperor, and a dynastic struggle agitated Brittany where Duke Conan's tutor had taken over the government. The people of Rennes had freed Conan by force of arms but civil war among the clans continued and was to last for at least fifteen years.

The Duke now showed a degree of political acumen beyond his years and rare among princes in the eleventh century. He left Renouf de Briquessart and other refugees to themselves and returned to Caen. William of Poitiers was to boast, 'The Normans, feeling themselves mastered, all bowed their necks before their lord.' Yet the battle, decisive though it was, had been won by the King of France. William's power remained as it had been, precarious and limited.

In addition, the period immediately following the battle saw the rise of the power of Anjou. The expansion of Anjou had hitherto been southwards, at the expense of the Counts of Blois, allowing Anjou to hold the key to the Loire valley. The Count, Geoffrey Martel, now reaped the benefit of the achievements of his predecessors and by striving to push northwards became a formidable menace to Duke William. In the course of their struggle, one family, that of Bellême, could not be ignored, as it held the key to essential lines of communication.

After the Battle of Val-ès-Dunes order returned to Normandy though civil peace was not yet firmly established. The true architect of the victory had been King Henry I of France, though to William's biographers it was the young Bastard who was 'chief of the avenging host'. But the Duke at the time simply endeavoured to seize the opportunity presented to him by his overlord. Apparently aware of the more long-term implications of his situation, he preferred diplomacy to revenge, leaving Renouf de Briquessart and other refugees to allow the impact of their defeat to sink in.

5

THE DEFEAT OF THE RICHARDIDES

Returning to Caen, having left forces around Brionne to confine Guy of Burgundy and prevent any further action on his part, the Duke, realising perhaps the limitations of his unsupported ducal authority (which had required the intervention of King Henry to restore it) and possibly remembering the initiative of the Peace of God taken by Archbishop Mauger in 1042,[1] convoked an assembly of ecclesiastical vassals, supported by the presence of lay magnates. This was a few weeks after the battle and the Council met at Vaucelles near Caen where it proceeded, after much debate, to proclaim the 'Treuga Dei' or Truce of God, in the name of the Church and, significantly, of the Duke. William had taken a calculated risk in summoning the bishops, since a number of them were themselves Richardides who had thought little good could come from intervention by the Church. But in the new atmosphere created by the victory, the idea of a Truce of God was accepted.

The lords who were present were required to swear solemnly to observe it, on the relics of saints brought especially for this occasion from many churches. William had most likely chosen to hold the Council in Lower Normandy in order to strengthen his hold on it. The relics were displayed for veneration in the church of Rots and the procession which carried them there was interrupted halfway on its journey by messengers sent by the Duke. He made it clear that he wished to carry the relics the rest of the way on his own shoulders, so demonstrating his own piety.

It is odd that neither William of Jumièges nor William of Poitiers makes any reference to the Council. Knowledge of it is derived entirely from hagiographical works, such as saints' lives, which discuss the reasons for the movement of the relics of Saint Ouen to Caen. There are manuscripts that talk about the 'Synodal Decree of peace commonly called the Truce of God instituted by Duke William and the Bishops of Normandy'.[2]

The Council is further dated by a curious incident concerning a local priest. He had brought some flax to sell at a fair. But his flax was stolen and then recovered when the robber was – miraculously – identified at the chapel where the relics were on display. The fair in question was that held at Saint-Denis in 1047.

The Dukes of Normandy had, of course, claimed the right to maintain public peace as part of their singular prerogative, but the power to do so had been weakened by Duke Robert's astonishing decision to abdicate and go on pilgrimage, leaving the duchy to be ruled by a nominated group of guardians on behalf of his young son.

Among the leading figures at the Council were William's cousin, Nicholas, Abbot of St Ouen (son of Duke Richard III), and Archbishop Mauger. Both men were well aware of the preaching of the 'Peace of God' by the charismatic Richard of Saint-Vanne. Mauger also knew that his church, the Archbishopric of Rouen, was the only one with sufficient prestige to tackle the difficulty presented by endemic private warfare with any chance of success. The wily Archbishop naturally tried to turn the situation to his own advantage by seizing the initiative, demanding that the Council should decree the Truce of God in the Duke's name since that would make it obligatory.

The Truce of God had originated out of the Peace of God movement, which had come principally from the great reforming Abbey of Cluny towards the end of the tenth century. That had been intended to bind warriors to a code of conduct that would protect certain classes of unarmed persons from the violence of private warfare, protecting clergy, the peasantry and merchants. It was to be effective during Holy Week and during periods of penance such as Advent and Lent.

The Truce of God went much further than the Peace. It forbade, under penalty of excommunication, all military action from Wednesday evening until Monday morning from the beginning of Advent until the Octave of the Epiphany (13 January) and from the beginning of Lent (Ash Wednesday) until the Octave of Easter. It also covered the period from Rogation Week (during which penitential litanies are sung), which is the week before Ascension Day, to the Octave of Pentecost.

Excommunication, which cut a man off from all Church services and the Sacraments, was the main ecclesiastical penalty for breaking the Truce and the secular penalties included banishment for up to thirty years. A man who had not completed his period of exile could be refused Christian burial. There were penalties for offences against property which were less severe, such as compensation for the injured party. Merchants and foreigners were to be specially protected, matters which were the concern of public peace rather than the Truce itself. Public peace was also strengthened by the extension throughout Normandy of the edict of 'Couvre Feu', later introduced into England as the curfew. Priests were expected to pray for the observance of the Truce at all Sunday Masses and on all feast days, and there were curses (anathemas) placed on those who broke the Truce. If anyone claimed that his offence was not intentional he had to prove it on oath and by ordeal of red-hot iron,[3] which was believed to put the matter of guilt or innocence in God's hands when men were unable to discover the truth. Taking the ordeal tested the sincerity of the oath and there was a penalty of seven years' penance if guilt was established.[4]

But the real political importance of the Truce lay in the fact that the Church's legislation did not bind the Duke himself, who could employ force against malefactors at any time of the year. He became, in effect, the supreme maintainer of Law and Order, a power usually found in the hands of kings. It was a calculated risk for the Church to sanction this, but the Norman clergy really had no option but to put their trust in the Duke. The decree of 1047 was reiterated twice before 1066, in 1061 and 1064, and the Truce became the fundamental legal basis for a Paix Normande (or Pax Normanica).

The Duke could pursue offenders and abandon them to the judgement of the tribunals of the Church. This suggests that in 1047 William was prepared to accept, or even was convinced of, the superiority of ecclesiastical jurisdiction. This worked, in practice, as long as he retained the appointment of bishops in his own hands, allowing him to favour the extension of ecclesiastical competence throughout his reign. Thus the Church filled the gap left by the absence of a ducal power of legislation. But the day was to come when he found the judgements of the Church too lenient and he began to summon cases before his own ducal Court where he could impose harsher penalties.

William's experiences during his minority, the terror and anguish at witnessing the murder of the Steward Osbern and his wandering life necessitated by the need to escape mortal danger, had taught him to judge men and discern their intentions towards him. It had certainly bred in him a degree of courage and boldness, even bordering on recklessness (as when he plunged into the heart of the mêlée at Val-ès-Dunes). What in a young man had seemed thoughtless impetuosity became shrewd political prudence. Witness his lenience towards Guy of Burgundy and both de Briquessart and Saint-Sauveur. The latter was only exiled for a few years and both vicomtes were restored to favour by 1054.

The Truce enabled William to guarantee normal economic and social life and the functioning of most institutions during most of the year. Both the peasants and the merchant class benefited from this as well as the Duke. But it did risk creating confusion between the domain of the Church and that of lay authority. The idea of warfare as a permanent right inherent in lordship did not disappear and was to persist into the twelfth and thirteenth centuries.

The Duke's final act in 1047 was to build a chapel to house the relics used in the ceremony. It was on the banks of the Orne on the outskirts of Caen and was known as All Saints and Holy Peace. He had now seen the need for a focal point for ducal authority in Lower Normandy, a political and military rallying point. For this, Caen, situated in the valley of the Orne, was the logical choice. Major trade routes led to it, from the south through the Loire valley on to Argentan, Alençon, Le Mans and Tours and north to the Cotentin, the valley of the Seine and Upper Normandy; a crossroads of strategic value. Although sources claim that William installed a formidable row of fortifications along his frontiers to protect the Norman people,[5] the truth was otherwise. Had he concentrated only on the frontiers, he would have left the interior devoid of protection, so, to fill the void, he developed Caen. In doing so, he followed the example of Baldwin of Flanders, who, faced with a similar problem, had created Lille at about the same time, or a little earlier than, William built up Caen.

Private warfare was reduced and became regarded as antisocial but could not be entirely eliminated. The Duke gradually limited its range during the times of the year when it was not actually forbidden. He banned the holding of prisoners to ransom, the robbery of defeated enemies, the burning of houses and mills and all general plundering.

Disputes that might be expected to be settled in the ducal court could always give rise to private warfare. Lords could expect their men to fight for them or perform castle guard on occasions such as 'if the lord shall have war in respect of the land … given to him with his wife' as William Paganel was to record in a charter.

On coming to independent power, William had found himself surrounded by a number of strong comital families, which were, without any exceptions, all linked to the ducal house itself. The first to have been so styled had been Rodulf of Ivry, a half-brother of Duke Richard I around AD 1000. After that, there came that Duke's sons, who received the Counties (Comtés) of Évreux, Brionne and Eu. This custom had been extended after 1027 into Lower Normandy. By the reign of Duke Robert, a son of Richard II, namely William, Count of Arques, occupied the territory called the Pays de Talou. It was from this man that trouble was now to arise.

In the immediate aftermath of victory, if William of Poitiers is to be believed, the barons began to put pressure on William to marry. That would have been because they saw the need to ensure the continuation of his dynasty. But it was the very nature of William's marriage that was to cause serious dissension, and it could be that the prospect of the continuation of the dynasty was not universally welcomed by the Richardides. It was discussed in or shortly before 1049 and, according to the *Chronicle of Tours*,[6] Baldwin V of Flanders, married to King Henry's sister, had given support to the young Duke, fearing that the anarchy in Normandy might spread to his own county. It is possible that the project of a marriage between William and Baldwin's daughter Matilda arose at this time.

The only certainty is that the marriage had not taken place before Pope Leo IX, at the Council of Rheims, had forbidden it, ordering Count Baldwin not to give his daughter in marriage to the Duke. The Pope had dealt with other lords guilty of marrying within the forbidden degrees, Counts Ingleran of Ponthieu and Eustace of Boulogne, and condemned Hugh of Brionne for repudiating his wife. No overt reason was provided for the banning of William's marriage though it is probable that this was on the grounds of a too close family relationship.

The ban indicates that William's intention to marry was well advanced by the autumn of 1049 and perhaps even that there had already been a betrothal.[7] The reason for the ban might have been clear enough in the eleventh century but Church Law has changed since then and it is now very difficult to identify the reason for it. In that century it was forbidden to marry within the seventh degree of relationship and remained so until the Lateran Council of 1139 changed it to the fourth degree.

As for the marriage itself, it remains unclear which party took the initiative. William of Poitiers, following his usual policy of enhancing the Duke's career, attributes the first move to Duke William. He says that the Duke had learned that Baldwin had a daughter noble in spirit and of royal descent who was strong in body. Where else could William have learned this than from the Count himself? William is then said to have asked for her hand in marriage.

Despite the papal ban, William, probably towards the end of 1051 or early 1052, went ahead with the marriage.[8] Count Baldwin brought his daughter to the Norman frontier, to Eu, and the couple were married attended by a great company of knights. But there were none of the usual public festivities and none of the great lords were in attendance. The Richardides kept their distance, but they were hostile anyway. There is no mention of the presence even of Robert of Eu, whose castle was used. It was William's mother, Herleva of Conteville, and her husband Herluin who acted as hosts. That might explain the absence of the Richardides, who lost no opportunity to show their disdain for Herleva. It was, one might say, 'a quiet wedding'.

The cause of the trouble lay in the history of the papacy in the mid-eleventh century. This precise period saw the beginning of the reform and revival of the prestige of the popes, which parallels the rise of Normandy. As it began to reassert its authority, Rome had need of support in Italy itself in order to free itself first from the influence of the local Roman nobility, which had been controlling the election of popes for some considerable time, and then from reliance on the support of the German emperors. They turned to the Normans of Southern Italy (many of whom had been driven out of or were exiled from Normandy between 1036 and 1042) as a result of William's success in 1047.

On 12 February 1049 Bruno of Toul became Pope Leo IX, put into office by the German Emperor, Henry III, and supported by reformers, especially the powerful Cardinal Humbert of Moyenmoutier. Leo promptly held a synod during which he condemned simony,[9] deposing several bishops judged guilty of it. He moved the Papal Court onto French territory and held a synod at

Rheims (3 and 4 October 1049) attended by some seventy bishops, including several from Normandy; Hugh of Avranches, Geoffrey of Coutances, Yves of Sées, Hugh of Bayeux and Herbert of Lisieux as well as Lanfranc, Prior of the Abbey of Bec. Archbishop Mauger, quite deliberately, in fear of being disciplined, refused to attend.

Simony was again condemned and several bishops were disciplined for falling under suspicion of it, one of whom, Geoffrey de Mowbray of Coutances, was able to clear himself of the charge. But more importantly, as far as Duke William was concerned, the synod issued decrees concerning matrimony, including decrees against incest (marrying within the forbidden degrees of kinship) and abandoning an existing spouse in order to marry another. Count Baldwin was instructed not to permit the marriage of his daughter Matilda to William of Normandy, though no grounds for this were given.

Historians have debated the possible basis of the decree. One argument advanced is that, as William and Matilda were both descendants of Rollo of Normandy, they were cousins of the fifth degree. But the descent is questionable. Also, it is probable that Rome was not aware of it. It is argued by some that it was because Richard II's daughter, Eleanor, had married Baldwin IV of Flanders. But, Baldwin V, the father of Matilda, was not the offspring of that marriage but of a prior union with the Anglo-Saxon Princess Aelfgiva (a descendant of Alfred the Great), so there was no actual consanguinity. But it did create an affinity[10] between Matilda and William and such links were taken seriously. An alternative argument claims that William and Matilda were cousins in the third degree, through the marriage of William's uncle, Richard II, to Adèle of France; but that marriage was never consummated either. Nonetheless, that marriage had created a relationship of affinity between William and Matilda which, if strictly interpreted, did pose an obstacle to their marriage, possibly requiring a Papal Dispensation. It remains uncertain whether any of this created the obstacle. Certainly a dispensation could easily be given if it were, unless politics dictated otherwise.[11]

But Canon Law in the eleventh century was not always rigorously applied unless the Church had other reasons for wishing to forbid a marriage and refuse a dispensation. Nor were churchmen often in a position to act against men like William. Norman sources make no reference to any grounds in Canon Law for the ban. This suggests that there were, in addition to an affinity, other grounds, possibly political, for the papal veto. The fact is that Leo IX still needed the support of the German Emperor in order to carry out his programme of reform.

But in 1049 Henry III of Germany was in conflict with Baldwin V; it was a dispute over territory, the location of the border between the Empire and Flanders. Lands east of the Scheldt were in dispute and, in 1047, Baldwin had burnt the palace of Nijmegen. The *Anglo-Saxon Chronicle* and Florence of Worcester record how King Edward the Confessor acted in support of the Emperor, blockading with his fleet the Flemish ports, and they report the presence of Pope Leo with the Imperial forces during 1049. The Pope is known to have held a synod at Mayence where he met the Emperor. So he was certainly between a rock and a hard place and simply could not have consented to a marriage alliance between Flanders and Normandy! He could not afford to damage the Emperor's authority and was in any case hostile towards Norman activity in southern Italy.

William could, especially when faced with papal opposition, have found a wife elsewhere among the daughters of counts of more remote countries, but clearly preferred to seek one close at hand. An alliance with Flanders certainly strengthened Normandy's position and was to prove extremely useful. Both Normandy and Flanders faced a similar political situation. Count Baldwin is known to have sought a marriage alliance with the Godwinesons (Earl Tostig married Judith of Flanders in the autumn of 1051) and both Flanders and Normandy had commercial links with England and were rivals for trade with London. But King Edward had supported the Emperor against Baldwin and that could explain the Count's desire for a Norman alliance.

Better still, Matilda was the niece of King Henry I, William's overlord to whom he had turned in 1047 and whose aid he still needed to protect his frontiers. But none of this was of any help in dealing with the Pope, who was a German and an Imperial supporter. King Henry himself was unpopular at Rome, for ignoring the decrees of Rheims. The King was said to have been more simoniac than Simon Magus himself![12] But the Norman attitude to all this remains unknown, William of Poitiers remains silent and discreet and other writers preserve an embarrassed silence. If William had hoped for the support of the Norman bishops who had attended the synod, there is no sign that he got any. Archbishop Mauger, who had discreetly held his own synod at which simony was condemned, seems to have tacitly approved of the papal ban on the marriage, which might explain the Duke's hostility towards him. Lanfranc, an authority on Canon Law, also agreed with the ban.

Of Matilda herself surprisingly little is known. Sources record only the conventional praise for her beauty and grace and she was said to have been stout and majestic in bearing. The eighteenth-century paintings in the Abbaye-aux-Hommes reflect this description. Her tomb, in the Abbaye-aux-Dames, was opened in 1512 and again during the French Revolution. A surgeon of Caen made an inventory of the contents in 1819, making an 'anthropological' examination. He reckoned she was less than 1 metre 50 centimetres tall, that is about 4 foot 11 inches.

Various legends gathered around Matilda in later years. One alleges that on being told that she was to marry a Norman she had refused to do so, insisting vehemently that she had no wish to marry a bastard! William is said to have been told of this and to have immediately hurried off to Flanders where he brutally assaulted the young woman, throwing her to the ground, cutting her with his spurs. This violent wooing naturally overcame her reluctance and she agreed to marry him! This was one of the thirteenth-century fables possibly created as an anti-Norman satire. Contemporary sources paint a picture of their mutual respect and affection for each other.

So the Bastard and the Count ignored the papal ban, as they needed to consolidate their authority and make rival rulers fear them. The impact appears to have been minimal. No Norman writer even mentions the Pope's reaction to the marriage. Only Orderic Vitalis, in his additions to the text of William of Jumièges, claims that Norman clerics reproved William for marrying his 'cousin', and that he sent envoys to Rome to seek papal advice. Orderic maintains that the Pope, aware that to order a separation would cause a breach between Normandy and Flanders, chose to grant a dispensation, absolving the couple for their fault and imposing a penance. He does not name the Pope involved. If this did happen, then the building of the two abbeys at Caen was thought to be in fulfilment of the penance. More reliably, as William of Jumièges testifies, Pope Nicholas II recognised the marriage, requiring only that William and Matilda build four hospices for the poor at Rouen, Caen, Bayeux and Cherbourg.[13]

A more detailed story emerged in about 1130. Milo Crespin, Abbot of Le Bec, came up with the assertion that Normandy had been placed under Interdict[14] and William himself was excommunicated.

This remained in force, it was said, until 1059, when Lanfranc obtained the lifting of the Interdict and excommunication from Pope Nicholas II, on condition of the building of the two abbeys. But the story is very late, recorded seventy-five years after the event, and lacks any contemporary corroboration. Scholars remain sceptical about its truth. If there had been an Interdict, then the Norman bishops would seem to have ignored it. The two abbeys were certainly built, which suggests the possibility that this was a penitential act, but there is no direct evidence to prove it had anything to do with an Interdict, let alone an excommunication (which no other source mentions). The story might reflect tradition at Bec, where Lanfranc had been Prior, so there could be an element of truth in the story. But in the absence of corroboration, it remains doubtful.

The marriage did give rise to tension between Rome and Normandy but there is no evidence of a complete break. Abbot John of Fécamp, for instance, visited Rome in the early 1050s, as his letter to the Pope proves, though it does not explain the reason for his visit.[15] There is no sign of any answer to the letter. Shortly afterwards the Pope moved against the Normans in Southern Italy and was defeated at Civitate in 1053, becoming a prisoner for six months.

As a result there were negotiations and a settlement was arrived at; Leo pardoned the Normans and blessed them, recognising their possession of the lands they had conquered. What more natural consequence could there have been than to drop his objection to the Duke's marriage? William himself had up to then ignored the ban, knowing that Leo was fully preoccupied with the Norman problem in the south and unable to do anything to enforce his ban. He could not have taken action against William while seeking an agreement with his Norman captors.

The Duke's case had probably been consistently raised at the Papal Court which was visited by prominent Norman clerics. In the years after 1053 relations with Rome do seem to have been normalised. They never seem to have been that bad, both Lanfranc and Bishop Geoffrey of Coutances visited Rome in 1050. In 1055 the Norman Bishops held a synod at Lisieux, over which the Duke presided, and Victor II, Leo's successor, sent his Legate, Ermenfrid of Sion-en-Valais. This demonstrates that there was no Interdict in force in 1055.

William also appears to have had supporters among the Normans in Italy, who could well have been able to see to it that he was not subjected to the kind of sanctions applied to other princes. There were also connections with ecclesiastics in northern Italy, from which had come William of Volpiano and his nephew John of Ravenna. Suppo, Abbot of Mont-Saint-Michel had come from northern Italy, as, of course, had Lanfranc (from Pavia).

It does look as though the couple had escaped any real sanctions under Leo IX. But, in 1058, the more rigorous Nicholas II became Pope, a man closer to the position of the quarrelsome Cardinal Humbert than to the more moderate Cardinal Peter Damian. Nicholas broke with the anti-Norman policies of his predecessors, forging a Concordat with them in 1059 and legitimising their conquests. He styled them Protectors of the Holy See. It could be that as a result the question of the validity of the Duke's marriage was formally concluded and that Nicholas extracted the promise to build the two abbeys as the price. That could have been either at the Lateran Council of 1059, or during 1060.

During this whole period, from 1047 onwards, Duke William had found himself concerned with settling the problem of the Richardides. The causes of their hostility towards William are not readily discerned. He was, after all, a Richardide himself, which ought to have given him access to the solidarity of those of the same lineage. Nor was his bastardy a real problem since many of the Richardides were also illegitimate or descended from others who were bastards. That could only have been a pretext. William had, of course, on coming to power, placed great confidence in members of his mother's family, especially his half-brothers. He had raised Odo of Conteville to the bishopric of Bayeux on the death of Hugh d'Ivry in 1049, a move which indicates a preference for close relatives and possibly a lack of confidence in any Richardide candidates. Most of the Comtés were still in the hands of Richardides, promoted as trustworthy by previous dukes, but William of Jumièges nonetheless hints at their systematic hostility to Duke William. That created a dangerous situation since the Counts were responsible for the protection of Normandy's frontiers.

A serious confrontation came in 1050 with William Warlenc, Count of Arromanches and a great grandson of Richard I. A young knight of his, Roger Bigot by name, came to see the Duke. Like many young men of aristocratic lineage, he despaired of ever gaining land and power. He told the Duke that, as he wished to go to Italy, to seek fame and fortune, he had approached his lord, William Warlenc, seeking his permission. The count had wanted to know what on earth had put such an idea into his head and, when told by Roger that it was because of his own poverty, told the young man that if he believed in him, his lord, he should stay in Normandy because within eighty days there would arise in Normandy a movement as a result of which he would be able to put his hand with impunity upon everything he could desire.

Shortly after that, on the recommendation of some of his relatives, Roger had entered the Duke's service and he now told him the content of his conversation with the Count. William promptly called the Count to him and demanded to know the meaning of this extraordinary statement, but he was unable to furnish a convincing explanation. William immediately accused the Count of having broken the peace by fomenting sedition. He exclaimed that it was a case of treachery, aimed at deposing him, the Duke, and that the Count had offered hope to his poor knight by holding out to him the prospect of ill-gotten gains from pillage and robbery. 'Nonetheless,' said the Duke, 'with the help of God, peace will be maintained! As for you, you must leave the country and never return while I live!'

William Warlenc was accordingly dismissed from office, his fiefs were forfeited, and he was condemned to a miserable life in exile at Pouille with the company of a single squire. The Duke then gave the Comté to his other half-brother, Robert, with the title of Count of Mortain. So yet another member of William's family had replaced a Richardide. The rest of the lands of the Comté of Arromanches were placed under a vicomte.

It remains quite impossible to show that there had ever been a real conspiracy and no other direct evidence has survived to prove that there was one. The sentence of exile was much resented and held to have been far too severe for a careless pledge.[16] William of Poitiers has no record of it. Orderic Vitalis makes a brief reference to it: 'for a single remark the duke dispossessed William Warlenc the Count of Mortain'. The dismissal was one of the grievances brought up against William by those involved in the 'Revolt of the Earls' in 1075. It remained a long-lasting stain on William's reputation as far as his enemies were concerned.

The appointment of his half-brother Robert to Mortain, a remarkable promotion, struck contemporaries as at least unfortunate and could have made many conclude that William was following an anti-Richardide policy. Orderic Vitalis was to comment some sixty years later that William had harshly humiliated his father's proud relatives while 'elevating with signal honours the modest family of his mother'. But at the time no one dared say so openly. The policy seems an obvious one; William was putting comital power into the hands of those he felt he could trust and the removal of William Warlenc was essentially the naked exercise of arbitrary power to this end.

Orderic was, in his interpolations into the text of William of Jumièges, deliberately compensating for that writer's calculated discretion. So it is Orderic who records the treatment meted out to William Busac, Count of Eu, another Richardide, grandson of Richard I and uncle to the Bastard. He was accused of aiming to snatch power out of his nephew's hands and reported to have made threats, conduct which repeatedly provoked Duke William to anger.

William Busac's grievance is alleged to have arisen from Duke William's treatment of his mother, Lesceline, widow of William of Eu, son of Richard II. He had expelled her, and her sons, from Eu (they took refuge at Rouen in the abbey of La Trinité-du-Mont). William Busac then seized the opportunity in 1052, in either summer or autumn, to return secretly to Eu. According to William of Poitiers, he then proclaimed himself Duke of Normandy.

Corroborative evidence for his alleged treason is lacking, as in the case of William Warlenc. Nonetheless, the Bastard took action against him, laying siege to his castle of Eu and forcing him to surrender. He was then exiled. The use of exile as a punishment for rebels was increasingly common among rising Scandinavian monarchies[17] (and was the usual policy in England) and it now became a formidable weapon in the hands of the duke.

William Busac took refuge at the French Court where he was well received and granted the Comté of Soissons. He could well have worked on King Henry to turn him against his Norman vassal. The Duke took care not to further offend the wider ducal kin by transferring Eu not, this time, to a member of his mother's family, but to William Busac's brother Robert who signed as count in a charter of 1051. Robert of Eu was to turn out to be a faithful adherent of the Duke, and his possessions remained the property of his descendants. The third brother, Hugh, was made Bishop of Lisieux, and it was his servant, the Archdeacon of Lisieux, William of Poitiers, who became a ducal chaplain and wrote the *Gesta Guillelmi*.

It is William of Poitiers who provides a full account of the Duke's dealings with Count William of Arques, taking great pleasure in blackening the Count's reputation. This man had been Count of Talou (Pays de Caux) since 1038 and had constructed a formidable castle on the confluence of the rivers Varenne and Béthune. This had a great wall

of stone flanked by many towers, which could be entered only at ground
level through a tower gatehouse. This great work stressed the wealth and
power of his family, and housed a formidable military household. William
of Talou then chose to name himself Arques, the name of his new castle.

Archdeacon William attacks the Count, calling him chief
orchestrator of opposition to the Duke, acting both openly and in a
covert manner to unite the Richardides against him. He is reviled as
the cowardly and perfidious offshoot of an illustrious clan who could
not be restrained by any law, human or divine. William of Poitiers
was, of course, a master of invective.

William of Poitiers further accuses William of Arques of defying
ducal prerogative by denying the Duke William entry to the castle
of Arques and refusing to perform service owed to the ducal army.
He boasts that the Duke, had he not been fully engaged in other
matters, would have dealt with this defiance when it first occurred.
He says this because it was not until 1052 that William took action
against the Count by seizing the castle of Arques and installing in it
his own garrison. William was hostile towards the Count because,
as William of Poitiers asserts, he had deserted William's army at a
critical moment in the siege of Domfront.

Technically, Duke William had been within his rights to do this
because Arques was not an inherited benefice but a fief granted to
William of Arques in virtue of his office as count. But the Count
responded by winning over the garrison so that it allowed him to
reoccupy the castle. He then made preparations to face a long siege.

The Bastard's response was prompt. He came directly to Arques,
though accompanied by only a handful of men, riding so swiftly that
most of the horses collapsed. He crossed the Seine, entered the Pays
de Caux and swiftly sized up the situation. The local population had
been panicked by the garrison's defection from ducal service and
treachery was feared from all sides. A troop of 300 knights from
Rouen had decided to oppose the Count's action but, on reaching
Arques and being confronted with its grandeur, their nerve failed at
the prospect of taking on a garrison of a thousand men.

William of Arques seized the opportunity to make a sortie against
them, but, on realising that the Duke himself had arrived, hastily
retreated within the walls and closed the gates. All this comes from
William of Poitiers' vivid narrative.

Duke William is then reported to have surrounded the castle,
intending to take it by storm. But, on finding that it stood at the

crest of a steep slope, decided against a direct attack. The ramparts could only be reached from one side, that defended by the gate tower, which seemed impregnable. William therefore settled down for a siege. He set up a siege tower to prevent the defenders of the castle from receiving either supplies or reinforcements and then, satisfied with his arrangements, withdrew.

He had learned that King Henry I had allied himself with the Count and was approaching at the head of a relief column. That does look like a prearranged move. The Duke moved part of his force to Saint-Aubin-le-Cauf, which he made his base camp. He had insufficient forces at his disposal to consider engaging the King in a pitched battle and so resorted to a series of ambushes by small groups of men, harassing the French column. That did not work. The royal army withstood the attacks and repelled them, killing the commanders of several of these attacking groups, most notably Enguerrand II, Count of Ponthieu. It was now the end of October 1053.

In the confusion following the defeat of the Duke's attacks, Henry forced his way through and entered the castle. Having delivered reinforcements and supplies, Henry, satisfied that he had achieved his major objective and not bothering to attack the besiegers in force, was then compelled to withdraw. Duke William, learning of this, took charge of the siege in person, camping directly below the walls. The siege continued, and in January 1054, William of Arques finally ran out of supplies and had to surrender. His garrison and the French reinforcements were in a distressed condition and William of Poitiers gloats over the 'sad spectacle' they provided and their 'lamentable end'. Once more the Bastard had seen off a serious threat to his authority, but it had come from the highest level of Norman society and the King of France had meddled in Norman affairs. The siege had been a long one and had cost many lives. But the fortress of Arques, so essential to the governance of Upper Normandy, was now in William's hands.

William now acted as he had done in the case of Guy of Burgundy. He offered his uncle an honourable settlement; he could remain in Normandy and enjoy his vast possessions provided he resigned his Comté. If he did so he would not be exiled. But the Count was a stiff-necked, proud man so he refused, preferring exile and taking up residence with Count Eustace of Boulogne.

King Henry's intervention had poisoned relations between Normandy and France, increasing Norman dislike and distrust of the French. But the Bastard now seemed to have dealt the final blow to Richardide opposition, with the sole exception of Archbishop Mauger. He too was a son of Richard II, like William of Arques, and his enmity towards Duke William was well known. He had given no help in the matter of the Duke's marriage and could well have been one of those who adopted a rigorous interpretation of the canons regarding marriage. If so, then it had been opportunism rather than principle since Mauger himself was no model prelate. He is accused of avarice and of misappropriating the revenues of his church to fund a luxurious lifestyle. Duke William was said to have rebuked him repeatedly, both publicly and in private, to no avail.

Mauger had been rather casual in his dealings with the papacy, refusing to attend the synod of Rheims, and Leo IX had responded by denying him a pallium. William of Poitiers hints at many other vices but does not specify them, alleging that it was pointless to do so. Wace, a native of Jersey where Mauger spent the last years of his life, is less reticent. He reports that the Archbishop had a liaison with a woman called 'Guisla' (perhaps Gisela) and even had children by her. A legend about the Archbishop accuses him of having dealings with a little demon called 'Toret' whom he could summon at will.

All this laid Mauger open to attack. At the Council of Lisieux in 1055, in the presence of a papal legate, he was condemned as unfit to hold office, deposed, and went to Jersey. The Duke replaced him with Maurilius, Abbot of Fécamp, who had been trained in Italy, at Santa Maria in Florence, and was an advocate of reform from the party of Cardinal Peter Damian. In doing this, the Duke broke with the long-established tradition of giving bishoprics to members of the ducal family without consideration for their spiritual qualities or experience of ecclesiastical life. Maurilius had also contributed to the struggle against the heresy of Berengar of Tours. Duke William was now posing as the champion of orthodoxy and the cause of ecclesiastical reform. This was in sharp contrast to the behaviour of Henry I and Geoffrey Martel of Anjou (the latter had supported Berengar). Normandy was to find itself in conflict with both of these rulers.

The rebellion of William of Arques had been connected with the reconciliation between Henry I and Geoffrey Martel which took place between the capture of Domfront and the battle of Mortemer in 1054. The rebel Count had certainly appealed to the King for help. The rebellion had thus followed on from the dispute between Duke William and Count Geoffrey Martel over Domfront and Alençon, to which attention must now turn.

6

FOREIGN AFFAIRS 1047–1061

In the years following the victory of Val-ès-Dunes in 1047, and while the Duke found himself engaged in an internal struggle against his own powerful relatives, Normandy had also found its frontiers under constant threat. Earlier in the century the threat had come mainly from the south-west but that source had been stabilised. However, there remained one obstacle to stability. Bellême lay between La Perche and the town of Domfront. Its main overlord was the King of France, but Domfront was held as a fief from the Count of Maine while Alençon was held from the Dukes of Normandy. That allowed the lords of Bellême to play one overlord off against another in an effort to secure their own relative independence.

These years were no longer a mere welter of mayhem, as no revolt had any serious effects, but they were nonetheless a period of continuous crisis. William certainly had to secure control of Brionne, and it took him three years. Thus he did not re-enter Rouen until 1050, after he had finally re-imposed his authority on the duchy and defeated Guy of Burgundy. He used most of that time to extend his authority over Lower Normandy.

Since 1030 Bellême had been held by the dreaded William Talvas I. Under him, the lordship had extended its influence over Maine, even influencing the choice of an archbishop for Le Mans, although the nomination was in the hands of the King of France. Through a series of marriage alliances the Talvas family had even extended its influence to the Archbishopric of Tours. Then, in 1050, Mabel, daughter of William Talvas I, had married Roger of Montgomery, a leading supporter of Duke William, a move which signalled that Bellême was moving into the orbit of Normandy, although the then head of the family, Yves, Bishop of Sées, still sided with Geoffrey of Anjou. It was not until much later that Bishop Yves is found witnessing ducal charters in Normandy, evidence of a change of allegiance on his part.

By the 1050s it looked as though a major conflict was looming over Bellême between Normandy, Anjou and Maine. King Henry of France was seeking to maintain the balance of power. Then, possibly towards the end of 1049 or early in 1050, King Henry called upon William as his vassal to render assistance in his operations against Anjou, which was pushing northwards. Maine now became the area at issue but Le Mans, the main town and seat of the bishop, was not finally occupied by Count Geoffrey Martel of Anjou, at the request of the citizens, until 28 March 1051. The Duke, like a dutiful vassal, had broken with Anjou and joined King Henry. Thus he repaid him for his earlier assistance. The King's objective was to take the castle of Mouliherne.[1] Geoffrey Martel had moved into the valleys of the Sarthe and the Loire, so disquieting King Henry, who intervened on behalf of the inhabitants of Mantes.

William of Poitiers, who had studied in Poitou, reports that men often remembered the campaign and especially the part played in it by the Norman contingent. As was his custom, he magnifies the rôle played by his hero Duke William. He boasts of how the King consulted the Duke rather than his other counsellors, and criticises William for his rashness in exposing himself to danger, reporting how he went into battle with just twelve companions, and tells a tale of how the young William and only four companions attacked a group of fifteen enemies. Duke William is said to have driven his lance into one man, throwing him to the ground and breaking his hip, whereupon the other fourteen knights fled! William and his men pursued them and took seven prisoners. From this he got possession of warhorses from the Auvergne and Gascony. William of Poitiers is no doubt exaggerating, yet it is likely that Duke William distinguished himself by his valour in action.

Geoffrey Martel had intervened in person in the conflict, entering Maine in 1051, following the death of Count Hugh IV, and freeing the Bishop of Le Mans, who then took refuge in Normandy. Geoffrey had taken control of Hugh's infant son, handed over to him by Herbert II, who was now claiming to be the heir presumptive. Herbert's son had then been made to do homage to Geoffrey. The Angevin then occupied the castles of Domfront and Alençon and was in a position to threaten Normandy. The men of Alençon had rebelled against Bellême and now sided with Anjou. That Geoffrey did not invade Normandy is probably to be attributed to his wish to control the two buffer zones of Bellême and Maine. He also captured Count Theobald of Blois and occupied Tours.

Geoffrey Martel's growing power on Normandy's southern frontier was now an obvious threat to the young Duke William. It is thus not surprising that he launched a campaign to recover Domfront. The castle was held by a garrison led by one of the escaped rebels defeated at Val-ès-Dunes. The Duke had hoped at first to recapture it by means of a surprise attack, reconnoitring the situation accompanied by a contingent of fifty men. But his move was betrayed to the garrison by one of the great men of Normandy, or so William of Poitiers claims, though he does not name him. It has been argued that he was referring to William of Arques since it is known that Count William left the Duke's camp rather furtively and without permission. If so, it would explain the Bastard's distrust of the Count.

Domfront stood on a rocky escarpment and was enclosed within formidable stone ramparts. It could only be entered through an immensely strong Gate Tower. Unable to take it by surprise, William resorted to a siege. The Normans at this period were well versed in siege warfare and William himself was a capable exponent of it. He surrounded the castle and the town to prevent any relieving force getting through or the defenders getting out. Siege works were constructed, consisting of motte-and-bailey castles positioned to target the fortifications by means of machines termed 'ballistae' which threw heavy rocks at the walls. The siege was maintained from October 1051 through winter into 1052.

Geoffrey Martel attempted to end the conflict by challenging the Duke to single combat and sent his herald to Domfront. Two of William's lieutenants, Roger of Montgomery and William fitzOsbern, were out on patrol and met the herald. They were informed that the Count would arrive early next morning and told exactly what horse and arms and shield he would use! They responded in kind, informing the herald what equipment Duke William would use. But next day, just as he was approaching Domfront, Count Geoffrey was informed that King Henry was approaching Tours at the head of an army, accompanied by the Count of Blois. Geoffrey promptly abandoned his intended challenge, leaving Domfront to its fate and returning to the Loire valley.

Duke William did not find it necessary to remain permanently at Domfront and took the opportunity to launch an attack on Alençon, which is about 45 miles away. He easily covered that distance over a winter's night, only to find that the garrison was on the alert and his ruse had failed. Some inhabitants had occupied one of the towers, from which they had hung the freshly tanned hides of animals, which was often done to protect fortifications from fire. But the Alençonnais insolently beat the skins with sticks, like tanners, and shouted insults at the Duke. Neither William of Jumièges nor William of Poitiers dared record what they said. Even Orderic Vitalis, writing after William was safe in his grave, only says that they referred to Herleva's father (the tanner of Falaise). Wace, in the twelfth century, ventured to record that they cried out, 'The Skin, the Skin, the Tanner's skin!', a direct reference to Duke Robert's mésalliance with a tanner's daughter and so to William's dubious birth.

One can easily imagine that their genial banter enraged their enemy, and it backfired badly. In a fury William launched a violent attack and took the town by storm. Entering the stricken city, the Bastard seized thirty-six of the men captured on the ramparts and had their hands and feet cut off, one of his best attested acts of gratuitous cruelty. He then installed his own garrison and returned to Domfront, which surrendered towards the end of spring 1052. The whole surrounding area, called the Pascais, was annexed to Normandy. William had substantially strengthened his frontier in this first serious confrontation with Anjou. He went on to build a castle at Ambrières on the confluence of the rivers Varenne and Mayenne, a little way south of Domfront and within the lordship of Mayenne, whose lord, Geoffrey, was a vassal of Maine.

William's success had now alarmed King Henry, who was concerned about the balance of power between the Seine and the Loire, which now seemed to have tilted too far in William's favour. William attempted diplomacy, visiting the King at his court, at Vitry-aux-Loges, in September 1052. It is possible that he was aware of negotiations between Henry and Geoffrey Martel that resulted in a treaty between the two on 15 October 1052 that was aimed at Normandy.

The King carefully concealed his hostility, contenting himself with receiving at Court various lords hostile to the Duke. William of Poitiers hints at intrigues conducted by Count William of Arques. He seems to have formed part of a coalition against William.[2] Several rebels, secure in their cosy refuge, were still hoping for armed intervention by the French King which would inflict a decisive defeat on the Duke. King Henry still hoped to secure Normandy for himself so that he could make it a fief for a French prince such as his brother Odo. If William of Poitiers is right, then William Busac, the Richardide Count of Eu, returned to Eu secretly in the summer of 1052, and even announced that he was the rightful duke. William therefore besieged Eu and banished Busac, who took refuge in France.

The outcome was that towards the winter of 1053/54, two armies, one French and the other Angevin, converged on Normandy. Henry's brother Odo, aided by the Counts of Valois and Clermont, crossed the River Bresle, passing through the Pays de Bray (on the plateaux of the Caux) and up the Seine valley towards Rouen. A second army, led by the King, accompanied by Geoffrey Martel and his Angevins, crossed the River Avre into Évreux with the intention of linking up with Odo at Rouen. The royal armies had adopted the classic pincer movement intending to converge on Rouen and force the Duke to accept a pitched battle.

Duke William accordingly divided his forces into two, taking personal command of the one raised in Lower Normandy. He advanced along the left bank of the Seine while his second detachment, led by Robert, Count of Eu, and Walter Giffard (son of the lord of Bolbec) advanced from Upper Normandy. So, as February became March of 1054, William had worked out the strategy of his enemies, dividing his army into two divisions which could be rapidly deployed where needed. He now adopted a novel solution to his problem, and it is by no means certain that any of his predecessors would have managed to avoid a pitched battle. Such battles were rare in the eleventh century: William himself fought only two, Val-ès-Dunes and Hastings. In both cases the type of combat was dictated by the adversary.

Through spies, William kept a close watch on the invaders, allowing him to choose a favourable moment for an attack. His plan was a typical Norman ruse, of the sort used by their Scandinavian ancestors. The Vikings were adept at such tricks, making great use of mobility in warfare to create in their opponents an illusion of ubiquity. William was to conduct operations in England in a similar manner.

In March the French army on the River Bresle encountered no opposition and were lulled into over-confidence. They came to a village called Mortemer where they found that such fortifications as there were had been abandoned by the Normans. Yet Walter Giffard and his men were not in fact far away. The French drank heavily and fell into a deep and alcoholic sleep, forgetting to set a proper watch.

During the night the Normans advanced on Mortemer, blocking off all means of escape and then torching the village. The French, despite superiority in numbers, tried desperately to escape. Many died and most of the others were taken prisoner as Giffard and the local people swarmed upon them. Wace was to claim later that there was no Norman of such modest status that he was unable to take a Frenchman prisoner or seize two or three fine warhorses. Count Odo himself was among the first to be captured. It was a total victory and the details survive in epic form in the *Roman de Rou*, corroborated by brief remarks in other sources. Public opinion and ducal propaganda agreed on magnifying the importance of the victory.

Meanwhile the Duke was advancing along the left bank of the Seine. Learning of Giffard's success, he now sent a herald, Ralph de Tosny, to inform the French King of Odo's defeat. Climbing a tree on the summit of a nearby hill, Ralph announced, in his stentorian voice, 'Frenchmen, Frenchmen! Rouse yourselves. Hurry to bury your friends slain at Mortemer!' The French listened in stunned surprise, as it was generally before a battle that a herald delivered a speech in the name of his lord.

King Henry soon learned from the remnants of his brother's army the extent of the disaster and, refusing to give battle, ordered a precipitate retreat. Duke William did not even bother to pursue him, preferring to consolidate his hold on that section of his frontier which faced the rivers Avre and Eure where the French held the castle of Tillières. That castle had threatened Normandy for years, so William now built another fortress in the same area, at Breteuil, which directly opposed Tillières. It was put under the custodianship of William fitzOsbern.

A truce was negotiated, either towards the end of 1054 or early in 1055, and Henry secured the release of the captives from Mortemer who filled the Norman prisons. He had to recognise William as the legitimate holder of the Pascais, and Ambrières was taken from Geoffrey Martel. King Henry promised neutrality as between Normandy and Anjou and to return Tillières to Normandy. All this formed the basis for peace. Nonetheless, the King remained concerned about the growing power of Normandy and never in fact gave up his Angevin alliance. Geoffrey Martel also never lost hope of recovering his lost territory. When he failed to fulfil the peace terms, William invaded Maine and seized the castle of Ambrières. But William, knowing he would have difficulty in consolidating his hold on the area, put his own man in charge as castellan of the castle of Ambrières.

The Lord of Mayenne, Geoffrey,[3] was now forced to call on his overlord, Geoffrey Martel. Geoffrey of Mayenne said that he feared 'his land could lie at the mercy of the enemy'.[4] Count Geoffrey was only too pleased to respond, and Mayenne also had the support of Guy-William, Duke of Aquitaine, from whom he held part of his fief, and of the Breton Count, Eon de Porhouët of Penthièvre. The Angevin army joined forces with those raised by Geoffrey of Mayenne and laid siege to Ambrières. But Duke William, ever on the alert, forced the raising of the siege before his enemies could employ the ram they had brought with which they had hoped to breach the walls. The defenders brought into play a counter-ram which was much stronger and caused the enemy ram to fall apart.

Geoffrey of Mayenne was taken prisoner in this battle, but, having been taken to Normandy, he then received every sign of honour and respect, rather like Earl Harold in 1064.[5] The warmth of his welcome induced him to become the Duke's vassal. This setback gravely weakened Angevin power and prestige. In Brittany, Count Eon was at last defeated by his nephew, Count Conan. Anjou's only remaining ally was now the King of France, and the rapid decline of Angevin power caused King Henry to get involved once more.

The King came to Angers in March 1057 to persuade Geoffrey of Anjou to join in a new campaign against Normandy. This time the allies set out from Maine and invaded the Hiémois. Sticking to his previous strategy, the Bastard again refrained from barring their progress directly. He gathered an army near Falaise, knowing that the King had paused nearby, at the Abbey of St Peter of Dives. William bided his time, letting the French and Angevins pass north, pillaging and burning in the Bessin. The Duke simply held on to his castles, knowing that as long as he did so he could recover his lands and repair the damage.

The enemy then advanced down the valley of the Orne, bypassing Caen (though at that time it had neither a castle nor defences around the Bourg du Duc) and reaching Seulles. Then they turned east away from the Orne. The Duke was kept informed of their movements by spies and followed them at a distance. He saw that their freedom of movement was now much impeded by the vast quantities of plunder obtained from their pillaging, and realised that they would have to pass Dives at the bridge of Varaville, as their line of march was directed towards the lower Seine valley. William knew the area well and planned to take advantage of the marshes around the Dives near the forest of Bavent where the Dives Estuary reached well inland and the ebb and flow of the tide caused the little river to vary greatly in depth. The invaders had little knowledge of the whereabouts of the Norman army and could not rely on assistance from the local population. The Duke positioned his men close to the road to Varaville. Having reached Bavent, about three miles from the bridge, he encountered a crowd of local peasants and encouraged them to join him, armed as best they could with clubs and hunting spears and even shovels.

Allowing the French to cross the bridge, William suddenly fell on them from the rear, which was cluttered up with carts full of plunder. The invaders desperately tried to return across the bridge but such was the disorder that many of them fell into the Dives, where some were drowned because it was now high tide. The rest succumbed to the onslaught of the Normans.

Important prisoners were again taken, at Varaville, as at Mortemer, notably the Count of Soissons (William Busac) and Theobald, Count of Blois. From the other side of the river King Henry, from a small hill, watched the disaster unfold. His intervention, urging his men to return blow for blow, actually made things worse and caused greater losses until, as Wace reports, his household knights persuaded him that all was lost and he should retreat. Geoffrey Martel fled the scene. The King, full of anger and stricken with grief, having himself struck not a blow, returned to France, swearing never to set foot in Normandy again. The little hill, of Bastembourg, from which the King watched the defeat of his army, can still be seen, bearing silent witness to the annihilation of the French rearguard, though the Dives is now little more than a stream and very gentle.

It was a decisive victory won without heroics. What mattered to Duke William was success and not the means employed to get it. Although this was an age when great epic poems, such as the *Chanson de Roland*, circulated freely, Duke William seems to have been quite unaware of this sort of cultural ethic. His attitude was entirely different and he preferred ruthlessness to notions of romantic chivalry.

William of Jumièges claims that it was after Varaville that King Henry restored the castle of Tillières, in the Vexin, to Normandy, and certainly it was back in Norman hands after 1058. Norman power in the Vexin does not appear to have been under imminent threat, though the French-occupied area had been a thorn in William's side. The Duke had now moved his frontier forward almost to Dreux. In the spring of 1058 he took control of the castle of Thimert.[6] King Henry tried to recover it but had to give up a fruitless siege. Negotiations were opened for peace. Henry sent envoys to Normandy, the Bishops of Paris and Amiens, who met the Duke's representatives at Fécamp in 1060, though one source suggests that William took part in person, meeting the King near Dreux, possibly during the siege of Thimert.

Relations with Anjou remained very bad but Geoffrey Martel made no further attacks on Normandy, preferring to hold on to Maine despite the fact that his rights there had been seriously eroded by Geoffrey of Mayenne's allegiance to the Duke. Herbert II of Maine was encouraged by Duke William's success to renew his homage, and certain marriage agreements followed, sometime after 1055. William's daughter, Alice, was to marry Herbert, while the Duke's son, Robert Curthose, by then seven or eight years of age, would marry Herbert's sister Margaret, who was placed under the care of the Lord of Mézidon, who placed her in a convent to await her marriage. If Herbert were now to die without an heir, Maine would fall into the hands of Duke William.

Sometime during the winter of 1058/59 came the rebellion of Robert, son of William of Giroie. Geoffrey Martel was always ready to foster rebellion against the Duke so Robert of Giroie had Angevin help and fortified the castles of Saint Céneri and La Roche-Mabille. He held out against the Duke, who besieged him until he died, allegedly of poison, sometime during February 1060.[7] His father, William of Giroie, then also resisted the Duke, but William, 'the wily Duke, broke down his enmity with fair promises' (a gambit William was to use on other occasions), so Giroie submitted and renewed his homage.

Suddenly, in 1060, King Henry I of France died, on 4 August, possibly as a result of his exertions at the siege of Thimert and at Dreux, before he could fulfil his promise to meet the Duke. William had now lost a formidable enemy. Henry was succeeded by his son Philippe, who had been associated in the kingship and crowned in 1059, but he was only a minor – eight years of age. His uncle, Baldwin V of Flanders, an ally of the Duke, therefore became Regent. The King's death and the minority of his successor was a stroke of luck for William, as Baldwin was his father-in-law. William met the young King at Dreux, a few weeks after his father's death and, like a good vassal, was politic enough to perform the requisite homage.

The Duke's political situation had been steadily improving for ten years and the death of King Henry in 1060, followed so swiftly by the death of Geoffrey Martel, was to transform William's position dramatically.

At around the time of King Henry's death the Duke found himself at odds with several of his barons. A quarrel had broken out among them and the leader of one faction, Robert of Montgomery (who was a confidant of the Duke), persuaded his master to take his side in the dispute. William, quick tempered as ever, then took his wrath out on Ralph of Tosny, Hugh of Grandmesnil and Arnold of Échauffour and, according to Orderic Vitalis, banished them 'without any proof of guilt'.[8] The Duke's ill-humour persisted, and he objected to reports that Robert, Abbot of St Évroul, had made humorous comments about him. The Duke summoned the Abbot to appear before him at Court but he, discreetly, avoided facing the Duke's anger and, despite protesting his innocence of the charge, took the advice of Bishop Hugh of Lisieux and fled into exile, proceeding by way of France to seek the aid of the Pope.

In his absence he was replaced at St Évroul by Osbern, Prior of Cormeilles, without any reference to the Pope's wishes. Osbern was not welcomed by all of the monks. William had after all dispossessed Abbot Robert by the sheer force of his personality rather than by virtue of any lawful authority. Meanwhile, the Pope heard the Abbot's case and promised him his support and protection. He sent him back to Normandy, as far as Lillebonne, accompanied by two cardinals, but the Bastard again flew into a tantrum. He would receive the cardinals, 'Legates of our common Father', but, he said, 'no monk of the duchy should dare to bring a plea against me or I will ignore his cloth and hang him from the highest tree!' Abbot Robert beat a hasty retreat to Paris. William then suggested that Robert and Osbern meet at Chartres, and put their case to the cardinals. Osbern agreed to this but, perhaps aware of the weakness of his case, did not turn up. Abbot Robert, supported by papal letters, excommunicated him! Some of the monks of St Évroul then left the monastery to join Abbot Robert, who had returned to Rome.

Orderic Vitalis, who was himself a monk at St Évroul, says that many other monks wished to do the same but that the sick and the very young could not, so that only the strong and free joined Robert. Pope Alexander II later gave them the use of the Church of St Paul the Apostle in Rome. It seems that many men felt that they could not rely on being justly treated at the Duke's Court. William was prone to treat bishops and abbots like secular vassals because the right he claimed to appoint them was itself a source of ducal power and, of course, cost him nothing. He also disposed of the rights of secular lords as he wished. Churches found it advisable to secure ducal confirmation, by charter, of their property and privileges. That meant that in the event of the removal of their immediate lay patrons, the Duke would still be expected to respect the rights of the church.

Duke William's position was strengthened still further by the death of another serious rival, Count Geoffrey Martel of Anjou, on 14 November 1061. Although he had been married three times, Geoffrey left no heir of his body and was succeeded by his nephew, Geoffrey le Barbu (the Bearded). Geoffrey Martel's death gave rise to fresh hopes of peace, William of Poitiers rejoicing that Geoffrey the Bearded feared God and did his best to earn eternal glory. But nothing happened.

Normandy was now beginning to take shape as a formidable state and all the factors were coming together which were to make the conquest of England possible. William had put an end to the drain on military manpower, preventing men from emigrating to Italy and elsewhere. New castles could no longer be built without his consent, and when vassals swore fealty for a fief from any subordinate lord, they had to reserve their overriding fidelity to the Duke. William had made good use of the ducal powers inherited from Carolingian times and could confiscate the wealth in movables and the fiefs of those who committed certain crimes of violence. He could certainly confiscate the fief of a vassal who failed to fulfil his obligations.

His ducal demesne lands were immense, extending into all parts of the duchy (partly as a result of confiscations) and taking in forests and whole towns. At Caen, Duke William had sold his half of the rights over salt deposits, fishing for sturgeon in the Seine, taxes on mills or on boats and ferries and taxes known as 'portuaires' (harbour dues), and 'octrois' (city tolls) to the local bishop, who already held the other half, and thereby increased the episcopal revenues. Also included were rights over vacant ecclesiastical offices, over wrecks and everything cast up on the coast, all hoards of treasure that might be found and even 'baleine', a tax on whales and other cetaceans.

There were four matters that fell under the Duke's mercy and which could incur discretionary fines. These were, firstly, attacks on men when coming to or going from the ducal court, secondly, attacks on men within eight days of the summons of the army, thirdly, for interference with merchants or pilgrims, and fourthly, offences against the Duke's money. He had a tax called moneyage, which he was paid for not making use of his right to alter the value of coins every three years. Fines were collected by the vicomtes, the only local officials.

Vicomtes derived their authority from being the deputies of the former Carolingian Counts. So they held castles as castellans for the Duke and probably 'farmed' the taxes.[9] But they could be removed from office if they offended the Duke and, in this period, one vicomte, Thurstan Goz, Vicomte of Exmes, was exiled. Another, the Vicomte of Arques, lost his office when William of Arques fell from power in 1054 (his lands went to the Vicomte of Rouen). Thus William was extending his grip on Normandy well beyond his control over major vassals and reducing the risk of rebellion.

According to a declaration of Norman custom made in 1091, the Duke already had jurisdiction over such offences as attacks on houses, arson and rape (rather like the royal pleas[10] in England). But, in contrast to the situation he found in England when he became King, William, as Duke of Normandy, was not the ultimate land holder in Normandy. Nonetheless, William tended to assume that he had the right to take homage from his vassals so that their lands appeared to be held from him as their lord. William's authority was further strengthened when he accepted an oath of homage from a returning exile. What really mattered was the personal character of the relationship between lord and vassal: that was what determined who was the real gainer.

Grants of land to vassals by monasteries do not appear to have disturbed the Duke's right to military service from those vassals, and there is no evidence that when lands and knights were granted to monasteries by the Duke, he was doing so in order that the abbeys could discharge the military obligations they already owed him. In Normandy the same word, knight (*miles*), was applied to warriors who fought for the Duke whether they held landed estates or not. To be a knight was essentially to be a professional soldier, and military service was not yet dependent upon land tenure. Nonetheless, it does look as though fiefs were being created on lands that had owed military service to the Duke ever since Carolingian times, and so the connection between the granting of a fief and military service to the Duke was strengthened. William's most effective achievement seems to have been that he ensured that all military service owed to the Duke was actually performed.

From 1047 to 1066 William does not seem to have tried to recover any ancient ducal rights or property, but to have slowly but surely eliminated his enemies, the Richardides in particular, and then to have given the lands which fell vacant to his supporters, such as the Giffards and the Warennes.

7

THE DUKE IN CHURCH ... & STATE

Although Duke William might be thought to have been thoroughly preoccupied after 1047 with the protection of his frontiers from the ambitions of Geoffrey Martel of Anjou and with dealing with the final revolts of the Richardides and their removal from positions of influence, this is not entirely the case.

After Val-ès-Dunes, seizing the opportunity thereby given to him, the Duke had set out to present himself as the champion of the Church, and especially of the reform element within it. He had summoned and presided over the Council that launched the Norman version of the Truce of God at Caen in 1047, which had effectively put him in a position from which he was free to use force in maintaining public order when no one else could do so without incurring the wrath of the Church.

Duke William then established himself at the centre of reform opinion, sponsoring a monastic revival undertaken by the Norman nobility and so permeating the Norman Church with his influence. This was underlined by his assumption of control over episcopal and abbatial appointments and his presence at provincial Church councils. He is recorded as present at Caen in 1047, Lisieux in 1051, Rouen in 1063 and Lisieux again in 1064. William of Poitiers insists that councils met 'at the command and with the encouragement of the duke' and that he was the arbiter of their proceedings. His policy has been well described as 'aristocratic, ecclesiastical and ducal'.[1] He oversaw a system of noble sponsorship of religious foundations, the charters issued being endorsed by ducal authority. They would be drawn up by the beneficiaries and then presented to the Duke for approval and he would add his 'mark', a cross. The monasteries naturally extolled William, presenting his virtues to the world as the protector of their churches and defender of their interests, a lord who intervened in their concerns.

His policies were often carried out by mere force of personality rather than by virtue of his ducal authority. He could treat bishops and abbots like secular vassals, and the appointments he made were themselves a source of ducal power that cost him nothing. If the immediate patron of a church was removed, as by exile, the Duke might still respect the monastery's rights and intervene in their disputes with lesser men. But ducal protection in itself was not particularly useful to the monks.

A baronial party favourable to reform coalesced around William, who had encouraged the formation of a group of confidants, and many foundations resulted. The new nobility, which, under previous dukes, had enriched itself at the expense of the Church, was now repaying its debt by developing Norman monastic life. On his deathbed, according to Orderic Vitalis, William had expressed the hope that it would be recorded in his favour in the eyes of God that the number of monasteries in Normandy had increased to thirty-six, twenty of them before 1066. Some of these foundations can be identified. But the endowments can be seen in another light, as enlightened self-interest, converting land into cash, as monasteries were often endowed with land in return for an annual payment to the 'donor'. Establishing a monastery, which exploited the lands it was given, actually increased the wealth of a noble lord, who received additional revenue without the expense of farming the estates himself. Also, some abbeys were established in areas in need of colonisation and exploitation, using the land for the raising of sheep and cattle. There was also the matter of an increase in the donor's prestige.

In 1050 William fitz Giroie and his Grandmesnil nephews gave the Abbey of Le Bec a priory, which, in time, developed into the Abbey of St Évroul. Roger of Mortemer founded St Victor-en-Caux. In 1056 Toustain Haldup and his wife and family endowed the Abbey of Lessay, and in 1059 Robert of Eu did the same at Tréport. In about 1066 William fitzOsbern founded Cormeilles, and Roger of Montgomery, the Collegiate Church of St Martin of Ecajeul at Troarn. But the Duke, like his ancestors, usually preferred to grant only lands or offices with a guaranteed income, rather than make new foundations, as for example when he gave the Provostship of Caen, worth one hundred pounds sterling, to Montvilliers.

Some of the foundations and endowments were perhaps a form of insurance, since many of the nobility, as they grew older, began to fear for their souls or perhaps for their lives and therefore chose to enter a monastery. Robert of Grandmesnil, for example, became a monk at St Évroul. The first abbot of that monastery had been Thierry de Mathonville and several other of its monks were of noble origin, such as Herbert of Montreuil. In addition, some became monks by necessity. William fitz Giroie, who had been castrated and mutilated by William Talvas of Bellême, had become a monk at Bec. He was joined there by three other lords who had fought at Mortemer.

But the endowment of monasteries and of other churches had a further purpose: the salvation of the soul of the giver, as the endowment became a form of penance for sins committed. Monks and priests were expected to offer Masses and their prayers for the spiritual welfare of their benefactor.

Robert of Grandmesnil, of course, became Abbot of Le Bec, until driven out by the Duke's enmity towards his family (on account of their involvement in revolt). Robert had continued to behave much like a baron, taking a lively interest in secular affairs. He and the new abbot, Thierry de Mathonville, quarrelled, and Prior Lanfranc, together with Archbishop Maurilius, conducted an inquiry into the cause, finding in Abbot Thierry's favour. But the latter preferred to resign and went on pilgrimage, being replaced by Robert of Grandmesnil. Secular affairs impinged on monastic life, and monasteries were by no means isolated from involvement in politics. St Évroul, like a number of others, became a barony owing, in this case, the service of two knights.[2] These monasteries were, with William's consent (for which read at his 'insistence') granted fiefs. The Abbot of Préaux had unusual jurisdiction over cases of arson and rape which elsewhere were reserved for the jurisdiction of the Duke.

Bishoprics, too, were disposed of in a manner that suited the Duke. The most obvious case was the appointment of his half-brother Odo to the See of Bayeux. This was not necessarily a bad choice at the time. William of Poitiers insists that Odo in youth was a suitably qualified and educated candidate. Though this may be mere flattery, it is true that Odo certainly improved the running of his diocese and built a new cathedral for Bayeux. A much better choice was the reformer Maurilius, who replaced Archbishop Mauger of Rouen. The Duke also influenced the choices for Lisieux, Avranches and Coutances. He sought to reform the Norman Church along lines drawn from the influence of the great Abbey of Cluny. That influence had arrived in Normandy by way of Dijon and influenced Fécamp. So the Norman Church became 'Cluniac' in spirit.

The Norman episcopate overwhelmingly reflected the secular aristocracy and its interests because the bishops were chosen from its ranks. Not all of these bishops were popular in reforming circles. The pace of change in ecclesiastical life certainly quickened after William was firmly established in power, that is, after 1055. The bishops, with William's support, set about creating a well-organised church, setting up archdeaconries and rural deaneries, a policy emanating from Archbishop Maurilius. Episcopal synods became a feature of church life as well as regular provincial councils. Even Archbishop Mauger had played a part with his summoning of the Council of Caen in 1047. He had stressed clerical celibacy and took steps to improve the conduct of parish clergy. He even acted against simony. The improvement in the church also led to the spread of 'Romanesque' architecture.[3]

But in other circumstances the Bastard's behaviour could, on occasion, be both erratic and theatrical. Orderic Vitalis saw him as ruthless, impulsive and unjust. He also charges him with vindictiveness because he listened to advisers to the detriment of justice. A fair trial could not be obtained in his Court. Men might be deprived of lands or office for trivial reasons. Abbot Robert of St Évroul thought it safer to flee rather than stand trial. Both William of Arques and Archbishop Mauger had, so Orderic insists, been loyal during the Duke's minority yet were probably expelled simply for resenting their replacement by favourites of William's own choice, or for disapproving of the Bastard's provocative attitude towards Geoffrey of Anjou and King Henry. William was known for seizing a man's son, brother or nephew as a hostage to ensure good conduct.

When he was making a grant at a feast, a man in his service, Hugh the Forester, objected to his action. William, who might only have been play acting but then again perhaps not, threatened to hit him with a large pig's bone. The monks of St Florent of Saumur questioned his views concerning a grant he had made but were scornfully dismissed by the Duke, who proclaimed, 'We are Normans and we understand such things because they should be done that way, and therefore, with God's consent, thus shall we do them!' Such tales of theatrical behaviour cast light on his character.

But much of his policy reflected a need to work closely with reforming churchmen in order primarily to cultivate good relations with the papacy (not least because of Pope Leo's attitude to his marriage), which led to the founding of Benedictine monasteries. He was careful to avoid the error of simony and sold no benefices.

It was during the early 1050s that William acquired the services of two men who were to be of great assistance to him. The first of these, an ex-fighting man, a 'miles' turned cleric, named William, came to Court in about 1050. He had received his education from the Abbey of St Hilaire at Poitiers and had been a pupil of the Chartrain Master Fulbert. He thus acquired a more secular education than other clergy, as his knowledge of classical authors such as Caesar, Tacitus, Virgil and several others shows. He became Archdeacon of Lisieux and a ducal chaplain and is known to historians as William of Poitiers.

His sole surviving work, the *Gesta Guillelmi* or 'Deeds of William', is a major source of information about the Bastard's career. It is viewed by many as a thoroughly biased work of propaganda[4] and by others as an invaluable source, claiming that he had no need to lie. He is sycophantic towards his hero, Duke William, and prone to exaggeration. His version of Earl Harold's oath cannot be accepted as it stands.

The Duke's most famous adherent was a man of very different character, Lanfranc of Pavia, who had come to Normandy during the 1040s. He was one of those who was critical of the Duke's marriage and came into conflict with him in about 1047 for criticising his choice of chaplain, a man called Herfast whom Lanfranc had exposed publicly as an ignoramus during a visit to Le Bec. William, furious, had set fire to one of the abbey's farms and then ordered the Abbot to expel this 'impertinent monk'. The Abbot had no option but to obey for fear of further consequences.

The next part of the story looks like a carefully staged act of reconciliation. The Abbot, so the story goes, gave Lanfranc a dreadful old nag on which to ride, and he set off to go into exile. But only a short while after he had started, he met the Duke, who had roared with laughter at the comical sight Lanfranc presented and made fun of his mount. Lanfranc, allegedly indignant, retorted that he was going as fast as he could, just as William had ordered, so if he wanted him to go any faster he should give him a better horse! William, amused by his defiance, then asked, 'Since when has the criminal completing his sentence demanded a gift from his judge?' The two continued to argue the toss until William was, apparently, won over by Lanfranc's ready wit.

The Bastard then conducted the monk back to the abbey, where Lanfranc's return was joyfully welcomed. So began a long and fruitful association between the two. During the succeeding decade Lanfranc went several times to Rome, and it is possible that he was pleading William's case for a recognition of his marriage with several popes. He was also a prominent supporter of church reform, intervened in the condemnation of Berengar of Tours, and used his influence to help secure the removal of Archbishop Mauger.

But the coming of Lanfranc had its effect on William. Lanfranc introduced him to ideas derived from Roman Law, which were foreign to feudal custom. But he was most valuable to William in the matter of the heretical views of Berengar of Tours.

Berengar was a former monk of St Wandrille who had moved on to teach at the episcopal school at Tours. He was a disciple of the philosophical teachings of the ninth-century scholar John Scotus Erigena, who taught that Reason should control all understanding of the doctrines of the Church, rather than the authority of Church Fathers. He believed that philosophy and religion, rightly understood, could not contradict each other since both were derived from the Divine Wisdom.

It was Berengar's application of this to the current doctrine on the Eucharist that caused the trouble.[5] Berengar's ideas did not bother ordinary worshippers who rarely thought about these matters. It never became a widespread popular heresy and Berengar never became a leader of a sect, a heresiarch. But different princes took sides for and against him. He was supported, for example, by Geoffrey of Anjou. Duke William proved to be more cautious.

Berengar sought support in Normandy to prevent his condemnation by the Church, as he had former colleagues and pupils there, even Lanfranc himself. But Lanfranc instead began a protracted controversy with Berengar over the doctrine of the Eucharist. Berengar was at Préaux near St Audemer in 1047–48, during the period of the siege of Brionne, and requested a meeting with the Duke. William let him speak but, lacking the ability to dispute the matter with him, referred the matter to a 'conciliabulum' or little conference of Norman clergy at Brionne. Lanfranc was not there, as he was in Rome for the synod, where he made Pope Leo aware of the concerns Berengar was arousing. Lanfranc presented a statement of his own giving his philosophical and theological views on the matter. The Pope raised the question at the Roman synod and at Vercelli in 1051.

At that council Lanfranc was instrumental in initiating proceedings against Berengar, who was summoned to appear before the Council. He refused. Lanfranc, on his return to Normandy, secured William's support, probably arguing it would win him support at Rome. Normandy never adopted Berengar's views. The Church never accepted Berengar's views. The affair rumbled on until his death.

Lanfranc had moved to Le Bec, eventually becoming prior, and in 1063 was made Abbot of St Stephen's, Caen, the 'Abbaye-aux-Hommes'. After the conquest of England, he replaced Archbishop Stigand at Canterbury.

Duke William maintained strict control over the Church, preventing bishops from also becoming counts and from usurping, as he saw it, ducal rights within their episcopal towns. Episcopal interference in legal matters was restricted and the bishops themselves were required to administer their dioceses through deans and archdeacons. Abbeys were protected but William never allowed the development in Normandy of the institution of lay 'Advocates', lay defenders of the abbeys. Such men were given a fief from the lands of the Church on condition that they protected the Church. The abbots were seen as ducal vassals and the knights enfeoffed by an abbey were held to serve the Duke directly and not by way of the abbot as intermediary. He granted abbacies in the same way as he created bishops. For example, when the Abbot of Mont-Saint-Michel died at Jerusalem, William designated a clerk as abbot, Renouf of Bayeux. In another case, St Wandrille was given to a reformer called Gerbert, a friend of Archbishop Maurilius.

William was therefore successful in gathering around him a coterie of influential churchmen and powerful lords. In addition to Lanfranc there was the Duke's half-brother, Bishop Odo of Bayeux, and that stalwart of Norman government in England, Bishop Geoffrey of Coutances, though all of the Norman bishops had supported Duke William's rule from about 1055 onwards. Among the lay lords, in addition to fitzOsbern and Montgomery (who represented the House of Bellême) there were men like Richard fitz Gilbert (a descendant of William's guardian, Count Gilbert), or William of Warenne.

In seeking to extend his control over Normandy, William followed a policy of attracting personal loyalty to himself from among the members of the great families. He judiciously favoured the younger generation, his peer group as it were, of young warriors, the 'tyrones'. They became his special confidants and the support was mutual.

Before 1066 he could only endow them by impoverishing the ducal demesne or by disinheriting Richardides who 'offended' him. The advance against Maine, which William began in the early 1060s, was at least in part driven by the need to reward his supporters. It could be that his ambition to become King of England was also driven by a desire to enrich his loyal followers, as well as himself. He also allowed these followers to become wealthy at the expense of the Church.

He had used the weapon of disinheritance quite freely, as when he used it against William Warlenc in 1055/56 and then brought in his other half-brother Robert, as Count of Mortain. His attempt to recruit to his service his uncle, Count William of Arques, however, had proved something of a failure until the defeat of the Count in 1054 allowed the Duke to reward several of his supporters. An example of that is William of Warenne, younger son of a lord called Rodulf who held lands near Rouen. Warenne came into favour for his support in the defeat of William of Arques and was then given custody of the castle of Mortemer after Roger of Mortemer forfeited his lands. Warenne rose to a position of first rank thanks to William's conquest of England.

In Normandy before 1066 there is no real sign that many lords held their lands conditionally or in dependence on the Duke and there is no evidence of widespread specified military service. Although Count Guy of Ponthieu was required to serve with 100 knights, he is not an exception to the absence of examples of specified service in Normandy because he was not a Norman. There could have been cases of lands being held as dependent tenures, like the knights' fees of post-Conquest England, but that remains doubtful. What is true is that William's subordinate lords did themselves establish military tenures on their own lands, to protect their possessions and attract dependants (whereas in England although there was a development of commendation as men 'bowed' to a lord and established the relationship of lord and man, similar to but not identical with that of lord and vassal, commendation did not necessarily involve military service).

It was later, after the Conquest of England, that lords welcomed the definition of the terms of their service, such as the amount of 'relief' payable on the death of the holder of a fief, as a protection against arbitrary demands. It is likely that the 'servicium debitum', by which the number of knights a lord owed to royal service was strictly defined, arose for the same reason. In many cases the amount of service was defined by mutual consent after hard bargaining.

William could hardly have applied a policy of demanding specified military service before 1047, because of the continuous state of disorder and rebellion, but the various lords had been free to levy such service from their own vassals. Nonetheless, by 1066 it does look as though William had managed to get a legal claim to the military service of his major vassals recognised more generally than it had been in 1035. Service had by then also been imposed on all the older monasteries and on most of the bishops, but it remains unclear how far, if at all, it had been imposed on the lay magnates. Nor was the Duke in any sense seen as the recognised head of an established feudal hierarchy.

Orderic Vitalis, however, makes a compelling case for William having established himself as an effective ruler who made successful use of the arbitrary prerogatives of his office, as Count of Rouen and Duke of the Normans. He can also be credited with having brought peace to Normandy. He had done this in the absence of any central royal government in Northern France and had seen to it that neighbouring rulers could not provoke disorder among their vassals in Normandy. He used the machinery of war to impose law and order and so made his Normans an adventurous lot, which proved invaluable to him when he came to plan the invasion of England.

But it is questionable whether all the assertions by William of Poitiers about the justice of his rule and his own moral righteousness were the exact truth since much of it is not only one-sided, going uncontradicted, but mere propaganda. Yet he does seem to have taken the idea of justice seriously, even if his concept of what justice was might seem strange to modern readers. He punished wrong-doing savagely and protected the Church. It is, however, very true, as one historian has commented, that he was guilty of 'ruthlessness and shameless manipulation of facts to justify dubious enterprises'.[6] His methods could be brutal and corrupt and his faults included cruelty and avarice. He sounds distressingly contemporary.

He certainly developed the ducal Curia, composed as it was of bishops and counts and other men of high rank, the vicomtes and the household officers. It could try barons for crimes, take tithes from the land, settle disputes over rival jurisdictions and actions between lords, record agreements, translate relics (that is, move them to a new sanctuary or burial place) and it was, of course, a Council of

War. Ridding his Court of Richardides had the effect of giving it a more public character, as men from a more varied background were consulted. It met three or four times a year and generally at the three great feasts of Christmas, Easter and Whitsun.

The clerks of the Duke's chapel fulfilled some of the functions that a civil service might provide, as well as performing religious ceremonies. William appears to have divided his Chapel into two parts, so forming a proto-Chancery, though that might not have been completed until after 1066. There was no officer called a Chancellor, no Chancellery and no separate Treasury. Judicial functions were delegated to vicomtes and bishops or to a committee. The Duke had his own domestic staff and his Court, as was usual in the eleventh and later centuries, was peripatetic, permitting sensible use of local produce and resources from ducal estates.

During his period of dominance, both before and after the Conquest, his policies made possible an increase in the size and number of towns, with the multiplication of places called Villeneuve, Neuveville, VilleFranche or Ville l'Eveque. Some of these became 'bourgs' and the inhabitants secured borough customs including the right to hold property as 'tenancies en bourgage', as at Pontorson or Breteuil, evidence of the rise of a class of wealthy townsmen.

The Duke himself sponsored the growth of Caen in order to create a ducal power nexus in Lower Normandy. The 'bourg' there had been begun by Richard II; William extended it to the east and west by building his two abbeys and also built his 'Bourg le Duc' on a rocky spur which he enclosed with a rampart.[7] The sites of the abbeys became the 'Bourg l'Abbé' and the 'Bourg l'Abbesse'. Of course he put the building of these churches before the Pope as the fruit of a pious gesture (with political and economic benefits for the Duke). Caen became part of the military and political strategy of Normandy.

In military matters William sought to strengthen his hold on Normandy by forging for his own use a large number of highly trained and well-equipped knights, a 'precision instrument of warfare unique in Western Europe'.[8] He had, like his predecessors, a personal guard of household warriors but he turned this into a force of fully trained cavalry. Furthermore, in a bid to out-manoeuvre and isolate the Richardides, he multiplied the granting of fiefs raised from his own demesne lands, recruiting men from Italy, Spain and even Byzantium, mainly impoverished knights who readily performed military service. The ducal army had to serve, when summoned, for forty days a year and leading vassals levied forces proportionate to the size of their fiefs, generally, it would appear, in multiples of five or ten, later called a 'constabularium' (or conroi).

This gave the Norman army a degree of mobility and unity of command seldom seen in the eleventh century. William also organised a force of archers. The knights fought with sword (principally) and lance. Lances were of ash, some two metres long, with an iron head and used as a javelin. The couched lance was not generally adopted until the twelfth century when the rules of battle were codified and two sides would line up opposite each other and charge. One suspects that this evolved gradually and that earlier conflicts, in the mid-eleventh century, adopted the methods of the hunting field, particularly those of boar hunting. But fighting on horseback helped to differentiate the knight from other classes of warriors. Horses were expensive and a cavalryman needed several as well as weapons, armour and shield. It is not certain when the penetrative power of a collective charge developed but it depended on both sides charging at each other.

William's wars honed his skills as a commander and as a master of siege craft, and he attracted many knights to his service.

The Duke's use of the powers granted him by the Truce of God were always of great value. He learned from presiding over Church synods the value of keeping written records where he saw examples of how to legislate and devise administrative methods. The Truce itself was renewed in 1054 in a synod at Narbonne but ominously the synod condemned the shedding of the blood of Christians by Christians: 'A Christian who sheds the blood of another Christian sheds the blood of Christ.'

The Norman Church benefited from William's choice of Maurilius as Archbishop and won for him the approval of reformers such as the Deacon Hildebrand (who became Pope Gregory VII in 1073) and the influential Cardinal Humbert of Moyenmoutiers. Archbishop Maurilius himself was a disciple of the Cardinal Bishop of Ostia, Peter Damian. But it was Hildebrand who triumphed and became most influential after he master-minded the accession of Nicholas II in 1058. It was to be Hildebrand who won papal approval for William's invasion of England.

8

THE MATTER OF ENGLAND

The most peculiar aspect of the relations between England and Normandy between the end of the tenth century and the Norman Conquest is the strangely one-sided nature of the relationship. Norman sources display a fascination with England and English affairs, which is not matched by a similar level of interest in Norman affairs in English sources.

Little is said about Normandy in the major historical source, the *Anglo-Saxon Chronicle*. One version notes the death in 994 of Duke Richard I 'the elder' and the succession of Richard II, his son. Under 1002, the arrival of 'the Lady, Richard's daughter' is noted but that she came to marry King Aethelred goes unrecorded. The destruction of Exeter in 1003 is noted and blamed on the Lady's reeve, 'Hugh, the French fellow' (i.e. a Norman). Then, in 1013 it is noted that the Lady 'crossed the sea to her brother Richard' and that her sons Edward and Alfred also did so in the care of Bishop Aelfhun. Afterwards King Aethelred joined her there. The *Chronicle* relates also how Abbot Aelfsige of Peterborough, finding the monastery of Bonneval almost destitute, bought from the monks the body of St Florentine and took it to England.

Nothing more is recorded until 1024 when another Latin entry notes the death of Richard II and the succession and death of Richard III, who is succeeded by his brother Robert. The latter's death is also recorded under 1031 (correctly 1027) in a misplaced entry. King Edward's accession in England is recorded under 1042 with no reference to any part in it having been played by the Normans. Edward simply took immediate steps to secure the approval of the Witan, even before Harthacnut had been buried, as he wanted to restore the legitimate line of Cerdic after twenty-six years of Danish rule. He immediately became King, as one charter records: 'Ego Eadward rex regali fretus dignitate.'[1] He was crowned a year later.

Yet another Latin entry records, without comment, the Battle of Val-ès-Dunes (*Uallium Dunas*). *The Worcester Chronicle*, 'D', mentions the presence of Frenchmen in a castle, 1052 (for 1051), that is, those in Herefordshire. It implies that at that point there was only one castle in England. Then comes the famous entry recording the visit of 'Willelm Eorl' to Edward's Court, with no explanation of its purpose. There is no indication anywhere in the account that it had anything whatsoever to do with the question of the English Succession. The Worcester and Abingdon, 'D' and 'C', versions record the expulsion of the Archbishop, Robert, from England and of all the Frenchmen who had 'promoted injustice and pronounced unjust judgements and counselled evil within this realm' while Peterborough, 'E', blames the Archbishop and the Frenchmen 'for the discord which had arisen between Earl Godwin and the King', which had led to the expulsion then the return of Earl Godwin.

This is confirmed by the account of the quarrel in the *Vita Aedwardi Regis* in which Archbishop Robert is accused of poisoning the King's mind against the Earl, accusing him of plotting 'the ruin of even Edward himself'. There is still no hint of any connection with the problem of the King's childlessness other than Archbishop Robert's effort to get him to divorce his wife, for which the most probable explanation would be a desire to enable Edward to marry again in the hope of begetting an heir.

The chronicle conventionally attributed to Florence of Worcester[2] adds little to the above sources. It confirms that Emma came to marry King Aethelred and the subsequent flight of Emma and her sons. It also records the attempt of the Aethelings, Alfred and Edward, to return to England 'with many Norman knights in their company' to visit their mother, Emma, which resulted in Alfred's murder by Harold Harefoot. It records that Emma, driven out by Harold in 1037, took refuge in Flanders and not, as one might expect, in Normandy. He stresses the lineage of Edward, descendant of King Alfred, in recording his accession, as though to explain it. He does claim that Eustace of Boulogne had Normans in his company as well as men from Boulogne. He records the arrival in 1052 of 'Earl William the Norman' in the same terms as the entry in the *Worcester Chronicle*, 'D', which he would have consulted. He can name some of the Normans from Herefordshire: Osbern surnamed Pentecost, and his companion, Hugh, who surrendered their castles and went to Scotland. Others, favourites of the King, were allowed to remain:

Robert the deacon, Richard fitzScrob, Alfred the Horse-thegn and Anfrid Cocksfoot. None are from prominent Norman families.

None of these sources has anything to relate about internal Norman affairs, nor do they suggest that Normandy in any way figured in any solution to the problem of the succession. But they do point to a growing Norman presence in England, which is supported by the presence of Norman clergy. King Edward chose a Norman abbot as Archbishop of Canterbury and two Normans became bishops. Other Normans served in the royal household. A small number of Norman knights were settled on the Welsh marches in Herefordshire and constructed a few castles. They appear to have been under the command of the King's nephew Earl Ralph. What is lacking is any real evidence that Duke William was in any way responsible or involved in these decisions by King Edward.

The only reference to any event relating to Normandy, during the conflict between Earl Godwin and the King, is found only in one version of the *Anglo-Saxon Chronicle*. It records simply,

> Then soon Earl [Eorl] William came from beyond the sea with a great troop of French men and the king received him and as many of his companions as suited him and let him go again.[3]

Several historians have disputed the genuineness of this entry. Some do so on the grounds that it strikes the reader as an interpolation, possibly inserted after the Conquest. But that cannot be the case, as there is no reference to this alleged visit in any Norman source. A comparison of the three extant accounts[4] reveals that they give the same events in the same order; Earl Godwin flees the country and goes to Flanders and his son Harold goes to Ireland; Queen Edith is sent to Wherwell (D and E); William the priest (a Norman) is granted the Bishopric of London; Queen Emma dies 14 March 1052. But only the Worcester version mentions the Earl's visit, whereas one might expect to find a reference to it in one of the other versions. 'Florence' of Worcester naturally follows the D text and so is not independent testimony. He adds, ambiguously, that it was 'William the Norman' who came and that the company were given many presents.

But some point out the apparent resemblance between the entry about a Norman visit in 1051 and the post-Conquest notice of the death of William fitzOsbern. In the Worcester text and in

Peterborough, 'E', it says 'the king of the French and *Willem eorl* were to be his [Arnulf of Flanders] guardians'. It has therefore been conjectured, because of the phrase 'Willem eorl', that it was this man and not the Duke who visited King Edward.[5] Others have contended in addition that Duke William was too heavily engaged in war, besieging Domfront and Alençon, to have been readily able to leave the conflict and pay what some see as a state visit to England.

But neither William of Jumièges nor William of Poitiers even refers to any visit and neither makes use of such a visit to strengthen their case. William of Poitiers even has Duke William state that King Edward did not make the promise to him in person. He says rather that Harold's father 'and the others had sworn in my absence' to serve him as lord after Edward's death. The most probable solution to this problem is to accept that 'Willem eorl' was William fitzOsbern.

William of Jumièges devotes eight and a half chapters of his *Gesta Normannorum Ducum* to England and its affairs, mostly in Book 5 on Richard II. He explicitly states, 'We have woven these facts into our work to explain the origin of King Edward for those who do not know about it.' These chapters were added after the Conquest, around 1070, to justify Duke William's claim to the throne, and that is evidence of Norman anxiety to construct a plausible justification for the Conquest. William of Jumièges gathered information from Archbishop Robert, who had been Abbot of Jumièges and returned there when expelled from England. The writer also drew on the contents of the *Inventio et Miracula Sancti Vulfranni* composed around 1053–54.

Furthermore, William of Poitiers repeats Duke William's claim four times in one chapter. For example he writes,

> Edward king of the English by the Will of God, having no heir, had in the past sent Robert, Archbishop of Canterbury, to the Duke, William, to appoint him heir (statuens heredem) to the Kingdom given him[6] by God. But he also at a later date sent to him Harold ... so that he should swear fealty to the Duke concerning his crown and according to Christian custom pledged it with oaths.

He also states that King Edward ordered Earl Harold to swear fealty to William concerning the crown and that, in accordance with Christian custom, he pledged it with oaths.[7] The swearing of fealty might be genuine while the rest was embroidery added to that basic fact. The writer goes on to add that Harold, having so sworn, seized the kingdom, so breaking his oath and becoming a perjurer, then alleges that Duke William urged the Earl to keep the faith he had pledged by oath. There are no legalistic arguments such as are found in William of Poitiers. Instead, he depicts Harold as a man foresworn and nowhere calls him king or admits that he was crowned.

So this writer deems the whole kingdom to have been King Edward's property, which he then bequeathed to Duke William as if it had been an estate or other piece of property. This, as George Garnett has pointed out, is Norman not English custom. The effect of putting the claim in that form was that William only actually received his bequest when he had successfully put an end to King Harold's (alleged) usurpation of it and was anointed King.

There is no claim here that Edward's decision had been confirmed by the English magnates as William of Poitiers was to claim. The content of his story of the sending of Harold to Normandy is not corroborated by any non-Norman source either. The claim that Edward made Duke William his heir does not appear in the contemporary European chronicles such as those of Adam of Bremen or Saxo Grammaticus, although they frequently refer to pacts between kings concerning succession. These writers appear to have thought that many treaties included an agreement on the part of both parties that whichever of the kings outlived the other would have a claim to his throne. Both Magnus of Norway and Swein of Denmark are said to have thought they had a claim to the English throne in the event of Edward dying without an heir.

Scandinavian kings saw England as vulnerable, a soft target for invaders, and their interest in England can explain the similar interest on the part of the Normans. It must have occurred to Duke William, even before his interest was aroused by Archbishop Robert, that he himself could be said to have a tenuous claim to the English throne because of his relationship to King Edward, whose mother, Queen Emma, was William's great-aunt. Edward and William were distant cousins.

Thus the basic fact, the link, which brought about the Norman claim to the English throne derived from the marriage of King Aethelred to Emma of Normandy. It also meant that when Edward's brother, Alfred, was murdered in England in 1036, the Normans thereafter were able to blame Earl Godwin for the murder of Duke William's relative, transfer that guilt to his son Earl Harold, and use that as a justification for the Conquest.

That kinship between Edward and William, in Norman eyes, implied that he would have chosen his kinsman as his heir; William of Poitiers has Duke William claim explicitly, before the battle of Hastings, that 'my lord and kinsman King Edward made me the heir of his kingdom'. Having described William's coronation, he then writes, 'And if it be asked what was his hereditary title, let it be answered that a close kinship existed between King Edward and the son of Duke Robert whose paternal aunt, Emma, was sister of Duke Richard II, daughter of Duke Richard I and mother of Edward himself.'

Thus he glosses over the fact that William was not a descendant of Edward and ignores the fact that Emma, on the death of Aethelred, had married Cnut the Great and had another son, Harthacnut, by him. Her marriage to Cnut had been a better option for Emma than a return to Normandy with the possibility of being married off to some vassal of the Duke. In England she remained a Queen.

Her failure to return meant that, in the 1020s, she became something of an outcast, the subject of a satirical tale, and in the twelfth century, scurrilous stories were told about her. But in the period after the Conquest it suited the purposes of William of Poitiers to overlook the marriage to Cnut and emphasise that she was Edward's mother. Yet she herself, as William of Malmesbury testifies, 'long mocked the needy condition of her son and never aided him' (further proof if it be needed that Edward was not really so well provided for by his Norman relatives as William of Poitiers maintained). Emma is also said to have transferred her hatred for the father, Aethelred, to the son, because she loved Cnut.

The Normans also, by emphasising that Edward had no heir of the body, ignore the fact that in 1051 King Edward had two plausible heirs, the sons of his sister Goda, wife of Count Drogo of Mantes. The elder, Walter, succeeded his father as Count and the younger son, Ralph, came to England and was made Earl of Hereford. They also ignore the existence of the sons of King Edmund Ironside, who had been exiled to Hungary by Cnut the Great. King Edward was childless but he did not lack heirs.

It was William of Jumièges who produced a series of stories, after the Conquest, around 1070, some with an element of truth in them, intended to magnify the connection between England and Normandy. It remains an open question whether he embellished these tales with more details when he took up his pen again in the 1070s or whether they remain as he wrote them before 1054.[8]

He pictures Duke Robert as taking a close interest in Edward and his prospects, insisting that the Aetheling had been brought up to be thoroughly Norman and a protégé of the dukes to whom he owed gratitude for the refuge in Normandy they had provided for him. He says that Duke Robert welcomed Edward at Court, a fact supported by charter evidence from the 1030s.[9] There is no evidence that Richard II had done likewise, nor is there any sign that Edward had been endowed with any estates, without which he was merely a landless pretender. That the dukes consistently supported Edward is only a Norman gloss, part of the rewriting of history to justify the Conquest. One might wonder whether Edward had much reason to be grateful. Exiled princes in straitened circumstances are not known for gratitude to their alleged benefactors. They are more likely to nurse their grievances and seek to keep alive the hopes of their restoration.

It was also claimed that Duke Robert planned an invasion of England on Edward's behalf. William of Jumièges says that it set out for England from the vicinity of Fécamp, but that a storm blew it off course and it ended up at the Island of Jersey, from whence Duke Robert then sent it against Brittany. The writer then asserts that this happened because God had intended that Edward's succession to the English throne should be peaceful. But Fécamp is on the Channel Coast, facing Portsmouth, and Jersey is off the western coast of the Cherbourg Peninsula. It would have had to have been a very strange storm!

William of Poitiers, however, transfers Edward's gratitude to Duke Robert to his son William and, furthermore, claims that Edward and William had been boys together in Normandy! When William was born, Edward was a man of about twenty-four years of age. He is more likely to have known Duke Robert as a youth rather than his son. He certainly did not choose William as his heir, if at all, because they were such close friends. This gambit casts doubt on the story of Edward's gratitude to William and the 'singular honour and intimate affection' bestowed on Edward by Duke William! It should really be referred to Duke Robert, as the *Inventio et Miracula Sancti Vulfranni* had already asserted.

After the departure of Duke Robert on pilgrimage, both of the Aethelings returned, independently, to England after the death of

Cnut, apparently at the invitation of their mother, Emma.[10] Both were accompanied by a force of Norman knights. Edward landed on the South Coast and, despite claims of a local victory over English opposition, was ignominiously driven out. Alfred, having sailed from Wissant, similarly landed, accompanied mainly by Flemish knights, and was apparently ensnared by Earl Godwin. Alfred was handed over to King Harold Harefoot, taken to Ely and blinded, dying of the savagery with which it was carried out, while his men were variously killed, sold into slavery, imprisoned, blinded, mutilated or scalped.

There is no reason to suspect that either expedition was sponsored by ducal authority, and it is unlikely that the young Bastard's guardians would have done so, being more concerned with maintaining order in Normandy. The Aethelings had probably gathered support from landless adventurers hoping for reward. They were no threat to King Harold Harefoot and had no official Norman support, since Normandy had been rendered helpless by Duke Robert's death. Nor was the situation in Normandy much better by 1042.

In 1042 Harthacnut, Edward's half-brother, died suddenly, leaving no heir other than Edward. He had already been recalled to England by Harthacnut, and been welcomed as Aetheling by various of the Anglo-Danish nobility, to whom he pledged that he would maintain the 'Laws of Cnut'. He was now called upon to succeed Harthacnut as he was acceptable to the English as of the line of Cerdic, and descended from Alfred the Great, and to the Danish element as the half-brother of Harthacnut. The *Anglo-Saxon Chronicle* appears to suggest that Harthacnut had been, or was planning, to associate Edward with himself in his government of the country. One version reminds its readers that, although Edward had been exiled, he had been 'sworn in as king; and then he dwelled thus in his brother's court'. Perhaps he was referring to the story that in his youth Edward had been 'declared beforehand by the oath of the people to be worthy to be raised at some time to the throne of his ancestral kingdom'.[11]

William of Poitiers was to claim that Edward had been received by the English through the Bastard's 'aid and counsel'. He is said to have made 'just demands' for Edward's restoration and that the English had 'eagerly arranged Edward's return to them with only a small Norman escort to avoid Norman conquest if the Norman count should come himself, for they well knew his reputation in war'. William, a boy of about fourteen, had, as yet, no military reputation whatsoever and was in constant peril of losing his own life. The story is meant to explain why Edward had only a few Normans with him, in 1041, and the whole is coloured by the writer's knowledge of the events of 1066. English sources, of course, are unaware of any alleged Norman interference and Normandy in 1041–42 was in no fit state to wage war on anybody.

No more of English affairs is recorded in Norman sources until the ejection of Archbishop Robert of Jumièges from the See of Canterbury in 1052 as a result of Earl Godwin's triumphant return from exile. William of Jumièges was to assert that 'Edward, too, King of the English, by Divine dispensation lacking an heir, had sent Robert, archbishop of Canterbury, to the Duke to nominate him as the heir to the kingdom which God had given him.' No date is set for this but, if it happened, then the most likely time would have been in the spring of 1051 when the Archbishop went to Rome for his pallium. He could well have passed through Normandy on his way there.

Unfortunately for the truth of the Norman claim, there is no corroboration of this in English sources, or anywhere else other than the pages of William of Poitiers. In 1051–52 there was a quarrel between the King and Earl Godwin. The *Anglo-Saxon Chronicle* attributes it to the Earl's defiance of a royal order to harry Dover, which was part of his earldom, because of the fighting between Count Eustace of Boulogne and his men (some of whom may have been Normans) and the townspeople of Dover. They had objected to the high-handed manner in which the Count tried to billet his men on the town and seize control of the 'burh' on the cliff top. A citizen was killed on his own doorstep and a fight broke out in which there were about twenty casualties on each side. Eustace, as husband of Edward's niece Goda, had demanded that Dover be punished for its insolence.

Godwin refused and called up his sons and all his supporters. There was a stand off at first, as men were unwilling to risk civil war for such a matter. Godwin's support dwindled as the days passed and the King struck, condemning the Earl unheard for refusing to attend a hearing unless he was allowed a safe conduct and hostages for his security. The Godwinesons were expelled and Robert of Jumièges became the King's chief counsellor.

The *Vita Edwardi Regis* reveals that Robert, at the time Bishop of London, had poisoned the King's mind against the Earl, persuading him to reject Aethelric, the choice of the Christchurch Canterbury monks and a relative of the Earl, as Archbishop and to appoint Robert himself instead. The Archbishop and Earl Godwin also then quarrelled over lands held by the Earl which had previously been Canterbury lands. Robert persuaded the King, so it was claimed, that the Earl was scheming to attack him, reminding Edward of Godwin's involvement in his brother's death. These charges too must have been made against Godwin as well as his defiance over Dover.

The basis of the quarrel is well documented and it clearly had nothing to do with the question of the succession, which had not yet been raised. Archbishop Robert sought to persuade Edward that he ought to divorce Edith, Godwin's daughter. Two motives are likely: to remove the last member of the Godwineson family from Court and to persuade the King to marry again in order to secure the heir Edith had failed to provide.

William of Jumièges and William of Poitiers maintain that the principal agent through whom the alleged promise was delivered to the Duke was Archbishop Robert. Jumièges asserts that Edward 'sent Robert, archbishop of Canterbury, to the Duke, with a message appointing the Duke as heir to the kingdom which God had entrusted to him'. Poitiers words his claim very carefully; he says that Edward 'as an appropriate gift resolved to make him (William) the heir of the crown obtained by his efforts. To this end with the assent of his magnates, and by the agency of Robert, archbishop of Canterbury as his ambassador in this matter, he sent him, as hostages of the most powerful family in the kingdom, the son and grandson of Earl Godwin'. There is absolutely no corroboration for this in any English source.

These two writers offer essentially the same story, derived no doubt from the same source, the official version of the Norman claim put out by the Duke himself. It remains necessary to provide a credible explanation of how William came to believe that King Edward had so designated him as his heir. Exactly why the Normans expressed the claim in that particular form, an act of formal designation of William as his heir, to take effect when the King died, is best left until an account is given of exactly how the Duke described what had been done after he had become King.

If Archbishop Robert was the agent through whom William came to accept that he was Edward's heir, then there are only two possibilities. Robert could have been instructed to convey a message to the Duke in spring 1051 when he went to Rome in order to obtain his pallium.[12] He could easily have passed through Normandy and visited William. The Norman sources assert that the consent had been obtained of the three great earls, Godwin, Leofric and Siward, and of 'Archbishop Stigand'. There are difficulties about accepting this. There is no reason to accept that Earl Godwin would have agreed, let alone the other earls, and there is no record of such an agreement in English sources, even though the Anglo-Saxon Chroniclers are very well informed about events at Court between 1049 and 1052. There is no hint of such an arrangement anywhere. A lesser point is that Stigand was only Bishop of Winchester at the time, though calling him 'Archbishop' may reflect only that he had become so in 1052. But it would have made more sense for the Normans to have claimed the consent of Archbishop Robert in association with the three earls.

It has been suggested that the message, if it existed, was conveyed by Archbishop Robert when, in late summer 1052, he and other Normans hastily fled when they learned of the triumphant return of Earl Godwin. While those with castles or lands in Herefordshire fled west, or north-east to 'Robert's castle' in Essex,[13] the Norman clergy, Archbishop Robert, Bishop William of London, Bishop Ulf of Dorchester and their companions, fought their way out of London's Eastgate, injuring many young men who tried to stop them, and left England in a leaky old tub of a vessel.

The Chroniclers gleefully relate that the flight was so precipitate that Robert left his pallium behind. He 'abandoned his pallium and all Christendom here in the land just as God wanted it, because he had earlier obtained the honour just as God did not want it'.[14] Canon Law actually condemns bishops who desert their sees in this manner. But Archbishop Robert, who went off to Rome to complain, successfully convinced the Pope that he had been driven out of his see rather than, as the *Chronicle* insists, having deserted it. Neither in 1052 nor in 1066 was any attempt made by Rome to seek evidence from England.

It has therefore been suggested that Robert, smarting from his loss of the see and the wealth and prestige that went with it, sought to exact his revenge. It could be that it was at this point that he had seized the son and grandson of the Earl and taken them to Normandy. Those who tried to prevent him leaving London could have been trying to recover the hostages.[15] If so, then Robert could now have produced them as evidence of the truth of his statements and have assured Duke William that he was Edward's chosen heir. As the King had no heir in 1051, it is only too likely that, once Earl Godwin was out of the way, the Archbishop had discussed with the King various possibilities (including divorce and remarriage) and had pointed out the advantage of selecting his kinsman as his heir. King Edward might well have allowed the Archbishop to assume that he approved of the idea. The Archbishop is said to have had so much influence over the King that if he said a black crow was white, Edward would have trusted the Archbishop's mouth rather than his own eyes.

It remains a possibility that King Edward had in fact made diplomatic noises to the effect that Duke William was his chosen heir since Duke William was convinced that Harold's father, Earl Godwin, 'and other aforesaid magnates had sworn in my absence' that they would receive him as lord.

None of these Norman claims surfaced until after the Conquest was an established fact. The Duke had made no attempt to visit his relative in England, or seek an invitation to do so and, according to the Norman story, made no public mention of it until Earl Harold fell into his hands, most likely in 1064. The date remains uncertain because neither of the Norman writers cares to give a date and there is no confirmatory reference to the affair in English sources.

While Duke William had been busy consolidating his hold over Normandy between 1054 and 1060, affairs in England had continued without any reference to Normandy. If there had been some sort of promise by King Edward, conveyed to the Duke, the return of the Godwinesons appears to have nullified it. There had been an immediate anti-French backlash in 1052 after Earl Godwin returned. The major Norman clergy had been expelled. Only William, Bishop of London, was allowed back since he was a favourite of King Edward and politically harmless. The 'Frenchmen in the castle' led by Osbern Pentecost[16] sought the permission of Earl Leofric to pass through his earldom of Mercia and seek refuge in Scotland, where they took service with Macbeth.

All the Frenchmen were outlawed 'who earlier promoted illegality and passed unjust judgements and counselled bad counsel'. Only those whom the King 'liked to have about him, who were faithful to him and all his people' were allowed to stay. The *Chronicle of Chronicles* of Florence of Worcester[17] names a few: Richard fitzScrob, Robert the Deacon, Alfred the King's Marshall, and Anfrid

'Cocksfoot'. Nothing more is said about them. The King's nephew, Earl Ralph of Mantes also remained. Archbishop Robert was deemed, in the opinion of a monk at Canterbury,[18] to have abandoned his see. He comments that Archbishop Robert had gone 'oversea immediately, forsaking his pallium', which, he says, was 'God's purpose ... since he had obtained that dignity against His Will'. The King then appointed Stigand, Bishop of Winchester, who had acted as intermediary between the King and the Godwinesons, to Canterbury.

Archbishop Stigand was a pluralist, continuing to hold Winchester and other ecclesiastical offices while Archbishop, and accepting Canterbury without seeking papal approval, so he was rejected by Pope Leo IX and all subsequent reforming popes. Rome had accepted the account given by Robert of Jumièges, who lodged an appeal there against his ejection, so Stigand was regarded as having become Archbishop in an uncanonical manner. Only the anti-pope, Benedict X (who was rejected by the reforming cardinals), had sent him a pallium (seeking endorsement of his election). That was in 1058, and it was only for a short time afterwards that Stigand consecrated bishops. Then Benedict's replacement, Pope Nicholas II, annulled all his predecessor's acts and Stigand's pallium lost its validity. Nicholas did, however, grant Ealdred, Bishop of Worcester, a pallium as Archbishop of York, in 1062, while denying one to Stigand for Canterbury.

But in 1054 action had been taken to discover the whereabouts of the sons of King Edmund Ironside, nephews of King Edward, driven into exile by Cnut the Great. William of Malmesbury attributes this initiative to King Edward himself, claiming that he sent a message to 'the king of the Huns' (i.e. the Holy Roman Emperor who was King of Germany) asking him to send Edward the Aetheling and all his household to England. So Bishop Ealdred was sent to Cologne, to Emperor Henry III, seeking his help and that of Archbishop Heriman of Cologne to bring back to England the elder of the two, Edward (known as the Exile). There is also evidence that Earl Harold, who had succeeded his father in 1053, went abroad in 1056, to Flanders, where he witnessed a charter issued by Count Baldwin in that year. While in Flanders Harold met other leading European rulers, especially the Regent, Agnes and her young son, the Emperor Henry IV, and Pope Victor II. It is possible that he used his powers of persuasion to secure the return of the Aetheling Edward and that it was possibly then that Earl Harold went to Rome, perhaps in the entourage of the Pope.

In 1057, therefore, Edward the Aetheling returned from exile, only to die shortly after his arrival, even before he could meet King Edward, and was buried in St Paul's Cathedral. The Worcester Chronicler laments his death as a 'cruel fate and harmful to all this nation'. His wife, Agnes, and his children, Margaret, Christina and Edgar, also returned at this time, and they remained in England. Edgar settled at Court, his sister Margaret eventually married Malcolm Canmore, King of Scotland, and his other sister, Christina, became a nun. William of Malmesbury recorded that Edward had lost 'the hope of his first choice' and therefore 'gave the succession to William, Duke of Normandy', though he gives no details as to how or when this might have happened. He can only point to Harold's sojourn in Normandy, but that came seven years later.

9

WILLIAM CONSOLIDATES HIS HOLD ON NORMANDY: HAROLD BECOMES HIS PRISONER

After the deaths of Henry I of France and Geoffrey Martel of Anjou in 1060, William of Normandy continued to keep his own counsel about any ambitions he might have had regarding England. Events conspired to reinforce and consolidate his power. Count Baldwin of Flanders, his father-in-law, became regent for the young French King, Philip I. Brittany was weakened by internal civil war. Anjou became less of a threat under Geoffrey the Bearded. That left William free to deal with Maine. There he set about securing a position of dominance by methods that curiously foreshadow those he applied to England.

In Maine the heir of Count Hugh (who died in 1051), his son Herbert, had been driven into exile by Geoffrey Martel. Count Herbert apparently turned in desperation to the Norman Duke, who was quick to see the advantage to be gained by promoting his claims. As a result, a matrimonial pact was arranged, sometime around 1055. Herbert promised to marry a daughter of the Duke, while his own infant sister, Margaret, was affianced to William's eldest son, Robert. What seems to have been the usual diplomatic agreement was reached, to seal the bargain, by which William, in the event of Herbert dying without children, would inherit the Comté of Maine. Herbert was thus in effect William's protégé, if not his vassal, and William enjoyed the prospect of possibly adding Maine to his dominions.

The parallels with the case of England are clear. William was to be heir and possess Maine by inheritance should Herbert have no children, just as he was to claim England as heir of the childless Edward. There was a double marriage alliance, just as Earl Harold allegedly agreed to marry a daughter of the Duke while Harold's sister was to marry a Norman of suitable rank. William of Poitiers

1. A drawing of the Abbaye aux Hommes in Caen.

Below: 2. Normandy during the reign of Duke William.

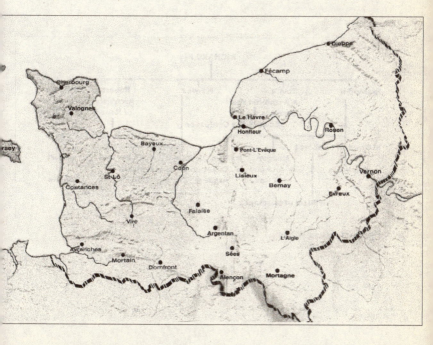

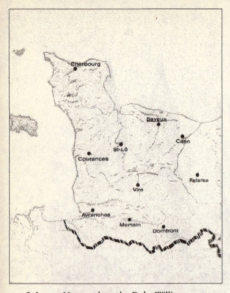

3. Lower Normandy under Duke William.

4. Upper Normandy under Duke William.

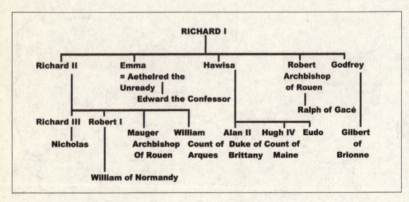

5. The uncles of Duke William.

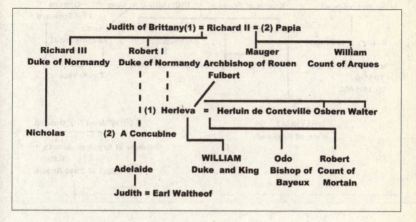

6. William's immediate family.

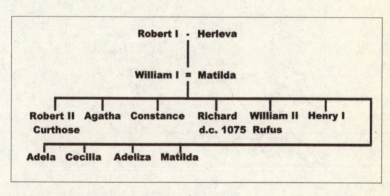

7. The sons and daughters of King William.

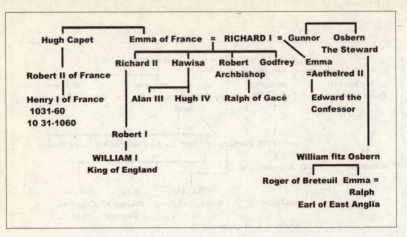

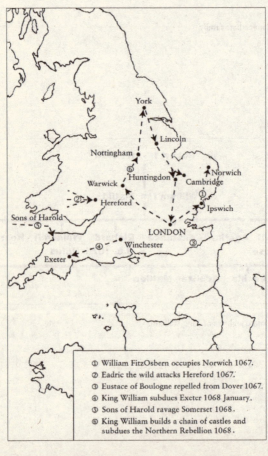

① William FitzOsbern occupies Norwich 1067.
② Eadric the wild attacks Hereford 1067.
③ Eustace of Boulogne repelled from Dover 1067.
④ King William subdues Exeter 1068 January.
⑤ Sons of Harold ravage Somerset 1068.
⑥ King William builds a chain of castles and
   subdues the Northern Rebellion 1068.

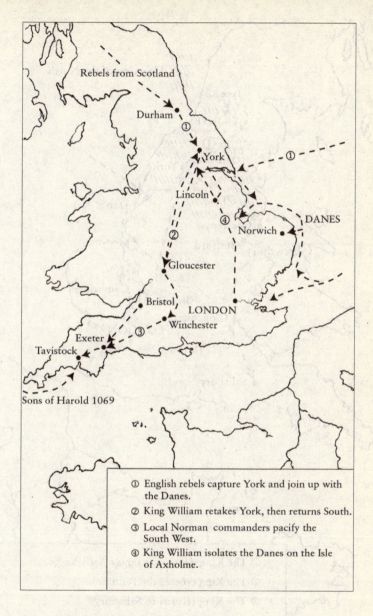

① English rebels capture York and join up with the Danes.

② King William retakes York, then returns South.

③ Local Norman commanders pacify the South West.

④ King William isolates the Danes on the Isle of Axholme.

Above: 10. The Risings of 1069 - 70.

Opposite top: 8. Other relationships of Duke William.

Opposite bottom: 9. The first stirrings of revolt.

① The King drives out Edgar Aetheling.
② The King crosses the Pennines.
③ The King returns to Salisbury
④ King William v. Hereward.

11. The crushing of rebellion.

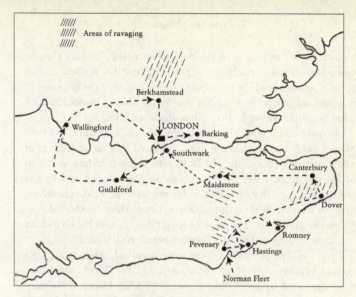

12. The Normans overawe London.

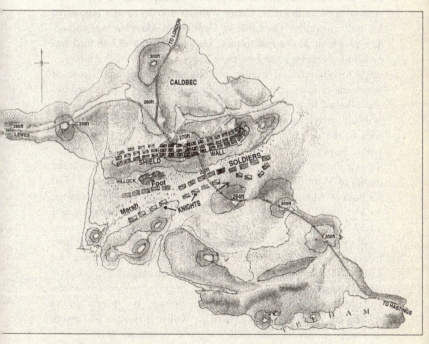

13. The battlefield of Hastings; 1066.

himself draws attention to the parallel involved; he says that he wished 'to record as truthfully as possible, how this William ... was to take possession of the principality of Maine, *as of the kingdom of England,* not simply by force but also by the laws of justice'. Exactly what the writer meant by that will be discussed later.[1]

The pact concerning Maine had little significance while Geoffrey Martel lived, but his death in 1060, followed by that of Herbert in 1062, precipitated a crisis. The Duke now claimed Maine on behalf of his son Robert but in Maine resistance developed, led by the border lord, Geoffrey of Mayenne. He put forward a rival candidate, none other than Walter, Count of the Vexin, elder brother of Earl Ralph the Timid, and a nephew of King Edward, with his own claim (which he never sought to vindicate) to the English throne.

Two disputed territories were now involved: Maine, a battle ground between Anjou and Normandy, and the Vexin, which had been contested by both Duke Robert and King Henry I. Norman troops harried the Vexin and the Duke himself invaded Maine. Hostilities continued into 1063. William captured Le Mans and strengthened its defences. Count Walter surrendered and renounced his right to Maine. The castle of Geoffrey of Mayenne was sacked. The people of Maine had to meet Duke William, 'call him lord and prostrate themselves and bow to his dignity' (just as the English were made to do in 1066). William of Poitiers even calls him 'victor' of which the primary meaning is 'conqueror'. Geoffrey surrendered but was allowed to keep his lands and castle on condition of accepting William's overlordship. The castle had allegedly been captured by a trick of the sort William was accustomed to practice. He paid two young boys to slip secretly into the castle and start a fire and so distract the garrison. It is likely that at this time the Duke rebuilt the castles of Mont Barbet and Ambrières to strengthen his defences and his hold on Maine. By the beginning of 1064 William was its master. So Maine had been subdued by a combination of force, trickery and intimidation.

All this made the Duke secure against any attack on his southern frontier from northern France should he wish to venture overseas. Count Walter and his wife, Biota, who had been taken into 'protective custody' after the fall of Le Mans, died in suspicious circumstances, and there were the usual rumours of poison, as Orderic Vitalis reports. As Sir Charles Oman remarks, 'William's enemies had a way of disappearing, either into endless captivity or into the grave.'[2]

At about this time Duke William also dealt with the last flickers of opposition to his rule within Normandy. Robert fitz Giroie, who held the castles of Saint-Géneri and Roche-Igé, revolted so William moved against him, besieging him at Montreuil-l'Argillé. Robert held out until his wife, Alice (a cousin of the Duke), gave him an apple to eat and he died of it. The usual rumour spread that he had been poisoned. He was replaced by his heir, Ernault fitz Giroie, but he too was accused of plotting rebellion in conjunction with Ralph de Tosny, and Duke William banished both of them, confiscating their lands.

Ralph went off to Italy but Ernault concealed himself in the 'maquis' around Chartres and carried out raids on the Pays d'Ouche. His aim was to regain possession of his castle of Échauffour but the ducal garrison beat him off. He too then fled to Italy. Several magnates, including Hugh de Montfort and William of Breteuil, interceded on behalf of the two exiles. They were worried about the loss of manpower caused by renewed emigration to Italy. The Duke was persuaded to recall both and restore them to his favour.

Having mastered Maine, the Duke now turned his attention to Brittany. There, Duke Conan II, hoping to repulse Norman ambitions, had directly challenged William, who had been stirring up trouble for Conan among the Breton lords. The Duke now launched an expedition during 1064. It had limited aims, more of a punitive expedition than an invasion, intended to give support to one of Conan's rebellious vassals, Ruallon, Lord of Dol, as William of Poitiers reports, as a means of punishing Conan for his temerity.

This was the expedition on which William was accompanied by Earl Harold, who was enjoying – if that is the right word – ducal 'hospitality' after having fallen into William's hands after a mysterious Channel crossing.

The Norman force crossed the River Couesnon, where Earl Harold, as the Bayeux Tapestry shows, rescued two men from the treacherous quicksands in a remarkable feat of strength. The Normans went on to raise Conan's siege of Dol, threatening to cut off his supplies and his means of retreat. The Bretons hastily retreated into the interior but the Duke was too wily to risk pursuing them. He was running short of supplies himself so turned back into Normandy. Conan, in alliance with Count Geoffrey the Bearded of Anjou, then rallied his men and pursued the Normans as far as the border. William promptly about-faced and defied his enemies but neither side was prepared to risk open battle. The affair then just petered out as both sides ran out of supplies and withdrew.

What this did accomplish was to provide both William and Harold with an opportunity to observe one another on campaign and form an opinion of their relative strengths and weaknesses. The *Vita Edwardi Regis* comments that Harold had 'studied the character, policy and strength of the princes of Gaul' and this would have been one of the occasions when he was able to do so. Poitiers has William observe, 'We know Harold's cunning very well.'

How, then, had Earl Harold come to be in William's power? The Norman version of events is beguiling. It is asserted, though without a shred of independent evidence to support it, by both William of Jumièges and William of Poitiers, that he had been sent to Normandy by King Edward for the express purpose of guaranteeing the crown 'to the duke by his fealty and confirm the same with an oath according to Christian usage' (Jumièges) and 'he despatched Harold to William in order that he might confirm his [Edward's, that is] promise by an oath' (Poitiers).

Both assert that Harold was either 'borne along by the wind' to or 'only escaped the perils of the sea by making a forced landing' on the coast of Ponthieu. The Bayeux Tapestry, without explicitly saying so in its captions, confirms this account visually. Harold is seen to take leave of the King, set sail from Bosham, the wind is 'full' (*plenis*), and he lands in Ponthieu. Thereafter he is apprehended by the men of Ponthieu and delivered into the hands of its Count, Guy, a vassal of Duke William, to whom he surrenders his sword. This is done at the castle of Beaurain on the border of Ponthieu farthest from Normandy. The Count thereupon throws him into prison along with his retinue (according to both writers). The one thing Count Guy does not do is to treat Harold as a King's Envoy. William of Poitiers comments that the local people, in 'an abominable custom', imprisoned and maltreated strangers, especially rich ones, who fell into their hands. Their fate was worse than that of actual shipwreck as they could be tortured 'even to the point of death' or be sold into slavery (presumably if they were unable to provide a ransom). This is added to the account to underline Harold's debt of gratitude to Duke William for what followed.

William, when he heard of this, sent messengers to Count Guy and secured Harold's release 'by prayers and threats'. Guy delivered him to the Duke at the castle of Eu. It has been likened to a small-time gangster being called to order by a more powerful operator.

There is little doubt that the Earl was now in William's custody and beholden to him for his release from imprisonment. William of Poitiers is careful to stress that Guy could 'at his pleasure have tortured or killed him'. In view of the fate of other captives held by Duke William, Harold's new position was little different.

But the Duke was determined to play out a theatrical performance of magnanimity. He purported to rejoice, 'to have so illustrious a guest who had been sent to him by the nearest and dearest of his friends', that is, King Edward. So dear were these friends that they had made little or no contact since 1041. He insisted that Harold accompany him to Brittany, displaying him in the role of a 'fidelis', as though he had done homage and become his man.

The comedy was played out before an audience of magnates and William, no doubt professing admiration for his strength and bravery, rewarded Harold with a gift of arms, a suit of armour and a banner.[3] Some suggest that William conferred knighthood on Harold but this remains uncertain. It is not clear that such ceremonial knighting existed in 1064 or that it would have been acceptable to an English earl. There then, according to the Norman account, followed the famous oath.

In Eadmer of Canterbury's version of events[4] it is made clear that the first Earl Harold learned of William's claim to the English throne was when the Duke himself told Harold that he had been promised it by Edward when he was a young man in Normandy. William then demanded Harold's co-operation in securing the throne, offering, as an inducement, the hand of one of his daughters in marriage. Eadmer further asserts that upon Harold's return to England the King said to him, 'Did I not say that William would get the better of me and that this journey of yours would bring many problems to the realm?' This implicitly denies that Harold had been sent to Normandy. Eadmer is also portraying King Edward as capable of foretelling the future.

William of Jumièges simply records that Harold 'performed fealty to him [the Duke] in respect of the kingdom with many oaths' and was sent back to England. Perhaps Harold did and, if so, plainly did so under duress to secure his freedom. Canon Law lays down as a basic principle that no oath taken under duress is binding.

That the Duke made some demand of Harold to which he agreed is clear. What is not so evident is the exact nature of it. One aspect of the matter that is given little prominence in most accounts is that

Harold and William had agreed to a two-fold marriage alliance. This is one of the few aspects of the story that is corroborated from other sources, some of which make it the main bone of contention between them.

According to Scandinavian tradition,[5] Earl Harold, having set out on a sea voyage to 'Bretland', was caught up in a 'perilous storm' and ended up at Rouen. 'Bretland' is Old Norse for Wales, an unlikely destination for Harold. (It probably crept into the story because Harold had been in Wales in 1063 with a fleet.) Harold's sojourn is set in the autumn of the year and he is said to have remained with Duke William until winter approached. If that is so, then suggestions that he was in Normandy in 1065 are implausible since the autumn of 1065 was when the Earl was involved in dealing with the rising against his brother Tostig.

Harold is described as living as the 'jarl' William's guest, entertained by his wife, Matilda, with whom he had long discussions. He is presented as at last approaching the Duchess with the request for the hand of one of the Duke's daughters in marriage. This reflects the customary practice in the eleventh century for marriages to be arranged by the women of the family. He then raised the matter with the Duke and was duly betrothed to one of the daughters. Winter being over, the Earl went back to England, parting with William on terms of 'the greatest friendship'. But it is pointed out that Harold never returned to claim his bride.

The story cannot be accepted in this form, as the source is hopelessly confused about other affairs in England. But it is substantiated to a certain extent by other sources. The *Chronicle of St Andreas of Cambrai* attributed Duke William's anger and decision to invade England to Harold's refusal to marry his daughter. The *Annals of St Bertin* at St Omer, in Flanders, say that Harold was slain because he was the man 'who had refused to accept the daughter of William himself in marriage'. William of Malmesbury states that Harold was given the hand of the Duke's daughter 'and the whole of her inheritance' in return for an oath confirming the Duke in possession of the castle at Dover (that is, the fortified burh) and, after Edward's death, the Kingdom of England.[6] This is certainly derived from the text of William of Poitiers. A variety of sources make the marriage a subsidiary issue while others elevate it to a primary role. Henry of Huntingdon[7] says that Harold, whom he asserts was on his way to Flanders when driven by a storm to Ponthieu, 'swore to

William, on many precious relics of the saints, that he would marry his daughter and after Edward's death would preserve England for William's benefit'.

Orderic Vitalis alleged that Harold had made a fraudulent claim that he had been offered William's daughter in marriage (which contradicts William of Malmesbury). He uses this to assert that Harold, on his return to England, told the King that the Duke had promised him his daughter and had transferred to the Earl his rights to the throne of England. This is pure fiction intended to depict Harold as a liar. It is meant to show that Harold 'stole the honour of the diadem' after Edward died. Orderic also records[8] that William promised Earl Harold his daughter, who is named here as Adeliza, together with half the kingdom! This is romance, of course, not history, but does testify to the existence of the proposed marriage alliance.

William of Poitiers, determined as usual to justify the Duke's actions, says that William 'did not desire his [Harold's] death but wished to increase for him the power of his father Godwin and give him in marriage to his own daughter'. These repeated references to a marriage offer cannot be lightly dismissed. William had used the same ploy in staking his claim to Maine.

It is not certain which daughter was meant; Orderic names Adeliza, others identify her as Agatha, most give no name because the marriage never happened. But such betrothals were certainly sworn to in this period and that would explain the public ceremony displayed so vividly in the Bayeux Tapestry, which does not state what the content of this oath actually was.

One possibility is that this woman, shown in the Bayeux Tapestry and named Aelfgiva, is Harold's sister, who was to marry a Norman lord, and if so the scene relates to the marriage alliance which forms part of the story. Alternatively the woman could be the daughter William had promised to Harold. If so, then she is named 'Aelfgiva' as the name by which she would have been known in England, just like Queen Emma. However, the Tapestry, here as elsewhere, assumes that the viewer would be able to fill in the details for himself. Viewed by a Norman these scenes reflect the story told by the Norman Chroniclers; viewed by an Englishman, or impartial observer, other interpretations become possible.

The Bayeux Tapestry is a major source of evidence for understanding what happened between William and Harold but the manner in which that evidence is presented, with significant omission of any attempt to spell out clearly the meaning of the scenes, reveals what could well be a deliberate effort to undermine the 'official' account of Harold's sojourn in Normandy as presented in other Norman sources.

This attitude on the part of the designer of the Tapestry is quite subversive. He was working for the patron who commissioned the work, Bishop Odo of Bayeux, the Bastard's half-brother. The Tapestry was preserved for most of the Middle Ages in the treasury of Bayeux Cathedral and a number of persons depicted in its scenes have been identified as vassals of the Bishop.

Yet at points where he could have been much more explicit about what was going on, the designer appears to have deliberately avoided doing so. Plate one[9] shows Harold taking leave of the King, but does not name his destination nor state that the King is 'sending' him anywhere. Instead he remarks, unnecessarily, that Harold and his men went to Bosham! He puts the Earl on the same level of status as the Duke. Harold is Duke of the English and William, Duke of the Normans. Harold then merely puts to sea, with no destination mentioned. One scene[10] shows William bestowing arms and armour on the Earl but there is nothing explicit to suggest that the Duke was making him a knight. In the most crucial scene of all,[11] nothing is said about the content of the oath that Harold swears yet such a phrase as 'about the crown' (*de corona*) could easily have been added.

King Edward's deathbed is shown, exactly as described in the *Vita Edwardi*; he is surrounded by figures representing Earl Harold, Queen Edith and Archbishop Stigand, and is supported as he tries to sit up by a figure that probably represents Robert fitz Wymarc. Here the designer avoids the issue altogether; Edward is merely said to address his vassals, yet his hand and that of the Earl are almost touching.

The most subversive element in the construction of the Tapestry is found by studying the figures in the lower border. At several points the birds and beasts depicted are not merely decorative. They portray scenes from the Fables of Aesop which warn of danger to the crafty or deceitful and to the unwary; they show the Fox and the Crow, which illustrates deceit and flattery and occurs twice; the Wolf and the Lamb represents deceit again, as does that of the Wolf and the Crane. A lion is shown who cheats his companions and eats all their prey. To a Norman observer it is Harold who flatters the

Duke and deceives him with false promises, to others it is a general warning about deceit and suggests that William is not to be trusted. The charge of perjury against Harold is intended to cover up the weakness of the Norman claims.

During the exchanges which took place between the two rivals early in 1066, William is more than once depicted in written sources as demanding that Harold fulfil his oath to marry his daughter, to which Harold is reported to have observed that the daughter he had been promised was dead and that in any case he could not marry a foreign bride without the consent of his magnates, that is, the Witan. He also insists that any promise to hand over the kingdom to William is invalid. As for the other part of the agreement, that his sister should marry a Norman, he remarks sardonically that she too was dead; 'If you, Duke, still wish to have the body, as it is now, I will send it to you, lest I be judged to have broken the oath I swore.' It almost looks as though Harold was saying that only a marriage alliance had been agreed. This is much in the style of the Norse sagas, which present conflicts between princes as personal quarrels.

The Norman version insists that the oath was concerned with the succession to the kingdom which had been bequeathed to the Duke by his kinsman King Edward. If that was an accurate account of the Norman case and if, but only if, such a bequest could be made, then William the Bastard was the rightful heir to the English throne and the English, in resisting him, automatically became rebels and could be treated as such. But it is by no means clear in what sense William of Poitiers thought that the Duke could be given such a bequest. Nor is he any clearer about how the Duke could, during King Edward's lifetime, have made a gift to Harold by promising him continued possession of everything he already held in England.

A comparison with the account, in William of Poitiers, of how Herbert of Maine behaved is significant here. He was said to have 'come as a suppliant … and given himself to the Duke with his hands and received back from him everything of his, like a knight from a lord'.

William of Poitiers seems to be influenced by what he saw happening in England after the Conquest. He notes that Earls Edwin and Morcar 'surrendered themselves and all their possessions' to William and he 'restored to them all that they possessed'. He attributes the ceremony by which lands were conferred on knights to the cases of Herbert and Harold. He had not witnessed either ceremony.

It is likely that after the return from Brittany, the Duke revealed to the Earl his claim to the English throne and began a campaign, probably of veiled menace, aimed at securing from the Earl a pledge to support his claim when the appropriate time came, that is, after King Edward's death. Inducements were offered. Harold was assured that he would retain his position in England and all his estates, possibly even that these would be increased, and a double marriage alliance was proposed, just as in the case of Herbert II of Maine. The prospect was dangled before Harold of the release of one of the hostages, either his youngest brother Wulfnoth or his nephew, Tostig's son Hacon. These unfortunate men are thought to have been taken to Normandy by Archbishop Robert when he fled in 1052, but there is no direct evidence for this.

Later commentators, seeking an explanation for Harold's journey other than that he had been sent by King Edward, which no subsequent Anglo-Norman writer really endorsed, thought Harold's real purpose had been to secure the release of the hostages.[12] The weakness of that is that there is no apparent reason why he should suddenly have decided to do so. In fact only one hostage, Hacon, appears to have been released, as William still had Wulfnoth as his prisoner after the Conquest.

Sources disagree as to where the oath-taking took place; Bonneville-sur-Touques, Rouen and Bayeux are all mentioned. Bonneville is the more probable site, as it was in the diocese where William of Poitiers was archdeacon. Orderic mentions Rouen with which he had connections and the Tapestry names Bayeux, the see of its patron. It matters little which was the actual location. But Harold was most likely paraded around Normandy in his capacity as the apparent vassal of the Duke. All Norman accounts insist that the oath-taking included an oath of fealty and, of course, that the oath was sworn by Harold of his own free will and employed 'the sacred ritual recognized among Christian men'. It has been commented that Harold was under obligations to William as a captive to his deliverer, as a guest to his host, as a soldier to his commander and (if the Norman story be accepted) as vassal to his lord.[13]

This has all the hallmarks of another of the Duke's theatrical showpieces designed to impress on the minds of observers that he had achieved an ascendancy over his captive guest, who was plainly displayed as the Duke's 'fidelis' or faithful man. As such, whether he actually swore what the Norman writers asserted that he swore was in practice irrelevant. Harold was displayed as the Duke's 'man' and as such owed him the services of 'auxilium' (his aid) and 'consilium' (his counsel). His aid had already been given by military service in Brittany. He was thus bound, in Norman eyes, to do nothing that would injure the rights of justice of his lord nor make it difficult for his lord to do anything he might wish to do nor do any wrong to his lawful possessions.

William of Poitiers is plainly deducing his statements from what might be expected of a faithful vassal. It was known in Normandy that a small number of castles had been built and garrisoned in England, mainly in Herefordshire, with one at Clavering in Essex, the latter being held by a Breton servant of King Edward, Robert fitz Wymarc. At least two, Osbern Pentecost's castle, known as Ewias Harold and that of Hereford were in Earl Harold's hands, possibly since 1052.

William of Poitiers, in this famous passage, spells out what he thought was entailed by Harold's oath. What he says is that Harold agreed to be the Duke's representative ('vicarius'; deputy, proxy, delegate) at King Edward's Court and to use all his wealth and influence to ensure that, after the King's death, William would be confirmed as King. Also the Earl would garrison the 'castle' at Dover (which before 1066 was simply a walled burh) with a number of the Duke's knights and furthermore place other such garrisons elsewhere in England, at his own expense.

His assertions are frankly quite incredible, not least because Earl Harold never made any attempt to comply with the conditions he lists. Even Norman readers valued William of Poitiers' work less than that of William of Jumièges. The latter's work has survived in several copies; it was reworked and interpolated by Orderic Vitalis, who inserts matter the writer was too discreet to include and tones down all attempts to enhance Duke William's reputation. William of Poitiers' work survives in only one incomplete text, though Orderic shows signs of having read its missing ending.

Harold was then released and allowed to return to England. As he was eventually defeated and killed at Hastings, eleventh-century opinion concluded, inevitably, that he had been in the wrong in taking the throne of England and had incurred the wrath of God by doing so. The sin he had committed was then identified as the breach of his oath, perjury. Yet later writers have found it hard to accept, denying whatever they could safely deny, either by omission or by creating other explanations for his presence in Normandy. They implicitly deny that King Edward actually sent him there. William of Malmesbury invents his own explanation, a fantastic tale of Earl Harold having gone fishing in the Channel until forced to land in Ponthieu. Eadmer of Canterbury suggests he was seeking the release of the hostages. Henry of Huntingdon, who could just be right, says he was off to Flanders, which he had previously visited in 1056, and where Count Baldwin V ruled, half-brother of Earl Tostig's wife Judith.

William of Malmesbury presents his account of the affair in a judicious manner. Having apparently accepted that the King 'gave the succession' to the Duke (but only after the death of Edward the Exile), he then discusses Harold's visit to Normandy. He says that 'some say' that he was sent to Normandy by the King. That phrase is William's way of putting forward a view while disclaiming responsibility for it. He goes on to claim that others 'more familiar with his secret intentions' say Harold was driven to Normandy 'against his will by the violence of the wind' and that he, Harold, invented a story to protect himself. Malmesbury then tells the tale of the 'fishing trip' and says further that Harold was ready to pay ransom for his release, but not to 'an effeminate' like Guy of Ponthieu. Malmesbury himself neither affirms nor denies the story, but says it 'looks very close to the truth'.[14] Similarly, Eadmer of Canterbury, seeking to deny that Harold was sent to the Duke, prefers to allege that he went seeking the release of the hostages.

To deny, as William of Malmesbury seems to do, and others certainly did, that Harold was sent to Normandy is to deny the supposed purpose of that mission, that is, to deny that he was expected to confirm the promise of the succession. To deny that comes close to denying that there was such a promise at all. No one directly does that, perhaps because to do so would be to deny William's assertion that he was King Edward's heir, a dangerous thing to do even during the reigns of his sons, William II and Henry I.

Some historians believe that the promise to Duke William was invented by Archbishop Robert when he returned to Normandy in 1052, as that would be the more probable origin of William's belief and explains why it remained unknown by anyone beyond William's closest associates. Robert of Jumièges could have invented the tale to enhance his status and dignity after his ignominious flight.

Harold had certainly sworn enough to obtain his release from captivity and would have been able to secure dispensation from his oath, on the grounds that he had been under duress, from one of his episcopal supporters, either Bishop Wulfstan of Worcester, who supported Harold in 1066 when he went north into Northumbria to secure the assent of that region to his accession, or Archbishop Ealdred of York, who officiated at his coronation.

It could have been known in his immediate family circle that he had been obliged to take oaths in Normandy. The *Vita Edwardi Regis* says that he was 'rather too generous with oaths' in the context of an account of the Earl clearing himself of the charge of having instigated the rebellion against his brother Tostig. But this source at this point is prejudiced against Harold because the writer thought that he did too little to help Tostig.

Much is often made of the fact that the *Anglo-Saxon Chronicle* for this period is all blank for the year 1064. Some allege that they could have been too embarrassed to record what had happened to Harold. But that does not explain the silence of the *Vita Edwardi*, which is not afraid to criticise him. Nor does it explain the huge gap in the *Abingdon Chronicle*, 'C', from 1056 to 1065. It is simpler to apply Occam's razor and suggest that the other two versions omit 1064 because they knew of nothing significant to record.

Nothing particularly significant is recorded in Norman sources either after 1064. They pass immediately to their version of events in 1066. The English sources are full of the consequences of the rebellion against Earl Tostig. Even the Abingdon scriptorium was moved to record the events of 1065, though it ceases completely in 1066 with a record of the battle of Stamford Bridge. All three versions of the *Chronicle* deal with King Edward's death and the accession of King Harold. The Abingdon, 'C', and Worcester, 'D', versions both say that Edward 'entrusted' the kingdom to Harold. Only Peterborough, 'E', (written up early in the twelfth century) uses the word 'granted', but even so stresses that he was 'elected thereto', that is, chosen by the Witan. Florence of Worcester (also twelfth-century) says Edward 'appointed' Harold 'successor to the kingdom' and that he was 'elected to the royal dignity by the magnates of the whole kingdom'. William of Normandy recognised the significance of 'election' and included a ceremony in the Coronation Ritual in which all present signified their consent to his kingship.

King Edward certainly knew about Harold's adventures in Normandy, and it is possible that it was his alarm at the prospect of a threat from Normandy (note his alleged prophecy that 'within a year and a day, Devils shall stalk through all this land') that moved him to make a deathbed decision to entrust the kingdom to Harold and so encouraged others of the Witan to do likewise.

Two processes can be seen operating during the period 1064–74. From the moment Earl Harold fell into William's hands, the Duke had been at long last able to reveal his belief that King Edward had designated him as his successor. The claim, possibly known only to a few of William's closest associates, had been made public and used to bring pressure to bear on the Earl to swear some sort of oath which could be interpreted as an agreement to support the Duke's claim. Harold had reached some sort of compromise over the claim, which won him his freedom. It is William of Jumièges who provides the most straightforward claim. He says that Edward had sent Harold to Normandy so that he could 'swear fealty to him [William] concerning Edward's crown and confirm it with Christian oaths'. He makes this claim twice, stressing that the fealty concerned the kingdom.

It appears, then, that Harold did swear fealty to the Duke, under duress and solely in order to secure his release, but whether he explicitly did so concerning the crown remains doubtful. However, if he was not actually sent by the King to William (which is also doubtful), then he had no power to make any promises regarding the crown. The Normans, and presumably Duke William himself, as the text of William of Poitiers shows, were applying the example of ducal designation of successors to create a supposed designation of Duke William by King Edward. William of Poitiers was especially concerned to show that the deathbed bequest to Harold should not supersede the prior designation of the Duke. (Yet William himself was to make exactly the same kind of deathbed bequest to his son William Rufus, so implicitly recognising the force of a deathbed bequest.)[15] In fact, any promise, supposing that there had been one, by King Edward to the Duke, lapsed when the King died precisely because he had made a deathbed bequest to Harold. All that William of Poitiers could do to strengthen the case for the legitimacy of the Conqueror's succession was to accuse Harold of perjury in accepting Edward's deathbed bequest. Norman sources do not deny that there was such a bequest, only that it could not cancel out William's prior claim. So they assert that, by becoming King, Harold had broken his oath.

When the King died and Harold calmly asserted his own claim and was readily accepted as King by the English magnates, the Duke first attempted to prevail upon him to fulfil the agreement as it was understood by the Normans and then, when that failed, appealed not only to opinion among the feudal princes of Western Europe but also to the Pope. It is likely, in view of the passages earmarked in his *Collectio*, that Lanfranc became the originator of the legal brief, outlining the Duke's case for the condemnation of Harold as a perjurer and usurper, presented to Rome.

The works of William of Jumièges and William of Poitiers are probably all that survive of materials, which circulated between 1066 and 1076, justifying William's claim to the throne of England. Lanfranc again could well be the influence behind these and other works.

William of Jumièges might well have inserted his digressions into English affairs into his text after the Conquest, carrying out what has been described as 'a crude cut and paste job' in the late 1060s. It ends with William's crowning by the Legates, Easter 1070. The interpolations, as they can easily be described, fit uneasily into his text and disrupt the flow of the narrative. In doing so the writer was clearly rewriting history. Several of his assertions are quite incredible and most are without a shred of confirmatory evidence in English sources, and are in fact contradicted by them.

William of Poitiers wrote after the Conquest, completing his work in about 1077. He too interprets events in a markedly biased manner and his version of the oath which he alleges was sworn by Harold has been rejected by many historians as quite unbelievable. Both writers seek to justify the Conquest on the same grounds, which may be those put to the Pope at Rome, that Harold was a usurper and a perjurer.

Even Domesday Book, produced twenty years later, is not the impartial record that historians have thought it to be.[16] All of its judgements concerning Harold's 'depredations' are made in the light of the Norman assessment of the legality (or rather illegality!) of his accession. To them and to the scribes of Domesday, Harold was not a legitimate king and all of his actions were unlawful. He is even accused of having usurped the kingdom. Consider, for example, the entry in the record for Kent: 'Through Harold's violence, Alnoth Cild stole from St Martin [Dover] Merclesham and Hawkeshurst, for which he granted the Canons an unequal exchange.'[17]

It was not until the twelfth century that dissident interpretations of the Conquest could be, and were, written. The Norman line received much less credibility elsewhere in Europe.[18] Eadmer was unable to restrain his anger in about 1120 when he wrote to the monks of Glastonbury, ridiculing their claim that their predecessors had stolen the body of St Dunstan from Canterbury. Sarcastically he asks them why they had not consulted 'men from overseas' who 'know better how to make up such stories'. He adds, 'you could even have paid someone to make up a plausible lie'. His scepticism about the veracity of Norman writers is very obvious.

The emphasis was all on William's 'hereditary right' in the sense that King Edward had made him a hereditable gift of the succession by means of a *post-obitum* bequest. That had to be asserted to explain why William had made no claim to anything in England while Edward lived. What is never explained is why Edward should have wanted as his heir William, the son-in-law of Count Baldwin of Flanders, who was regarded by Edward as an enemy. The inheritance of the kingdom is treated like a gift after death to a church. So William of Poitiers imposes on England, retrospectively, the Norman custom of ducal succession. Orderic uses the same concept when he discusses the position of Robert Curthose as William's heir.

The succession, it was claimed, had been conceded to William, although it gave him only an expectation of inheritance. It still had to be made good. Norman dukes expected the barons to swear fidelity and do homage to the heir, and that explains why the sources insist that Stigand and the three earls had sworn an oath and given pledge of hand in consenting to Edward's 'bequest'. They were said to have promised to receive William as their lord when Edward died. That was why it was necessary for Harold to renew the ceremony, presumably on behalf of all the English magnates! It remains doubtful whether they did and whether they would have done so in the Norman manner. William of Poitiers strains the reader's credulity in boasting that he never went 'a single step beyond the bounds of truth'.

10

THE DUKE VERSUS THE KING

While nothing is recorded about events in Normandy until after the accession of King Harold Godwineson, in England there had been, in the autumn of 1065, a great upheaval resulting in the exile of Earl Tostig of Northumbria. Earl Harold on behalf of King Edward had renewed the 'Law of Cnut', as demanded by the Northumbrian rebels who also obtained their other major demand, the elevation of Earl Aelfgar's remaining son Morcar in Tostig's place.

The effect on King Edward of this, involving as it did the exile of Earl Tostig, who was apparently highly favoured by the King, was disastrous. King Edward had been in good health up until the autumn of 1065, certainly fit enough for Earl Harold to have built a hunting lodge at Portskewet in Wales to which he hoped to invite him. The *Vita Edwardi* records that the King 'spent much of his time in the glades and woods in the pleasures of hunting' and that he did this throughout his reign. He was also much involved in the design and construction of his great Abbey Church at Westminster.

The year 1065 had seen the consecration of the new church for the Abbey of Wilton, built by command of Queen Edith, shortly before the rebellion broke out.[1] The King is recorded to have then gone to a royal manor near the abbey, at Britford, where he took counsel with his Witan about what was to be done. There is no evidence that he was, as William of Poitiers liked to insist, on the point of death.

But 'changeable weather was already setting in from hard winter' and the King was unable to raise enough troops to put the rebellion down by force. He was horrified, as was the Witan, at the prospect of civil war, and raged against his counsellors. This caused him to be overcome by depression, 'a sickness of the mind' says the *Vita*, protesting to God and complaining, calling down vengeance upon his, as he saw it, disobedient counsellors. The King's condition had become worse after Earl Tostig and his family went into exile and Edward 'languished from the sickness of soul he had contracted'.

But his sickness became physical. He became 'drowsy because of his body's heaviness' and grew more and more fatigued, fell into delirium in which he was 'broken with age and disease and knew not what he said' and much of what he did say was unintelligible. He had hallucinations which those around him interpreted as visions sent by God. Queen Edith struggled in vain to warm his feet. Given the harshness of the winter, the evidence of hallucinations and periods of coma interspersed with periods of restlessness, it would not be unreasonable to suggest that, in his depressed state, he had contracted pneumonia and, in the absence of the possibility of treatment, died of it.

But before the end he rallied and achieved a period of lucidity. He gave instructions for his funeral, to take place in his newly consecrated Abbey Church (he had been too ill to attend the consecration), and made his last will and testament, verbally as was the custom, in the presence of his wife, Queen Edith, and servants, his household priests and three major witnesses, Earl Harold, Archbishop Stigand and the 'steward of the royal palace' Robert fitz Wymarc. That such last words or 'verba novissima' were binding on those present and inviolable, as William of Poitiers records, was asserted by King Harold in response to the Duke's demands.[2]

The Witan, consisting of earls, archbishops, bishops and abbots, kings, thegns and other notables, had already assembled in London, during December 1065, first for the consecration of Westminster Abbey and then to celebrate Christmas with the King. They would have remained when it became clear that Edward was not expected to live. Edward then died on 5 January 1066. Earl Harold, supported by witnesses to the King's last words, was therefore promptly acclaimed as King and a coronation followed.

All three versions of the *Chronicle* testify to Harold's acceptability to the Witan as King Edward's choice; he 'succeeded to the kingdom of England just as the King granted it to him', so the Peterborough 'E' version compiled in the twelfth century said. Both 'C' and 'D' (Abingdon and Worcester) say Edward 'committed [or entrusted] the kingdom to a distinguished man, Harold himself' and Florence of Worcester adds (basing himself on a now-lost text of the *Chronicle*) 'the subregulus [under-king] Harold ... whom the King had nominated [or appointed] as his successor, was elected King by the chief nobles of all England'.[3] He met the two essentials for kingship; he had been nominated by King Edward in effect as a member of the royal family, as Edward's brother-in-law, and mutual recognition existed between him and the magnates of their respective rights and duties, ratified by oath. He was then anointed and crowned by Archbishop Ealdred of York, not, as the Normans preferred to claim, by the schismatic Stigand. Norman sources of course alleged that Harold had made himself king 'by the adroit use of force' and testify to the fact that he made use of the Mass on the morning of Edward's funeral for his own Coronation Mass, being enthroned at the Introit of the Mass.[4] Harold had been accepted as king following English custom, before his coronation and not as a result of it.

William, a year later, was careful to have Archbishop Ealdred anoint and crown him, in order to erase from men's minds the spectacle of the coronation of Harold. But 'election' by the Witan was the essential act; it amounted to recognition of the person best fitted to be king and with the strongest claim. William of Normandy was to alter completely the basis upon which a man became king in England. He ignored the Old English process of submission and mutual pledging of oaths which constituted 'election' by the Witan.

As William of Poitiers implicitly concedes, the Norman attitude was that William could not begin to rule as king until he had been consecrated, whereas English kings began to rule as soon as they had been recognised by the Witan. William of Poitiers speaks of William 'setting aside the title of Duke' and he is shown as refusing to accept the crown (possibly in a display of false modesty) until urged to do so by the vicomte Aimeri de Thouars. The vicomte expressly admired William's modesty. William of Poitiers further distinctly asserts that William was hallowed King by Archbishop Ealdred after having been hailed as King by both English and Norman magnates. William then ignored his own promise to be a good lord. In fact, before the coronation, as William of Poitiers insists, William had already determined 'that he would avenge the injury [the English refusal to accept him] with arms and demand his inheritance with arms'. To William that was his 'just cause' because the English, by fighting for Harold, and because their magnates had confirmed Edward's designation, were to involve themselves in his guilt. They were to be treated as though they had been rebels even in the period before William had actually made himself king. Those at Hastings 'rebelling against him as ... king, deserved death'.

The attitude to the English is ominously anticipated by William's attitude to the people of Mantes. They too had 'rebelled' against the allegedly designated heir to Count Herbert. They were regarded as rebels even before they had actually accepted William as Count of Mantes. Yet only Herbert had bound himself to William, the people of Mantes themselves had not done so.

The *Vita Edwardi* grudgingly admits concerning Harold that Edward said, 'I commend this woman [Edith] and all the kingdom to your protection'. The author wrote what the Queen told him to write and she, as William of Poitiers claims, later allowed it to be understood that she wanted William to be King, probably in fact wanting anyone but Harold, whom she blamed for Tostig's fall. But the text cannot avoid reporting the commendation of the kingdom to Harold. The Bayeux Tapestry shows the deathbed scene exactly as the *Vita Edwardi* describes it.

William of Poitiers has to concede that Harold rebutted William's claim to the throne with the counter-assertion that King Edward had 'bestowed on him the Kingdom of England when dying'. That is how the Normans describe Harold's claim. Within about a month the news of the death of King Edward and the succession of Harold reached Normandy, perhaps as early as 17 January, probably through Norman sympathisers in England such as the monks of Fécamp living in Sussex or from Norman merchants who frequently crossed the Channel. William, it is said, was hunting in the forest of Quevilly, near Rouen, when the news was brought to him. The Duke returned to Rouen in fury and no one dared speak to him. Once in the ducal apartments he sulked for hours, contemplating his options. At length the trusty William fitzOsbern was persuaded to rouse the Duke and a council of Norman magnates was summoned. Supported by his closest confidants the Duke sent messengers to England to register his protest at Harold's audacity, as William saw it, in seizing the crown of England.

The Duke demanded that Harold 'fulfil the faith which he had pledged by his oath', or so William of Jumièges asserts. The Duke proceeded to craft his demands in a manner which would present him as the champion of feudal ethics, depicting Harold as a faithless vassal and a perjurer. He included in the demand not only that Harold surrender the crown but that he fulfil his promise to marry the Duke's daughter. Harold refused to acknowledge the Norman claims and what he probably said is used by William of Poitiers in formulating the speeches he puts into the mouths of Harold and William in the messages supposedly exchanged before the Battle of Hastings. It is likely that he had seen a draft of the brief which most authorities believe was presented to the Pope by Bishop Gilbert Maminot of Lisieux in the spring of 1066. He certainly led a delegation to Rome. William of Poitiers was Archdeacon of Lisieux and in a good position to know what the bishop did.

William proceeded to accuse Harold, quite unwarrantably, of having 'seduced all the English people away from obedience' to himself. There is no evidence that anyone in England was aware of any such obligation nor that King Edward had made any effort to bind his magnates and his subjects to obedience to the Norman Duke. But this claim remained a theme of Norman propaganda, and after Hastings, the Duke is described as having 'laid low a people opposed to him, which, rebelling against him, its King, deserved death'. The basic Norman claim was that Edward, grateful for the home he had been given in Normandy and the friendship of the Norman dukes, had bequeathed the Kingdom of England to Duke William, making William his heir, just as the Norman dukes themselves were accustomed to do for their sons and as Duke Robert had done for William and thus that William was the rightful King of England as soon as Edward died.

So England, according to Norman claims, had been bequeathed to Duke William by means of a 'post-obitum bequest', a form of will witnessed by clergy, as though England was his private estate, his private property. This shows ignorance of best English practice regarding the transmission of the crown from one king to another. English kings were expected to be chosen from amongst the close kin of the monarch, preferably the man best fitted, in the eyes of the Witan, to rule, and the chosen successor was then 'elected', most likely by acclamation, by the Witan. That sort of election amounted to recognition as king of the obvious candidate.

But in the eleventh century much of this had been forgotten under the Danish kings until restored with the accession of King Edward. He was welcomed as a member of the royal house and accepted by the Witan. What King Edward on his deathbed had done for Harold, in commending the kingdom to him, was to point him out to the Witan as the obvious successor. Edgar the Aetheling, still only a boy, possibly not more than ten or twelve years old, was not even considered. He had little support and less land and had not even acquired a following of commended men. The Witan really had no option but to recognise Harold's claim. He was the best available commander in war, brother-in-law of the late King and related by blood to the Danish royal kin. His maternal great-grandfather was Harald Bluetooth, King of Denmark.

William of Poitiers voices the Norman case in speeches attributed to Harold and William. For rhetorical purposes he appears to reverse the order of the Norman case and its English rebuttal, causing Harold to rebut the Norman claim before it had been put to him. It is more likely that Norman envoys were sent to Harold and that he sent English envoys in return. William is thus made to claim that 'my lord and kinsman' King Edward had made him the heir of his kingdom, in gratitude for the 'honours and rich benefits' conferred on him in Normandy 'by me and my magnates'. There is absolutely no evidence for this. English sources provide no confirmation. When Edward was in Normandy, down to 1041, William was a child. He could only have been about thirteen or fourteen years old by the time Edward left and was in no position to confer honours and benefits on anybody. Nor is there any evidence of such gifts from Norman barons. Yet Edward is supposed to have thought that William was 'best capable of supporting him during his life and of giving just rule to the kingdom after his death'.

The threadbare claim is trotted out that Edward's bequest had been consented to by the three great earls and by 'Archbishop' Stigand, who confirmed this 'by oath and pledge of hands', and that hostages had been sent to seal the bargain. Yet there is no reference to any of this in English sources. As for Harold, he is alleged to have made himself William's 'man' by a solemn act of homage, with his hands in those of the Duke, and to have 'pledged to me the security of the English kingdom'.[5] The last phrase is a curious one. How could Harold possibly have pledged the English Kingdom, of which he was not the lord, to William? There is no evidence that homage by 'immixtio manuum' was known back in England, where men 'bowed' (*bugan*) to a lord and then swore a hold oath, which was equivalent but not identical to the continental oath of fealty. The Bayeux Tapestry shows Harold swearing on two caskets containing relics; it does not show him swearing fealty by 'immixtio manuum'. Perhaps it was recognised in Normandy that Harold would not have performed ritual homage but could be compelled to swear on relics. William of Poitiers betrays fundamental ignorance of English practice. There was no homage in England, no ceremony acknowledging dependent tenure, men simply bowed to a lord.[6] Many were also free to 'go with their land to whatsoever lord they wished'.

Harold is then said to have been sent, probably in 1064, to swear in William's presence what his father and others had sworn in the Duke's absence. It all flies in the face of common sense. But Poitiers claims that he is recording all this in the Duke's own words! He adds 'for we wish posterity to regard him with favour'. There is no presumption that William was guilty of deliberate falsehood in making his claim. If it did depend on the assertions of Robert of Jumièges, then William probably believed what he had been told, having no reason to disbelieve the Archbishop. Similarly, William of Jumièges records what he had been told by 'sources close to' the Duke. William of Poitiers is guilty of fabricating much of his account.

Harold's envoy is described as rebutting all these claims. He announces that Harold 'bids you know, you have come into his land with arrogant temerity beyond comprehension'. Harold, through his envoy, is made to admit that Edward 'a long time ago decided that you would be his heir' and that Harold himself had given the Duke surety regarding the succession. It is highly unlikely that Harold would have said anything of the sort. He is more likely to have asserted that William had claimed these things, since the envoy next says, 'He knows that the kingdom is his by right, as granted to him by gift of that same King his lord upon his deathbed. For, since the time when blessed Augustine came into England, it has been the common custom of this nation that a gift made on the point of death is held as valid.' William of Poitiers added that Harold's envoy said that unless the Duke backed down 'he will break friendship and all agreements made with you in Normandy and place all responsibility for it upon you'. There, one suspects, one can detect the echo of Harold's own words. It does suggest that there was some sort of agreement under duress reached in Normandy that allowed Harold to regain his liberty and that Harold was denying that any agreement regarding the kingdom was binding upon him because Edward was his lord, not William. The Duke's envoy in all this appears to have been Hugh Margot, a monk of Fécamp.

William of Malmesbury states that Harold admitted he had taken an oath about the succession, but that the King had argued that it would have been presumptuous on his part to have done so without the general consent of his magnates and people. He is more likely to have said only that *if* he had taken such an oath it *would* have been invalid without consent, since Malmesbury adds that he said that 'so foolish an oath deserved to be broken'. Harold is also represented as comparing the situation to that of a maiden who takes an oath or vow to marry without her parents' knowledge, saying that a whole kingdom could not be disposed of without the knowledge of its people, especially if the oath was taken 'compelled by circumstances', that is, under duress.

These points are taken from the speeches crafted by William of Poitiers, who alleges that this was the substance of exchanges between the two men shortly before Hastings. It rather looks as though he has put together matter taken from the exchanges made in the spring of 1066 when Duke William demanded that Harold surrender the crown to him and possibly also from what was in the brief presented to the Pope, Alexander II, in Rome, together with the content of last-minute speeches of defiance before the battle. Only William of Poitiers reports all this and the curiously similar claims that had led to the acquisition of Maine in 1063.

At some point in early spring Earl Tostig, in the course of his wanderings in search of support for a bid to regain his earldom, arrived in Rouen and sought to persuade the Duke that he could help gain the crown for him if he should decide to invade. The Earl also rather audaciously reproached the Duke for allowing a perjurer to usurp the throne that rightfully belonged to him. Tostig was clearly flattering William, and the Duke seems to have realised this. He took advantage of the opportunity presented and urged the Earl to attack the English coast, leaving Normandy from the Cotentin, that is the Cherbourg Peninsula. In fact the Earl accomplished little and could not even reach the English coast 'because King Harold had covered the sea with ships and soldiers'. Adverse winds prevented a return to Normandy and the Earl went off to seek the help of King Swein of Denmark, unsuccessfully. Then he went to Harald Hardrada of Norway, whose ambition was stimulated by the Earl's flattery.

All sources are in agreement that William set about putting Harold in the wrong in the eyes of the princes and magnates of Europe. His last message to Harold was to the effect that 'quicker than he thinks he will know our designs, and he shall have more certain knowledge than he wants, for he shall see me in person', or so William of Poitiers asserts. The Duke is further reported to have said, 'Take back this message; tell him that if he does not see me within one year in the place which he now strives to make safe against my coming, he may rest quiet for the rest of his days and need fear no harm from me.' This he is supposed to have said to one of the English spies captured in Normandy. Harold, said the Duke, 'has no need to throw away gold and silver in buying the fidelity and fraud of men like you to come clandestinely among us to ferret out our plans'. The words are those of William of Poitiers but the sentiments expressed reflect the Duke's overweening confidence.

No English source attempts to explain why the Duke intended to invade. The *Chronicle* succinctly remarks that Harold had been told that 'William the Bastard would come hither and win this land'. It links the menace to the advent of Halley's Comet, as does William of Poitiers. Easter came and with it the comet. It arrived on Monday 24 April and was visible for at least seven nights, though some parts of Europe claimed to have seen it for much longer.

While King Harold gathered as large a land and sea army as he could, Duke William carried out a threefold campaign. From Count Baldwin, Regent of France, he secured consent for French knights to enlist in his service, a vital benefit for William. His Flemish and French borders were secure. From the German Emperor, Henry IV, he secured a vague agreement, some sort of diplomatic neutrality perhaps. Agents were sent out to recruit men from France, Brittany, Aquitaine, Poitou, Flanders and Burgundy. But most importantly, a legation was sent to Rome, led by Gilbert Maminot, Bishop of Lisieux. A case was presented to Pope Alexander II and his cardinals and the support was enlisted of Archdeacon Hildebrand,[7] who assisted the Bishop in the presentation of his case.

Despite the horrified murmurings of those cardinals who opposed Hildebrand's policies and were worried at the prospect of endorsing a war in which Christians would shed Christian blood, the Norman case was accepted. No effort was made to ensure that King Harold was told of the case nor was he allowed to put his side of it. It seems that William even placed a watch on the Channel ports to ensure that no news of the mission to Rome should reach England and that Harold would be unable to send anyone to Rome. English spies sent by King Harold were arrested and sent back to England.[8]

Strictly speaking, as Eadmer of Canterbury and William of Malmesbury[9] both hint, an oath taken under compulsion is ipso facto invalid. The *Gesta Regum* says that Harold, once crowned, 'did not spare a thought for the agreement between himself and William, declaring himself released from his oath because William's daughter, to whom he had been betrothed, had died before she was old enough to marry'. Harold is also said to have believed that 'William's threats would never be put into practice, involved as he was in fighting with neighbouring magnates'. This suggests that Harold's information about the strength of William's position was woefully out of date. The writer adds that the Duke continued to send messages of mild remonstrance, 'complaining of the breach of faith and mingling threats with entreaties'.

In view of the preparations made for invasion, the embassy to Rome and the care taken to ensure neutrality amongst his nearest neighbours, all of this was so much rodomontade intended to confuse Harold as to William's real intentions. At Rome the mission was successful. Convinced by the arguments put forward by the Normans, and which had most likely been drawn up by the wily and learned Lanfranc, a man 'skilled in human and divine law', the Pope blessed the Norman venture and bestowed on William a papal banner of the sort popes in this period had begun conferring on those carrying out campaigns acceptable to the papacy.

That Lanfranc was the probable author of the brief presented at Rome is supported by the discovery, in the *Collectio Lanfranci*, of his own copy of a collection of Canon Laws.[10] It has his own marginal notes next to a very relevant canon: Canon 75 of the Fourth Council of Toledo which anathematised usurpers and deals with the choice of a 'successor regni' by nobles and bishops on the death of a king. A usurper is declared excommunicate for 'tyrannical presumption' and for perjury. The relevance of this for Harold's case is plain to see. These are precisely the charges laid against Harold by William of Poitiers, who accuses him of perjury and calls him a tyrant. Addressing his corpse he says, 'You will be abominable to future generations.' He also three times justifies tyrannicide. But if Harold was, as the English held, legally King of the English, then it was William who was really the usurper and guilty of perjury. The possibility that men might say that had to be eliminated and that could only be done by securing a judgement from Rome.

So Rome was convinced, by Norman testimony, that Harold was guilty of perjury and was thus a usurper, crowned by an Archbishop who himself, in the opinion of Reformers at Rome, had usurped the See of Canterbury. Archbishop Stigand was furthermore condemned as a pluralist, in that he held several other high ecclesiastical offices (especially that of Bishop of Winchester)[11] in addition to Canterbury. He was also believed to be a simoniac, guilty of buying and selling office in the Church, though there is no concrete evidence that he did so. As Pope Alexander II had studied under Lanfranc, he would have been powerfully influenced by his advocacy. The Normans were later to claim that a Papal Bull was issued condemning Harold but if so no trace of it has survived.

The papal banner was sent to William.[12] It most likely bore the image of Crossed Keys, signifying the power of the keys derived from St Peter. With it went a ring said to contain a few hairs, relics of St Peter himself. Curiously, there is no clear sign in the Bayeux Tapestry of this banner though it was meant to be carried before the army into battle. Various banners and pennants are shown but none can be safely identified as papal. William does appear with a banner (Plates 53 and 54) but that bears only a cross with nothing distinctive about it.

Either while the embassy was doing its work or shortly afterwards, William summoned a council of his leading nobles at Lillebonne and put before them his intention to enforce his claim against England, demanding their support. This was probably at Easter since he then took six months to prepare his projected invasion. His hardest task was to persuade his own men to agree to such a risky venture. They could not be compelled to serve outside Normandy and had to be persuaded and cajoled into supporting their prince.

The basis of the claim was laid before them and they became convinced that Harold was a faithless vassal and a perjurer who had to be punished. But they were unhappy at the prospect of launching an invasion by sea. Some argued that the English had formidable forces at their disposal, no doubt aware of the strength of the English fleet. They did not believe that enough ships could be made ready in time or even that there were enough oarsmen.

The Bastard replied that Norman power would grow as time passed while Harold frittered away money and support. He promised to reward them out of the riches of England, saying that 'victory will go to he who can bestow not only what is his own but also what is held by the enemy', and promised that they would soon have a fleet large enough for the purpose.

'Wars,' he said, 'were won not by numbers but by courage. Harold will fight to retain what he has wrongfully seized, whereas we shall fight to regain what we have received as a gift and lawfully acquired.

Strong in this knowledge we shall overcome all dangers and win a happy victory, great honour and high renown.' But still the barons exaggerated the resources of Harold and minimised their own.

William was saved by the cunning of William fitzOsbern. Aware that rhetoric and argument had failed to win over a majority, he called the assembled lords to discuss the matter privately with him, away from the Duke, where they could speak freely. He allowed them to give free rein to their objections and promised to act as their spokesman and convey their sentiments to the Duke. In this way he allowed them to voice their concerns and relieve the pressure.

The Council was reconvened and, to the consternation of the assembled lords, fitzOsbern spoke only of their loyalty and love of the Duke and promised in their name to provide the ships and men required, personally promising sixty ships. The Duke's closest supporters backed him up. Bishop Odo and Count Robert of Mortain, the Duke's half-brothers, offered one hundred and one hundred and twenty ships respectively; the great houses of Eu, Montgomery, Beaumont and Avranches chimed in with sixty ships from each; Évreux, not to be outdone, offered eighty, de Montfort forty, and others lesser numbers. Some also pledged contingents of knights. The Duchess, Matilda, promised a great ship for William's personal use, to be called the *Mora*. In all 812 ships were pledged and a total of 280 knights.

Work on the ships began immediately and the Bayeux Tapestry in a number of vigorous scenes shows their construction and other preparations. Robert Wace, whose father was a witness to these activities, said in his *Roman de Rou* that in the end 776 ships were made available by early August. Some ships were not finished in time and others were lost at sea. After the move from Dives to St Valery there were 696. They were transport vessels, not fighting ships, and mainly of very basic design. Hugh of Fleury also provides a figure of 700 ships. He says William had 150,000 men, an obvious exaggeration, but perhaps a figure of 10 per cent of that might not be unreasonable. Not all of these were fighting men; there would have to have been non-combatants of all sorts: cooks, carpenters, blacksmiths, farriers, ostlers, servants, clergy and so on.

William devoted his time to supervising the preparations and organising his duchy in anticipation of his absence, even of the chance that he might not return. Meanwhile, King Harold made his own preparations, stationing the English army, the fyrd, along the

South Coast to keep watch and sending the fleet to sea for the same purpose. The English remained on the alert from May to September and the fyrd was probably called up in two sections. One could have completed its customary two months service by the end of the first week in July and a second served from then until early September when the harvest was drawing near, supplies were running out, and men had to be allowed to return home. By then Harold might well have begun to think that, as autumn approached and with it the end of the fighting season, William might not come.

There were some alarms and excursions caused by raids organised by Earl Tostig. Duke William based himself at the ducal monastery of Fécamp so that he could raise supplies from the fertile countryside around Caen, rich in cereal production and in hay as fodder for the horses. More supplies came from the Pays d'Auge and the fields and valleys of the Dives and Touques, which produced cattle. A blockade was maintained on the Channel ports and steps taken to arrest any English spies.

A Council of magnates was summoned to Bonneville-sur-Touques early in June, shortly before Pentecost, and another at Caen on 18 June. William attended the dedication of Matilda's church, St Stephen's, Caen, and the Duke confirmed Fécamp in its possession of Steyning in England in the event that God should grant him victory. (It appears to have been confiscated by King Harold after King Edward's death.)[13] Most of the major figures in Normandy were present at these events, and charters reveal that the Duke met his closest advisers regularly throughout this period. He was organising a series of rallies to maintain morale. His main aides were William fitzOsbern and Roger of Montgomery but he also consulted Count Eustace of Boulogne and the Vicomte of Thouars in Poitou, Aimeri.

At some point, possibly at Caen, the Duchess Matilda was in effect named as regent during the Duke's absence, and his eldest son, Robert Curthose, possibly not yet twelve years old, was associated in a regency council. He had already, in 1063, been designated as his father's heir to the duchy. It was a crucial point in 1066 when his father was about to embark on a hazardous enterprise from which he might not return. Robert was again proclaimed as heir and the magnates were required to swear an oath of fealty to him. He confirmed his father's gifts to the Abbey of Marmoutier 'at the request of his father who was then preparing to cross the sea and to make war on the English'. The unvarnished truth about this enterprise tends to leak out in statements found only in charters. Other Norman magnates made grants to various churches, especially Holy Trinity, Rouen, dated 'when the duke of the Normans set out across the sea with his fleet'.

That fleet began to assemble in and around the mouth of the River Dives towards the end of July and was fully ready by 12 August. More ships continued to be built, but it looks as though the idea was to launch an invasion on an auspicious day, 15 August, the Feast of the Assumption. But the fleet was delayed, ostensibly for lack of a favourable wind, 'for thrice five days', and did not in fact move for a month, which happened also to be when Harold had to disband the fyrd and move his fleet to London. It is recorded that the King had gone 'to Wight and lay there all summer and the autumn'. It is possible that the apparent delay in the launching of the Norman invasion fleet was a deliberate ploy made in the hope that Harold would be forced to discharge both his fleet and the fyrd, neither of which could be kept ready for war indefinitely, and to persuade Harold that William was not going to come that year. Information about English moves could be obtained from monks of Fécamp resident in England and other Norman sympathisers.

William then set out early in September, around the 12th, and it is possible that he had intended to make a direct crossing from the Dives towards Southampton or even the Godwineson family seat of Bosham. If so, then the Duke had miscalculated. The fleet was caught by one of the changes in the weather for which the Channel is notorious. The fleet, 'equipped with the utmost foresight,' says Poitiers, 'had long lain in the mouth of the Dives and the neighbouring harbours awaiting a south wind to take them to England' (that is, straight across the Channel) but 'it was blown by westerlies into the roadstead of St Valery [sur-Somme]'.

That this was a storm is only revealed by the admission that the Duke, 'whose spirit could not be broken by delay or contrary winds, by the terrors of the deep or by the timorous desertion of those who had pledged their service ... met adversities with prudence, *concealing the loss of those who were drowned* as far as he could by burying them in secret, and increasing the rations every day in order to mitigate their scarcity'.

These bodies of drowned men washed ashore could have been those of men slain in a sea battle. Both fleets appear to have been at sea during the storm. There had been losses in the Channel of ships, men and supplies. If Wace's figures are at all accurate the Duke had lost close to eighty ships, either at sea or by desertion. A charter for Holy Trinity, Rouen, records a gift by a knight called Bodes, worn out and injured during a storm involving the Duke's fleet. Another man, Roger fitz Turold, left a gift to Holy Family, Rouen, when William 'was going to sail across the sea' but died on the voyage and the gift was void. It would appear that this was the same storm which struck Harold's fleet during the move to London a few days after the Nativity of the Virgin, 8 September, when many ships perished before they could reach harbour.

The *Chronicle* notes that Harold had gone out against the Duke with his fleet and Domesday Book names Aethelric of Kelvedon, who 'died in a naval battle against King William'. Eadric, the 'Commander of King Edward's Ship',[14] was later driven into exile because he had fought against the Duke. The annals of Nieder-Alteich, on the Rhine, record how in 1066 the men of Aquitaine fought a naval battle against the English. There were certainly Aquitanians in the Duke's army. It looks as though there had been some sort of skirmish as the two fleets possibly intermingled during the storm, though most of the damage to both sides was caused by the storm.

The storm would have been one of the features of the weather in 1066, as in most years, when the Autumn Equinox would have fallen, under the Julian calendar then in use, on 16 September. This one was an equinoctial gale.

The sojourn of the army at St Valery was a miserable time. The Norman army was drenched by torrential rain and exposed to violent winds. The Duke's men began to despair and mutter against him in their tents. 'The man is mad,' they said, 'who seeks to seize the land rightfully belonging to others! God is against us for He denies us the wind. His father [Duke Robert] had the same idea[15] and was prevented in the same way. There is a curse on this family. Yes, it always conceives more than it can perform and finds God in opposition to it.' Such sentiments spread and weakened the resolve of the army.

The Duke took refuge in daily prayer, ostentatiously visiting the church of St Valery. He anxiously watched the weathercock on the steeple, waiting for a sign that the wind was changing. Throughout that August and into September a series of Atlantic lows had brought storms and rain until at last, on 27 September, a ridge of high pressure brought warmer weather and clear skies. Probably the Duke was alerted to the change by local sailors and fishermen well versed in what to expect.

Duke William now mounted one of his well-crafted public spectacles. In a last appeal to God and the saints, he ordered the bones of St Valery to be brought out of the church and a solemn procession held so that everyone might call upon the saint to intercede with God as they prayed for a favourable wind. To everyone's astonishment, but not, perhaps, to that of the Duke, a southerly wind began to blow and this was seen as God's response to their appeals. Hands and voices were raised in thanksgiving and a mad rush began to embark the army and launch the fleet.

Eagerly the knights and soldiers, scarcely waiting for a word from the Duke, who might well have primed their commanders in advance about what he hoped would happen, hastened to board their ships. Some were still calling for missing companions and others forgot to wait for them or for their provisions, eager not to be left behind. The Duke himself urged his men on, determined not to miss the evening tide. That is thought to have been due at about 3.20 in the afternoon so that the fleet needed to catch the ebb tide or it would be delayed another day. The voyage was to take place overnight so that the English coast could be reached next day at high tide. A landing in daylight was essential, as the shore was expected to be hostile and resistance was expected.

A herald was sent round to warn the captains of the ships to drop anchor when they reached open sea so that the whole fleet might set out at the same time. A light would be shone from the masthead of the *Mora* and a trumpet would sound and they would all weigh anchor. The Duke's ship led the way, piloted most likely by Stephen the Steersman,[16] who was skilled in the study of the winds and the stars. The crossing was about 55 nautical miles and undertaken mainly in darkness except for the light of a crescent moon.

Navigation was by dead reckoning; the Duke's pilot took the *Mora* as far across the Channel as he dared and dropped anchor somewhere off the English coast. The heavily laden transports full of men, provisions and horses wallowed across the Channel. They were of shallow draft, driven by a single forward-facing sail, and they fell well behind the Duke's well-appointed vessel.

After eight or nine hours they all dropped sea anchors and waited for the first light of dawn. That would have been at about 5.00 a.m. The Duke, when he woke, found the *Mora* alone on the sea with neither his fleet nor the English coast to be seen. He sent a man up the mast to act as lookout but he too could see no sign of the fleet. The Bastard calmly ordered his breakfast to be brought and ate it, washing it down with spiced wine 'as though in his solar at home'.[17] Having finished, he sent a man up the mast again and this time he reported four ships approaching and a little later on said that he could see so many masts that it looked like a forest of trees with sails approaching over the water.

The fleet was then borne by the favourable wind into Pevensey Bay, which in the eleventh century was a large lagoon stretching well inland. A landing was effected as rapidly as possible and a contingent of cavalry was sent out to secure the area. There was no resistance. King Harold was in the North with the English army. It was 28 September. The local thegns and ceorls kept well out of sight and sent reports as rapidly as possible to London. William himself disembarked, and it is claimed that in doing so he tripped and fell, causing a great cry of horror at this evil omen. With his customary panache the Duke turned it to his own advantage. Grasping two handsful of soil he scrambled to his feet saying, 'By the Splendour of God I have taken seisin of my Kingdom, the earth of England is in my hands.'[18] A nearby soldier seized a bundle of straw from a nearby cottage and gave it to the Duke who cried, 'I accept it, may God be with us!'

The Normans occupied the remains of the old Roman fort at Pevensey, Anderida, constructing a castle in one corner. They had brought with them the means of building a castle in easily assembled sections and soon erected that on a mound, or motte, with a surrounding ditch. The Duke then sent out foraging parties and reconnaissance men into the surrounding area, especially to the west. Domesday Book twenty years later still revealed the effects of the passage of the Norman army on the agricultural productivity of the area. They ravaged and plundered as far west as Lewes. Having seized the supplies they wanted, the Normans then destroyed the farms.

As an invader, William knew that he now had to live off the countryside as no more supplies could reach him from Normandy. He also knew that he would have to break out of his beachhead if he was to confront and defeat King Harold. Accordingly, on either 29 or 30 September he moved his army along the coast, ravaging as it went, and moved the fleet to Hastings once the army had occupied it. The trail of 'wasted' farms marks the route. There was still no sign of organised resistance. The local levies of the fyrd had been stood down as early as 8 September and many of the best of them would by now have gone north with King Harold. Hastings was a better base for the Duke, less exposed and with a natural harbour. The fleet occupied the Bulverhythe Estuary and Coombe Haven while the army billeted itself on the town. Another castle was erected within the burh on the cliff, which was located within the ancient Roman fort. Hastings was on the southern edge of a peninsula and the way north lay over the Ridgeway across Andredesweald (the Weald of Kent). The Duke would have to follow the road north if he wanted to reach London.

A review of the fleet revealed that two vessels were missing. It emerged that they had lost touch with the rest of the fleet and attempted a landing at Romney. The men of Romney had fallen on the crews of the two missing ships and had slain them. The Duke later ordered the systematic ravaging of Romney. This was part of a deliberate ploy to force King Harold to accept battle. Everything in the Norman line of march was destroyed and the unfortunate inhabitants slain. Parties of men now went out from Hastings to ravage to the north, especially targeting estates held by Harold or other members of his family or his commended men.

One man was reported to have been drowned during the crossing, a cleric who claimed the gift of prophecy. William remarked sardonically, 'A poor diviner he must have been who could not foresee the manner and time of his own death. Foolish would he be who put his faith in the words of such a soothsayer.' The unfortunate man had prophesied that William would be victorious without striking a blow!

William of Poitiers describes how there were messages exchanged between the two princes over the next fourteen days or so. His account includes material from the earlier exchanges between them and from the brief presented at Rome, but some of what he says suggests the content of shorter messages sent out before the battle. One story that bears the ring of truth says that Robert fitz Wymarc, the leading staller of Harold's royal household, sent a message of defiance to the Duke. He informed him of Harold's crushing defeat of the Norwegians at Stamford Bridge and warned him that Harold was approaching 'with all speed ... with innumerable soldiers all well-equipped for war'; in comparison with them William and his men were 'a pack of curs' and the Duke would be well advised to retire behind entrenchments and not dare to offer battle.

William, possibly believing the message was from, or inspired by, Harold himself, replied that it would be better 'not to mingle insults' with the message, that he would not seek the shelter of fosse or walls, and that he intended to offer battle as soon as possible. He boasted that he would do so even if he had only 10,000 men and not the 60,000 (*sic*!) he actually had, or so William of Poitiers asserts.[19] William of Poitiers claims that no one had told him what the Duke said in the days before the battle (he was not an eyewitness) and then, as was customary, proceeds to tell his readers in detail what was said. The speeches are of his own devising to illustrate the arguments he thought the Duke would have deployed, though possibly based on what others who were present told him. (This was in imitation of the methods adopted by classical writers such as Livy.)

William of Malmesbury praises Duke William as a shrewd and cautious commander and offers as proof William's strategy in forcing the English to offer battle and make King Harold come to him. He occupied Hastings, which offered better protection for his ships, and began ravaging inland estates including some held by Harold himself. This served two purposes. William was able to replenish his supplies from English farms, a necessity because his supplies were limited, and was able to provoke Harold into what English sources regarded as a premature move. William of Malmesbury regarded Harold as rash for moving too soon.

Duke William's strategy and tactics at Hastings were remarkable when one considers that he had never had sole command in a pitched battle. At Val-ès-Dunes he had been under the leadership of King Henry I and neither Varaville nor Mortemer was a set piece battle. William had, however, a great deal of experience in command of forces besieging castles.

One story related about events before Hastings bears the ring of truth and is typical of the Duke's penchant for dramatic flourishes. He is said to have offered Harold three choices of settling the dispute either under English or Norman law. Harold could abdicate in William's favour, or reign under William as his overlord or, in order to avoid unnecessary bloodshed, by single combat, saying, 'I am ready to wage my life against his that the English kingdom by right falls to me rather than him.' He could have known full well that trial by battle was not a custom known in England and that the offer would be spurned. Harold refused all three offers.

It was most likely then that Harold told the Duke that he had invaded 'with arrogant temerity beyond comprehension' and so, lifting his face up to Heaven, said, 'May God this day judge the right between me and William.' To Hugh Margot of Fécamp, William's messenger, he said, 'Return, thou fool! Tomorrow, with the Lord as arbiter of the kingdom, the rightful claimant shall appear! The Holy Hand of the Lord will deal justly!' Then, 'We march at once, we march to battle!' One suspects that his words have been doctored to emphasise how wrong he was since his defeat in battle showed God was against him.

Having settled affairs in the North, leaving the sheriff of Lincolnshire, Maerleswein, in charge at York, Harold had returned to London as swiftly as he had gone northwards, gathering further military levies as he came south and collecting still more over a period of a few days in the city. He then set off to confront the Norman army, probably hoping to catch it unawares as he had Hardrada. But the Normans had men out on reconnaissance who reported his approach. He was also said to have sent a fleet into the Channel to cut off Norman reinforcements.[20]

The Duke feared a night attack and ordered his men to stand to arms all night. His men had to watch with their arms and armour ready to hand. He then moved his forces to Telham Hill early in the morning.

Harold seems to have concluded that surprise was out of the question since his forces, ordered to gather 'at the hoary apple tree' (probably on Caldbec Hill, where three hundreds met), spent the night resting (and not, as William of Malmesbury was to assert, in drunken riotousness) after eating and drinking what they had brought with them. No doubt they toasted one another before settling down to try to sleep. Wace reports the toasts in use: 'Drinkail and wassail.'

The Duke and his men attended Mass, probably at dawn, and took communion. William is said to have hung round his neck the relics upon which Harold was alleged to have sworn his fateful oath, and the Norman clergy, led by Bishop Odo, and the army prayed before the battle. The Duke then led his men out from Hastings along the track leading north until they reached a location below the hill of Senlac (as Orderic Vitalis calls it, meaning an area called 'sandlacu' or the sandy stream).[21] The Normans assembled at the base of Telham Hill, near Starr's Green and Black Horse Hill.

11

THE BATTLE OF HASTINGS

Early on the morning of Saturday 14 October, Duke William, having reached the crest of Telham Hill, some 200 feet above sea level, while his men moved down into the valley below, observed the English moving into position below Caldbec Hill, which loomed higher at about 260 feet. The hill is the last spur of the Andredesweald, covered at that time by forest. It juts out to the south and blocks the road to London.

William would have noted how the boggy then rising ground would cause problems for his cavalry. It featured a ridge with a long lane at the top and forest behind it facing down into a muddy valley with a track running across it.[1] A location more unfavourable to an attacker could not have easily been found. The Bastard watched as the English emerged from the forest and the woods 'glittered full of their spears'. He viewed the vanguard, resplendent with the gilded banners of the fyrd, as it took up position on the brow of the hill of Senlac, forming a solid wall of shields.[2] An eagle-eyed soldier called Vital pointed out to the Duke where King Harold stood, the place marked by his standards, the Royal Standard, the Dragon of Wessex, and Harold's personal standard, the bejewelled banner of the 'Fighting Man'.

The Duke now donned his hauberk of chain mail, inadvertently putting it on back to front, again to the alarm of his men, who saw it as an evil omen. But he laughed it off, hastily reversing the hauberk and remarking that he would that day turn from a duke into a king. The Poitevin, Aimeri de Thouars, is said to have said, 'Never has such a knight been seen under heaven. A noble Count will become a noble King.' The Duke then descended the hill and issued orders for the battle lines to be formed.

The Normans drew up in three ranks and three divisions. In the front line the Duke placed his archers, men from Évreux and Louviers (some with crossbows rather than ordinary bows) supported by lightly armed skirmishers with slings. Behind them he placed his heavy infantry, in full armour, armed with swords or throwing spears and protected by shields and helmets. In the rear came the knights mounted on warhorses. These were not the huge stallions used later in the Middle Ages, ancestors of the shire horse, but trained fighting horses called 'destriers'. The Duke commanded from the centre surrounded by his elite knights. The army was further divided, as was customary, into a centre and two wings.

The Normans, commanded by the Duke, took the centre, the Bretons and possibly the Aquitainians, under Count Alan Fergant (Iron Glove) formed the left wing, and the French, including the men of Boulogne under Count Eustace, formed the right, commanded by Roger of Montgomery. William of Poitiers asserts that the papal banner was carried before the Duke, by Toustain fitz Rou. That was not the only banner carried at Hastings. William also had the banner of St Michael the Archangel.[3] The Duke is said to have urged on his men in a speech, so William of Poitiers claims, and no doubt he did say a few words, but not necessarily those attributed to him by that writer. They can briefly be said to have included warnings that there was no possibility of retreat, with the enemy before them and the sea at their rear, and so the Normans fought 'not merely for victory but for survival' and the assurance that their cause was just, and other suitable arguments.

On the crest of the hill before them waited the English army. Earl Gyrth probably commanded the right wing (he was involved in the fighting against the Bretons) and Earl Leofwine the left, with their brother, King Harold, in overall command in the centre. The King had most likely distributed his professional troops, the housecarls and king's thegns, among the shire levies to provide the necessary stiffening. Their arms and armour would have differed little from that of the Normans and their allies. But the English still fought in the traditional manner in a pitched battle, on foot, in the formation known as a 'shield-wall' or 'war-hedge'. The front line protected itself from arrows, spears and slingshots with shields and could form a wedge-shaped battle line to advance a few yards and repel the assault of an enemy. The phrase 'war-hedge' suggests that the line bristled with spears. Horses were not used in battle, being regarded as too valuable to be used so wastefully. The Normans were astounded to see the English deliberately send their horses to the rear, out of harm's way.

To the Normans their opponents appeared to be a dense mass of men, with wings possibly bent backwards to face out to right and left and prevent an outflanking manoeuvre. The slope down from their position and the boggy nature of the ground also prevented outflanking. The ground was then much steeper than it appears now, because the crest of the hill was flattened and lowered some years after the battle to permit the construction of Battle Abbey, and the spoil from these works was spread down over the slope.

There were banks and ditches scattered over the field of combat, even some sort of rough earthwork in the centre, halfway down, an obstacle to a direct approach. Wace reported the presence of some sort of structure in front of the English line (its form exaggerated in later years) made out of 'shutters and other pieces of wood'. So they could have heaped brushwood and timber and branches of trees in front of the line to deter horses.

Harold held lands in the vicinity, both north and south of the battlefield, and probably chose the site deliberately. The English stationed a squad of picked warriors off to their right, on a small hillock, so that flanking attacks could be made against the Normans. King Harold, like Ealdorman Byrhtnoth at Maldon, would have ridden along before the shield wall to encourage his men and urge them to hold their ground firmly, and then taken up his position on a slightly higher piece of rising ground from which he could survey the whole battlefield. One disadvantage would have been that the English had the early morning October sun in their eyes. But it is likely that the day was damp and misty and that the mist remained for a considerable time.

William of Poitiers is magnifying the Duke's achievement in defeating Harold while the Chroniclers seek to explain away the defeat by reducing estimates of the size of the army. They make much of reports that the English were ill-prepared for the fight and that William 'came upon him [Harold] by surprise before his people were in battle array' (which might just be an echo of the report about Stamford Bridge where Harold 'came upon them [the Norwegians] by surprise') or that 'one half of his army had not yet arrived' and so he fought 'before a third of his army were drawn up'. But William of Poitiers on the contrary insists that Harold had 'a vast host gathered together ... from all the provinces of the English' and Florence of Worcester resorts to claiming that the English 'were drawn up in a confined position' so that 'many deserted from him'.

It looks more as though the English continued to receive more and more reinforcements during the morning until the whole force was present and that there was insufficient space for all of them. William of Poitiers even claims there were reinforcements from Denmark!

It is almost impossible to state exactly how large the forces involved were. The received estimates have tended to accept minimal numbers, some 5,000 or 6,000 men on each side, but modern historians are tending to accept higher and higher figures. There are some clues. The *Chronicle of St Maixent* in Poitou claims that the Normans had 14,000 men, which is not an impossible figure compared with the typically exaggerated numbers found in other sources. That would include non-combatant support staff of all kinds and William probably had up to 12,000 fighting men. In that case, Harold would hardly have had many fewer and probably more.[4]

William of Poitiers says that the English had superiority in numbers, which would appear to be confirmed by the fact that the battle lasted until dusk, that is apparently for some seven or eight hours, and that in the end the English lost only because Harold was killed. Medieval armies did tend to disintegrate if their commander died.

The battle began at the third hour of the day, that is 9 a.m. when the Duke had trumpets sounded and ordered his archers and skirmishers forward to harass the enemy. As poets were accustomed to put it, 'the bows were busy and bitter was the onset of war'. The shield wall easily withstood this first assault, though the skirmishers rushed forward as close as they dared to discharge their weapons, only to be greeted themselves by a ferocious barrage of missiles of all kinds. The attack petered out as the skirmishers exhausted their supply of missiles and retreated.

Then the heavily armed infantry charged up the hill, hampered not only by their arms and armour, but by the marshy conditions. They too met a brutal mass of missiles, long throwing spears, javelins, rocks and stones and a kind of throwing stick with a rock tied to one end. Both sides gave vent to battle cries; the English cried 'Out! Out! Out!' and 'Holy Cross!' or 'God Almighty!' The Normans replied with 'Dex Aie!' (God helps[5]). The cries were soon drowned out by the groans of the wounded and the dying and the clash of weapons as the two lines met.

The job of the infantry was to weaken the enemy front line, if possible cutting a hole in it, so that the knights could exploit it. But the Normans found it impossible and were repelled by the use of the fearsome two-handed battle axes of the housecarls. That struggle probably took the best part of an hour as first the skirmishers and then the infantry were driven back. The whole English frontline could easily have moved a few yards forward, in a pre-arranged tactic in which they had been trained, to push the Normans down the slope (just as Earl Tostig's men had pushed back the English led by Earls Edwin and Morcar at Fulford). The two front lines became locked together in a desperate fight for mastery, the Normans thrusting with spears and shields or slashing with swords, the English responding similarly, hewing men down, chopping off heads, legs or arms. The Bayeux Tapestry vividly illustrates this.

The killing zone in front of the English line was an area about 30 yards wide, the effective range of a spear or javelin. A wedge-shaped column could cover that in less than a minute. But little of this kind of fighting is recorded by William of Poitiers. He is concerned with the exploits of the knights. He does describe the infantry as 'drawing nearer, provoking the English by raining death and wounds on them' and the English resisting valiantly. The English at this point had the advantage of the ground and preserved an impregnable front.

After the first assault by infantry came the first wave of knights. Their horses were unprotected by armour, though trained for war, standing about 14 hands high. Riding up the hill was no problem, but doing so against a wall of close order infantry with secure flanks was. Horses are easy targets for long spears and long-handled battle axes, as the Normans soon found to their cost. The shield wall braced itself to meet the knights as they loomed up at it. This was no shock charge of the sort that could be delivered in open countryside. The English were positioned along the steepest part of the hill and could rain blows down upon the horsemen. It is likely also that the English spears were set forwards at an angle, butts planted firmly in the ground, and aimed at the horses' chests. The knights could not have made their horses mount a sustained assault against naked steel blades. As Waterloo showed when French cavalry failed to break the British squares, horses cannot face cold steel.[6]

The knights certainly adopted a different tactic, to charge up to within striking distance of the shield wall, wheel to the side and strike at the enemy with spear and sword. Then, as a natural consequence of that manoeuvre, as the élan of the attack faded, the knights returned back down the hill to regroup. That could easily be presented afterwards as a prearranged tactical retreat, a feigned flight. William of Poitiers claims that this tactic was used several times.

But during one of the earliest assaults, the ferocity of the English countermeasures (volleys of missiles followed up by the devastating blows of the battle axes) broke the nerve of the Bretons on the left wing and they retreated pell mell back down the slope in a panic-stricken flight that threatened to become a wholesale rout. The Bretons in particular had perhaps never encountered that sort of response. Pitched battles of the sort fought at Hastings were rare in the eleventh century. William of Poitiers remarks that it was 'a strange kind of battle; one side vigorously attacking; the other resisting as if rooted to the ground'. He would have expected a battle in which both sides charged the other rather than one in which the Normans did all the attacking while the English stood firm in defence.

As a result, the whole ducal army threatened to fall back as the Bretons and all their auxiliary troops on the left wing were driven back and fleeing Normans protected their backs with their shields. A large part of the English right wing surged forward exultingly, and William saw that it was in pursuit of his men. So great was the disorder that many on the Norman side thought that the Duke himself had fallen, but William deliberately rode his horse across the front of the retreating Bretons and Normans, shouting and brandishing his sword. He removed his helmet to show his face and cried out that he still lived. 'Do you not recognise me,' he shouted, 'I am alive and, by God's help, I will be the victor'. William of Poitiers claims that the Duke rebuked them for cowardice and told them that flight would never save them: 'Those you could slaughter like cattle are herding and killing you!' Thus he stopped the rout and stiffened their morale, leading them into a counter-charge in which they surrounded and decimated the pursuing Englishmen.

That could well have been a turning point in the battle. The English had suffered heavy losses and the right wing was weakened. Some argue that Harold ought to have seized the moment and ordered a wholesale charge, but that would have meant conceding the advantage of the high ground.

The battle resumed as the English line stabilised and the English 'fought with all their might, determined above all to prevent any breach from being opened in their ranks'. But the Norman assaults continued under William's direction, unrelentingly, and breaches were cut in several places, causing heavy casualties. First the men of Maine and Aquitaine played a part, then the Bretons and French, and especially the Normans. William of Poitiers relates the exploits of Norman lords and especially of his hero, Duke William.

There were further tactical withdrawals, ordered by the Duke, who had perhaps been inspired by the idea of such a tactic by the results of the counter-attack after the flight of the Bretons. This enticed other groups of Englishmen to pursue the Normans, so inviting a counter-charge. These men were easily surrounded and killed. Whether these can rightly be called 'feigned flights' is a moot point; in the fog of war it becomes difficult to carry out manoeuvres that look so easy when practised in training.

Duke William is said to have had three horses killed under him, just like Robert Guiscard at the Battle of Civitate, but to have continued to lead the attacks in person, causing great death and destruction. He is described as surpassing all others by his courage and prudence and directing his men with great skill.

One story claims that he encountered Earl Gyrth in the conflict and that Gyrth speared the Duke's horse and forced him to fight on foot. William attacked Gyrth in the belief that he was Harold himself, saying, 'Receive from me the crown you deserve, if my horse dies I will revenge it on foot.' There could after all have been a family resemblance. The third brother, Earl Leofwine, was also killed towards the end of the day. Both were later found dead close to the body of their brother the King. After the fight with Earl Gyrth, William was given a fresh horse by Eustace of Boulogne. This horse too was killed under William, who turned to a knight from Maine and demanded that he give him his horse. The knight refused, so William simply struck him off his horse and took it for himself.

But English resistance seems to have continued to the bitter end. Evening was falling but the Normans could not yet overcome an army 'massed so strongly in close formation ... without severe losses'. The shield wall reformed again and again and prevented the Normans from breaking the line. Harold held on, expecting to hold the field until nightfall when he could make a tactical retreat if necessary. He could afford to retreat and renew the fight on another occasion, but William could not. He simply had to win the day.

The major Norman sources are curiously silent about exactly what happened, but towards the end of the day Harold was killed and the English line crumbled and fled. The *Carmen de Hastingae Proelio* provides its own solution, which, if this work was written soon after the battle, is credible enough. The text is somewhat difficult to interpret, because of some damage and wear, but the story is as follows. Harold, who had moved into the frontline of the battle, was seen by Duke William and by Count Eustace of Boulogne, and it was decided to send a small squadron of knights to attack him directly. The Bayeux Tapestry shows a group of four mounted knights making an assault on Harold's position.[7]

The *Carmen de Hastingae Proelio* is ambiguous and one reading includes William himself among the group. Yet no Norman source ever claimed that William took part in the killing of Harold; if he had done so, the world would certainly never have heard the last of it. More probably, the squad was led by Eustace of Boulogne and it included Hugh II de Montfort, Walter Giffard and 'the noble heir of Ponthieu'.[8] That can mean Enguerrand the Younger (he died in 1087) or Hugh II.[9] These four made a determined attack on Harold. The first man speared him through the chest, the second cut off his head, the third disembowelled him and the fourth hacked at his thigh. But there was something shameful about the last blow, and the man who delivered it was dismissed in shame from the army, though he is not named.

The *Carmen* uses the word 'coxa' and William of Malmesbury uses 'femur'. Both words refer to the area of the groin, and it is thought that Harold was in fact castrated. If so, that was a shameful act, especially as Harold was an anointed King.[10] The other sources agree that Harold's body was almost unrecognisable and that he was eventually only identified by secret marks on his body known only to his long-standing wife, Edith Swansneck. William of Jumièges says he fell 'covered with deadly wounds'. William of Poitiers says he could not be identified by his face. Neither of them describes his death or states who killed him.

William of Malmesbury comments on the two commanders. Both are praised for their bravery and King Harold is said to have carried out his task vigorously, often laying low horse and rider with one blow. Duke William encourages his men with his shouted commands, leading the charges in person and plunging into the thick of the enemy, never flinching. Three times he fought on foot, avenging the death of his warhorses and overthrowing several Englishmen with his shield. One of these is called 'the son of Helloc' but cannot be further identified.

Henry of Huntingdon claims that towards the end a squadron of twenty knights broke through the English line, seizing the standard. Then, as the English army dissolved into flight, it was pursued into the gathering gloom by the Norman army, some of whom were cut down by desperate Englishmen in the woods, valleys and ditches that abounded in the area. The battle had endured all that day and darkness fell at about 6.30 p.m. Hastings, like Waterloo in the eighteenth century, had been a close-run thing.

Duke William, now armed only with the stump of a broken lance, called Eustace of Boulogne to him as he was about to signal a retreat. Eustace urged William to advance no further, as he would only court death by doing so. At that precise moment the Count was struck violently between the shoulder blades from behind, so that the blood gushed from his mouth and nose and he had to be led from the field by his men.

The Duke then calmly had food prepared and brought to him there on the battlefield, and a tent was erected for him. He sat and ate and drank 'champagne', not the sparkling wine of that name, but the plain white wine of the region. He then spent the night in his tent. One story relates that Walter Giffard rode up and, finding the Duke there, was appalled. 'My Lord,' he cried, 'what are you doing? It is not fitting for you to remain here among the dead.' He told William that there were, among the dead, many wounded Englishmen and that some might be unhurt but had covered themselves in blood, pretending to be dead. They might seek to avenge their defeat before escaping. 'They do not mind if they die,' he said, 'so long as they have killed a Norman.' Nonetheless, William stayed where he was.

The Duke surveyed the battlefield, contemplating the extent of the carnage. He had Harold's body, once it had been identified, brought to his camp. Harold's mother, Gytha, tried to persuade William to release the body for burial, offering his weight in gold,[11] but the Duke ostentatiously refused, saying, according to William of Poitiers, that it was unseemly to accept money for a corpse and he was determined to prevent Harold's burial when so many of his own followers lay unburied on the field of battle.[12]

Then came one of Duke William's macabre jests. He affected to order William Malet, who had lived for some time in England and formed some sort of relationship to Harold, to take the body and bury it under a 'tumulus' or barrow[13] on the seashore so that Harold could guard the coast he had defended with such 'insane enthusiasm'.

In fact, the Duke later relented and allowed the body to be given to two monks from Waltham Abbey who took it away and buried it there.[14] King Harold's banner of the Fighting Man was preserved and sent to Rome as a gift for Pope Alexander II.

At first William might have been tempted just to leave the bodies of the English where they lay, to become the prey of wolves and vultures. The camp followers and common soldiers had been stripping the dead of arms and armour and had left the bodies to rot. But, posing as a Christian knight, the Duke then remarked that such a fate seemed too cruel and he allowed all who wished to do so to collect the bodies for burial. No remains of the battle have ever been found there as the armour and weaponry was removed as well as the bodies. Any surviving evidence was probably removed by the monks of Battle and any bodies buried when they landscaped the abbey lands.

William is said to have sworn on the battlefield that if God gave him victory he would build an abbey there, but that may be only the 'foundation myth' of the abbey. There is a Battle Abbey Charter, a forgery.[15] If genuine it would date to 1070, drawn up at Windsor in the presence of the papal legates. The forgery, which contains the story of the battlefield vow, may be based on a now-lost original. But William did grant land to the monks of Marmoutiers, and the abbey was built in the 1070s. The monks claimed that the idea was suggested to William by their abbot, William Faber. Duke William is said to have refused to allow it to be built in the valley, where there was a plentiful supply of water. He insisted that it be built on the hilltop, and that the high altar of the Abbey Church (long since demolished) should be built on the very spot where Harold was killed. That looks more like the construction of a war memorial in thanksgiving for victory than any act of penance. But the decision might in fact have been taken in 1070 as a response to the legate Ermenfrid's imposition of penances for the killing of Englishmen during and after the battle. Domesday Book records the abbey lands in Sussex, almost 65 hides worth 43 pounds, more than ten thousand silver pennies.

The tradition at Battle was that the 'fields were covered with corpses and all around the only colour to meet the gaze was blood-red. It looked from afar as if rivulets of blood, flowing down from all sides, had filled up the valleys, just like a river.'

The Duke waited in the vicinity of the battle and the Normans comprehensively ravaged the surrounding area, seeking supplies. The Duke waited, half expecting a new challenger and hoping for submission by the English. But neither came. It was by no means certain that those in London would accept the verdict of Hastings, let alone the men of the Danelaw and Northumbria. The latter might maintain their independence and enlist the aid of King Swein of Denmark. In fact he dithered and made no intervention until 1068.

The remnants of the Witan gathered panic-stricken in London and argued among themselves. Some wanted Edgar the Aetheling to be chosen as King, and so crowned. They were under no obligation to recognise any claims made by the Norman Duke and the Aetheling had not been condemned as a usurper by the papacy. He had a hereditary claim through his father Edward, son of Edmund Ironside. But he had little real support and was only about fourteen years old, unable to lead an army in battle even if one could be raised.

As against that, there was an ecclesiastical party who were arguing that the defeat was a sign of God's displeasure and a punishment for sin. They also wanted a strong King as soon as possible who would guarantee their possession of Church estates. Archbishop Ealdred of York and some of the London burgesses supported the Aetheling, while the Earls Edwin and Morcar and probably Archbishop Stigand, were more reluctant. The earls seem to have withdrawn to somewhere in Mercia. King Edward's widow, Edith, watched in trepidation from her estate at Winchester. She had no reason to support the Aetheling, although there was support elsewhere in the country. Abbot Leofric of Peterborough had returned, possibly wounded, certainly sick, from Hastings and was to die on 1 November. The monks then elected Brand, their provost, as abbot, and he sought recognition of his election from the Aetheling. That was to prove an expensive mistake.

So, in the fortnight after Hastings, the nobles and clergy in London dithered. The *Chronicle* remarks, acidly, 'Always the more it ought to have been brought forward, the more it got behind.'[16] But no Englishmen of any repute had yet submitted to the Duke, who grew impatient. He took reprisals against the men of Romney who had attacked two of his ships, inflicting 'such punishments as he thought fit for the slaughter of his men'. That had the desired effect, and the Norman army began moving along the coast, north of Romney Marsh where estates were sacked and Folkestone was ravaged. Dover, a major cross-Channel port, promptly surrendered. Despite that, the 'vill' was burned down and utterly destroyed. William now moved his fleet there and so established communications with Normandy.

The areas affected by the Norman progress are about 25 miles apart, suggesting the length of a day's march on alternate days. Dover's surrender came too late to prevent the destruction of the burh on the cliff top. William's control over his men seemed to leave much to be desired. News of the treatment meted out to Dover reached Canterbury, where the inhabitants 'shook with terror'. But the Duke could not enter the city. He was now, with his men, delayed by sickness, as the change of diet and plentiful rich food brought dysentery among them. Possibly mortified by his men's lack of discipline, and fearing that the disease was a sign of God's wrath, he compensated the citizens of Dover for the fire damage. That did not prevent him from driving out some of the inhabitants and billeting his men in their houses, a pattern to be followed in other towns and cities following their surrender.

EDVVARD REX : VBI hARO

14. Here King Edward grants Earl Harold leave to go on his proposed journey.

15. With his companions, Earl Harold rides to Bosham.

·VI·MILITES·EQVITANT·AD·BOS

HIC HAROL

16. The Earl feasts at Bosham. The fable of the Fox and Crow warns of deceit.

17. The Earl wades out to his ship. No destination is mentioned.

ROLD·MARE NAVIGAVIT·ETVE

18. The landing on the coast of Ponthieu.

19. Count Guy I of Ponthieu arrests Earl Harold.

AR OLD: hIC: APPREhENDIT: VVIDO:

Above: 20. At Beaurain, Guy admonishes the Earl who surrenders his sword.

Below: 21. The Duke returns to Bayeux after his campaign in Brittany.

Opposite: 22. The Duke confers arms and armour on Earl Harold.

23. Earl Harold swears an oath on two reliquaries containing saints' bones.

24. King Edward scolds an embarrassed Earl Harold after his return.

VARDI·REGIS·AD·ECCLESIAM·S
PETRI A

25. The funeral procession for King Edward's burial.

26. Above, the dying king stretches his hand out to Earl Harold. According to the *Vita Edwardi* he confided the kingdom to Harold's protection. Below, Edward lies dead.

INTECTO·ALLOQVIT·EIDE

ET·HIC·DEFVNCTVS·EST

Opposite: 27. Harold is enthroned as King.

Above: 28. A messenger informs the new King that a Comet shines in the sky and an amazed crowd views it.

Below: 29. A Motte and Bailey castle is constructed at Hastings.

30. Norman knights, using their lances as spears, charge into battle.

31. The charge continues, supported by others.

32. The charge reaches the English shield wall.

33. Horses and men fall as they are repelled from the shield wall.

34. Bishop Odo (with baton) encourages the younger knights.

35. The death of King Harold.

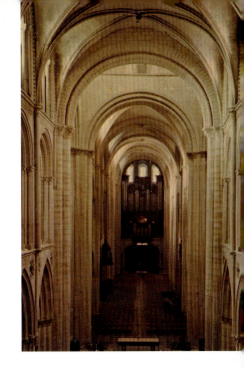

Above: 36. A page from the *Historia Regum* of Simeon of Durham.

Right: 37. The Abbaye aux Hommes at Caen.

38. The field of battle from Duke William's point of view.

QVI IACET HIC
REGNI SCEPTRVM TVLIT
HARDICANVTVS,
EMMÆ CNVTONIS
GNATVS & IPSE FVIT.
OBIIT A.D. JO42.

40. The resting place of Queen Emma and her son Harthacnut: Winchester.

Opposite page: 39. A fourteenth-century painting of Edward the Confessor as a saint.

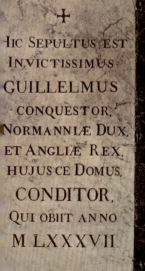

✝
HIC SEPULTUS EST
INVICTISSIMUS
GUILLELMUS
CONQUESTOR,
NORMANNIÆ DUX,
ET ANGLIÆ REX,
HUJUSCE DOMUS,
CONDITOR,
QUI OBIIT ANNO
M LXXXVII

Left: 41. King William's gravestone in the Abbaye aux Hommes.

Above: 42. Ely Cathedral: - note the militaristic design of the West Tower.

Overleaf: 43. A map showing the relationship of Normandy to England in the eleventh century.

12

COLLABORATION & CONTINUITY

On Sunday 29 October the Duke was at Canterbury, having left the sick and wounded to recover at Dover. Reinforcements had arrived from Normandy. All Saints Day was celebrated and a camp for the army was set up at a place called Broken Tower.[1] Perforce the Duke remained there until 1 December, a Friday, because he himself had contracted dysentery. While there he sent messengers soliciting submissions, especially those of Winchester and, more importantly, of Queen Edith.

Winchester and the Queen then surrendered, Edith sending gifts in confirmation of her submission. She was allowed to retain a respectable amount of land, suitable for a King's widow. She was later alleged, by William of Poitiers, to have declared that she wished to see William become King since he had been adopted as a son by her husband and made his heir. There is no support for this in the text of the *Vita Edwardi*, which ends the account of Edward's reign with a lament over Stamford Bridge 'where namesake kings had fought', leaving the River Ouse 'with corpses choked'. There is not a single word in it about Duke William or his claims, yet it must have been completed and converted into a religious life of the King in the early years of the Conquest. However, it suited the Duke's purpose to present her submission as acceptance of his claims.

The march on London was resumed and the Normans moved east towards Maidstone, still pillaging and destroying as they went. A force of 500 knights was sent to probe the defences of London while the main body moved on towards Epsom.

London was found to be strongly defended by men under the leadership of the wounded Staller, Aesgar. Messages were exchanged between him and the Duke and specious offers were made, promising that the Staller would be allowed to retain his office and his estates provided that he surrendered. The same tactic was to be used to persuade others to submit. But these talks between William and Aesgar came to nothing. The knights advanced as far as Southwark, threatening London Bridge, until forced to retire in the face of determined resistance. William of Poitiers relates that some English leaders were tempted to offer battle and that London had a numerous and formidable force. Some attempt might have been made to raise yet another army, perhaps by those who supported the claims of the Aetheling. They had announced that it was 'their dearest wish to have no lord who was not a compatriot'.

But others were losing their nerve, fearing the consequences of further resistance. All that could be achieved, therefore, was to deny the Normans entry to London. The Duke decided against any attempt to storm the city across the Thames and was deterred from attacking other heavily defended crossings, such as Southwark Bridge. He continued his march through Surrey and southern Berkshire, and was rejoined by the contingent of knights which had probed the defences of London somewhere around Walton-on-Thames. He avoided attacking Reading and swung in a wide arc around it until he reached Wallingford. Here, with the connivance of the local magnate, a king's thegn called Wigot of Wallingford, he crossed the Thames by bridge and ford and Archbishop Stigand came to him to submit, the first of many.

Stigand remained for the time being in office and in possession of his estates, 'because of the great authority which he exercised over the English'. He renounced all allegiance to the Aetheling, repenting of having 'rashly nominated' him. Other high-ranking clerics followed his example in the days that followed, all anxious to retain both office and lands. Collaboration with the Duke was becoming the order of the day.

William continued his march, following a wide curve north of London and cutting it off from the hinterland from which it obtained its food supplies and other necessities. Ravaging continued with the Normans rejoicing as more and more Englishmen submitted, and many 'flocked to submit like flies to a running sore', says William of Poitiers. But others still held back from submission to the Duke, William of Poitiers complaining that 'no one meant to come to him'. The Duke still kept to his 'slash and burn' progress as a deterrent to anyone attempting a further pitched battle.

As he approached London, another advance party of knights was sent into the city and was again met by fierce resistance. They inflicted 'great sorrow upon London by the death of many of her sons and daughters'. This perhaps finally persuaded the leading citizens to submit themselves and 'all they had, to their noble conqueror and hereditary lord', as William of Jumièges puts it.[2]

The Earls Edwin and Morcar are reported to have withdrawn to the North to await developments and to have submitted to William at Berkhamstead, yet they are also recorded as submitting at Barking. One possible explanation is that they sent word, by means of a herald, notifying William of their submission while he was at Berkhamstead and then made their submission in person at Barking, having concluded that it was both safe and prudent to do so. But events at this time were confused and Berkhamstead may be a simple error.

On arriving at Berkhamstead the Duke had received a delegation of leading Londoners and local thegns from Middlesex and Hertfordshire, who made their submission. They 'sought pardon', it was claimed, 'for any hostility they had shown and surrendered themselves and all their property to his mercy'. Those were obviously the terms upon which such submissions had to be made. The Duke then, magnanimously, 'restored all their possessions and treated them with great honour'. One of those who surrendered was the Abbot of St Albans. The delegation from London was led by the Norman Bishop of London, William, accompanied by Walter, Bishop of Hereford, Wulfstan, Bishop of Worcester and a number of others including Giso, Bishop of Wells. Yet these latter areas had not even seen a Norman yet. Even Edgar the Aetheling now, although 'proclaimed King by the English', came in and as he 'hesitated to take up arms ... humbly submitted himself and the kingdom to William'.

The motive of all ecclesiastics who so readily submitted was to retain their sees and abbacies and protect the Church's possession of its estates. Bishop Giso of Wells in his last testament was to insist on taking the credit for having not only preserved his church's property but increased it. He says that he found it impoverished when he received it, and that he recovered lands 'unlawfully' taken from it by Harold, Stigand and others (carefully skating over how Harold, when King, had restored lands to him 'as fully as ever he had them in King Edward's time')[3] and boasted of worming more land out of King William and persuading others to give or sell land to him. He also took care never to refer to Harold as king and to describe King Edward as William's immediate predecessor. He became, as bishop, part of the system by means of which King William controlled the West Country.

Archbishop Ealdred put his skills at William's disposal, organised his coronation and used his influence in southern England as a former Bishop of Worcester on behalf of the new King. Bishop Wulfstan recognised William as King, especially after his coronation, and used the resources of his see to ward off Welsh attacks. He had been won over by his desire to avoid further bloodshed and joined in the offer of the crown to Duke William. None of these men raised any objection to the prospect of William becoming King, despite the ancient tradition, first recorded at the Synod of Clovesho, 747, now apparently overlooked, that a bastard could not be King.

As for the abbots, most kept well out of political affairs. But Baldwin of Bury St Edmunds was a member of a 'bloc' of abbots who grew richer by supporting the new regime. He used his abbey's resources to defend East Anglia from the Danes and to combat disorder in the aftermath of the occupation. Aethelwig of Evesham, regarded as an 'archetypal quisling' by some,[4] redeemed his abbatial lands (as did Baldwin) by 'paying the appropriate price'. He rose to greater prominence in 1069 and received a commission with great administrative powers and jurisdiction over seven shires, mostly in western Mercia.

Most clerics preferred discreet submission to open rebellion and this set the pattern for collaboration with the enemy. They actually begged William to take the crown, saying that 'they were accustomed to obey a king and wished to have a king as their lord'. All law and order depended on there being a king who could enforce it. The Londoners sought the confirmation of their existing borough customs and, after the Coronation, a writ was issued confirming them. Other boroughs must have acted similarly later as the 'Judges' of York and Chester, the 'Lawmen' of Stamford and Cambridge continued in office, as Domesday Book records. Normans were, of course, added to their ranks. Similarly, men with the authority of 'Soke and Sake' over various shires continued to exercise their rights, but again these powers were also bestowed on Normans.

Leading lay lords also submitted in due course: Aesgar the Staller, Siward son of Aethelgar and his brother Ealdred, the Shropshire thegn Eadric 'the Wild' and the West Midland thegn Thorkell of Arden (who took great care to protect his kinsmen by allying himself to several of the incoming Normans), and the Lincolnshire thegn

Ulf Topeson. A special case was Edward 'of Salisbury', who still held over 300 hides in nine shires in 1086. These men submitted to William's overwhelming force, but others who submitted were real collaborators. Men like Coleswein of Lincoln (who made his fortune only after the Conquest) or Wigod of Wallingford, and Queen Edith's steward Wulfweard White. Most of these were or became royal servants. Their humiliation did them little good. Few Englishmen were allowed to retain the estates William re-granted to them (at a price), and only a handful can be found in the pages of Domesday Book with estates of any great size. Many early collaborators were to lose their lands through involvement in rebellions between 1067 and 1076.

One major collaborator was Copsige, who had been right-hand man to Earl Tostig in Northumbria. He certainly supported William and rejected efforts by others to win him over to opposition to the Norman. He was given the earldom of Osulf of Bamburgh, effectively becoming Earl in Northumbria, but was slain by that same Osulf, who had now rebelled.

A party was forming, determined to accept the Duke as King, so legitimising his rule. They wanted to ensure that he accepted 'the Law of King Edward', that is, English law as it was on the day, as the Normans put it, that 'King Edward was alive and dead'. The Normans clearly thought that resistance was at an end and Orderic Vitalis sums up the attitude, saying that 'by the grace of God, England was subdued within the space of three months and all the nobles of the realm made their peace with William, begging him to accept the crown according to English custom'. This was to prove to be an extended period of calm before the storm. William's policies towards the English were to provoke resistance and were compounded by the arrogant and exploitative behaviour of his followers.

William, in his usual facile manner, promised to be a gracious lord to the English, but they were to discover that one of his most prominent character defects was avarice. They no doubt thought that things would continue much as they had under previous kings, especially Cnut and his sons, so they submitted, bowing to William in the English manner (there is no explicit reference to homage), being taken under his protection then reinvested with their lands and honours. But they did not see themselves as being invested with a fief and becoming his vassals. Despite that, William was to take the view that England was now his to dispose of as he wished. After the

Coronation the mask began to slip and the English came to rue the day they submitted to the 'Norman Yoke'.[5]

The *Chronicle* records the shock experienced by the English magnates when harrying continued right up to the eve of the coronation. It complains that 'it was great folly' that they had not submitted sooner and so they hastened to give hostages and swear oaths of fealty, yet the Normans 'in the meantime harried everywhere they came'. That is why Archbishop Ealdred required William to give 'a pledge on the Gospels and swear an oath besides' before he would place the crown on William's head. Despite this, William was to allow his men to harry wherever they came after his return from Normandy, 6 December 1067.[6]

The Aetheling is described by William of Poitiers as having been given wide lands, but there is little trace of them in Domesday Book. He had a total of eight hides and one virgate, worth ten pounds (2,400 silver pennies) at Barkway and Great Hormead in Hertfordshire (which Edgar had not held in 1066, which had previously belonged to Aesgar the Staller and his sokemen!). Whatever lands Edgar had before 1066 remain unknown but, like so many surviving Englishmen, he most likely now held a great deal less.[7]

William now had to make himself king. This was essential to permit him to take control of the government and the legal system. There were already rumours of rebels lurking around, seeking to 'disturb the tranquillity of the realm'. Publicly, William let it be known that his preference was to wait until he could bring his wife Matilda to England, so that there could be a joint coronation. Privately, he was either exercising caution now that he was so near the summit of his ambition or was merely displaying becoming modesty. He waited for the offer to be made by the English themselves, conferring some sort of legitimacy on the process, and then tested the reaction of his followers.

He asked his closest advisers whether he should agree to the English request, saying how he was reluctant to accept while the country was still unsettled and had no wish to show undue haste. They naturally urged him to take the crown. Among them was Aimeri of Thouars, who overcame the Duke's hesitation by arguing that no one would urge him to seek coronation if they did not consider that he was 'in every way nobly suited to discharge his duties as King'. He added that hardly ever had knights been asked to express an opinion on such a matter and that William should take the crown as soon as possible.

Men were accordingly sent into London to erect a castle and prepare for the coronation, while the Duke himself calmly went hunting. He had displayed the customary modesty expected of him. The date fixed for the ceremony was Christmas Day, 1066. William would have known that Harold had been crowned on the Feast of the Epiphany and he now planned to erase that ceremony from men's minds by a new one held, as Harold's had probably also been, in 'the Church of St Peter the Apostle which is graced with the tomb of King Edward', that is, Westminster Abbey. So the Norman once more set about creating the image of himself as the legitimate heir of the Confessor.

As the Normans were to insist that Stigand must have conducted King Harold's coronation, and in view of the doubts that were held over his canonical position, the Archbishop of York, Ealdred, was prevailed upon to breach English custom again (which held coronations to be the traditional right of Canterbury) and crown William. Once crowned William would be able to demand that all freemen swear the hold oath and recognise him as king. This would enable him to 'make England his kingdom in a way in which it had never been Edward's'.[8]

The coronation, for which the third English Ordo is thought to have been used, followed the established pattern and was packed with religious and political meaning. It was, where necessary, suitably adapted to fit the peculiar circumstances of William's succession. He could not claim to be an Aetheling, having no English blood whatsoever, and could not refer to King Edward as his father. The phrase 'by hereditary right' was substituted for the usual phrases, and William claimed to be heir to an unbroken succession of monarchs. By hook or by crook, he was determined to stress a connection with English royal succession from Woden and Cerdic through Alfred the Great to Edward the Confessor.[9] So at the very beginning of his reign he made this spectacular claim of hereditary right, which governed his policy until his death. Of course, once William had been anointed and crowned the truth or falsity of his claim became irrelevant. William effectively established that royal authority was henceforth created by consecration as king.[10] The main change in the coronation rite was the introduction of a formal demand that the assembled congregation accept the new king. This was an innovation imported from France, which became an integral part of the ritual.

A third innovation was the introduction of a litany, which became known as the 'Laudes Regiae'. These had been sung in Normandy on the chief feasts of the Church (not as part of a coronation ritual, as Norman dukes were not crowned and anointed).[11] There is no positive indication that they had been used in pre-Conquest England nor that they originally had anything to do with coronations. They were used again at the coronation of Duchess Matilda, at Winchester, Pentecost 1068. William was to have them chanted before him during ceremonial crown-wearings, further evidence of his penchant for dramatic spectacle.

The form of the litany had changed. In pre-Conquest Normandy the Duke was named in the litany after the King of France and the saints invoked on his behalf came very low in the hierarchy of saints. Now, following an acknowledgement of Alexander II's contribution to William's elevation (the Pope is 'Supreme Pontiff and Universal Pope'), there was no mention of any King but William and the saints invoked were Our Lady, St Michael and St Raphael, as in Normandy. William was now saluted thus: 'To the most serene William, the great and peace-giving King, crowned by God, life and victory!'[12]

'Vita et Victoria' was an old Carolingian imperial formula as was 'serenissimus'. No eleventh-century ruler other than the German Emperor and the King of France was saluted thus. William was solemnly saluted by the Church as a 'Rex' and thus became one of the chief secular rulers of the age.

Thus, sanction was given to his kingship won by force of arms. Hildebrand (in a letter after he became Pope) mentions how he was criticised by other cardinals for having sanctioned great slaughter. Orderic Vitalis has William admit on his deathbed how he wrested his crown 'from the perjured King Harold in a desperate battle with much effusion of human blood'.[13]

Coronation also gave the sanction of the Church to this kingship won by battle, and glorified William's new status as King. But William and his supporters were never content to leave it at that. They now continuously argued, perhaps had to argue, that William was the legitimate successor not of Harold but of King Edward. Harold's reign was treated as an interregnum caused by his usurpation. William claimed to be King not merely *de facto* but *de jure*. This was done so that he could make use of English law to enforce the transfer of land from English into Norman hands.

The claim by hereditary right was buttressed, as William of Poitiers shows, by a stress also on right by blood (*jus sanguinis*) by a contention that the King's relationship to Queen Emma made him a blood relative of King Edward and so a member of the royal stock or *stirps regia*. That was an extremely weak argument and was soon dispensed with. William simply never ceased to insist that he had been formally designated by King Edward and was thus his legitimate successor, despite the fact that such designation, though it had been done for Harold, was not English custom. It was derived from Norman ducal custom; King Edward would probably have heard of this custom during his exile in Normandy.

William's position with regard to recognition by oath was equally equivocal. His acceptance as King, as at Berkhamstead and at Barking, by English magnates complied with recognised practice, but he had obviously been dealing by constraint with the representatives of men he had recently beaten in battle. To overcome that, the appeal to the congregation at the coronation had been introduced and was followed by the customary swearing by William of the coronation oath employed ever since the tenth century. He also had a special crown made for the occasion by a Greek craftsman, with an arc of twelve pearls, resembling that made for the Emperor Otto the Great.

The claim was that William reigned 'by the grace of God and by hereditary right' like King Edward, and the Norman was laying claim to attributes specially delegated to him by God. His royal state was subsequently surrounded by an aura of veneration, especially at crown-wearings. On one such occasion a foolish cleric was heard to cry out twice, 'Behold I see God!' Archbishop Lanfranc had the man whipped for it. William's reaction is not recorded.

The coronation did not run as smoothly as William wished. When the congregation responded to the demand by Archbishop Ealdred and Bishop Geoffrey of Coutances, in English and in Norman French, whether it was their will that William should be their king, the response was so loud and enthusiastic that the armed guards outside the abbey, put there in case of protests by disaffected Londoners, concluded that some mischief was brewing; they panicked and set fire to the surrounding houses. While some men tried to fight the fire, others began looting. The noise and the smoke from the fire then panicked the congregation, which rushed out of the abbey, leaving William alone and quaking in his boots. A handful of remaining clergy hastily completed the ceremonies, the closing prayers and a blessing from the Archbishop, as order was gradually restored. One can only wonder what it now meant to a man born in bastardy that he was acknowledged to be an anointed king.

Following on from the coronation further submissions were made on the part of the English. There was a round of them held at Barking Abbey, which William had adopted as his residence while awaiting the completion of the fortress he had ordered to be built for him in London – the Tower. He had retired to Barking on account of the hostility of the Londoners. Earls Edwin and Morcar made their submission there in person, which suggests that they might not have attended the coronation.

The new King now held a Council, the *Anglo-Saxon Chronicle* calls it a Witan, at which several decisions were taken. He took over the existing administrative machine as it had been under King Edward. So he was assuming the usual royal powers. The primary decision was an order for the levying of a heavy geld, probably, like most of William's gelds, at the high rate of two shillings on the hide.[14] William was demanding gelds paid in shillings not pennies. The penalty for non-payment was forfeiture of the estate, which was then sold to anyone who could guarantee to pay it. For example Ralf Taillebois paid the tax on Sharnbrook, which had belonged to Tovi the Housecarl, and was then able to grant it as a fief to one of his knights. Tovi had held the land but 'after King William came into England he refused to give gafol [tribute] from this land and Ralf gave the gafol and took possession of it in forfeiture.'[15]

William also issued a writ dealing with the case of Abbot Brand of Peterborough. The Abbot had made the error of seeking recognition as abbot from the Aetheling and William had been furious. But 'good men' interceded with the King on the Abbot's behalf and 'because the Abbot was a rather good man', William allowed his wrath to be appeased by the payment of 40 marks in gold. The writ now confirmed the Abbot in possession of his abbatial lands, especially those 'lands that his brothers and kinsmen held hereditarily and freely under King Edward'. Among the witnesses were Archbishop Ealdred, Maerleswein, Sheriff of Lincolnshire, William fitzOsbern and Ulf Topeson a relative of the Abbot, certainly some of the 'good men' who had pleaded for him before the King.[16]

Another early writ issued in 1067 was one confirming land granted to Regenbald the Priest at Latton and Eysey, a conveyance to him of land previously held by King Harold. Regenbald used his position in the royal household to secure the writ for himself. The writ therefore actually says that the estate was granted to him 'as freely as it had belonged to King Harold'. This early in the reign the decision to eliminate all reference to Harold as a king had not yet been taken, though it soon was. Very few references to Harold's title have survived.

Regenbald had been the Confessor's Keeper of the Seal and even, according to a rather doubtful writ, his chancellor. He retained his office under the Conqueror during 1067 and from him William learnt the use of the writ. Then he was replaced, possibly just after the end of the year, by the Norman Herfast, who became Bishop of Elmham in 1070, who was the first official to be called Chancellor. One might wonder whether Regenbald's incautious reference to Harold as 'king' was the cause of his removal from office.

William made use of the treasure that Harold 'had avariciously shut up in the Royal Treasury' to pay off the mercenary soldiers and to enrich Norman followers. He also gave a great deal of it to Norman monasteries. But the transfer of lands from English into Norman hands had now begun. Even before William returned for a while to Normandy, in the spring of 1067, he granted to Geoffrey de Mandeville the lands of Leofsunu at Moze in Essex; 'this manor King William gave when he stayed in London.'[17] Geoffrey was the 'heir' to all the lands in Essex of Aesgar the Staller.

The King himself took into the royal demesne almost all the lands of the Godwineson family, so vastly increasing the size of the demesne. Countess Gytha, Earl Godwin's widow, retained some lands, as did Queen Edith as Edward's widow, while a few estates were used to reward Norman followers and some of the collaborators. But the King was now far and away the largest landowner in the kingdom. William, now lord of all the land in the kingdom, also proceeded to dispose of land as he thought fit. That was a right that no previous English king had ever had. William's successors, William Rufus and Henry, were also incapable of treating the kingdom as in any way different from any other landed estate, an indication of their limitations.

Consequently, all land holders became the King's dependents, directly or indirectly. Even the language of inheritance vanished from post-Conquest England, except of course in the case of the King, and everything was ultimately held of him. This was a direct consequence of the Conquest. Eadmer of Canterbury quite rightly wrote that there had been 'strange changes' and 'developments which were quite unknown in former days'. That is why his work was entitled *Historia Novorum in Anglia*.[18] He deliberately abstained from commenting on William's laws in secular matters because his was an ecclesiastical history, but he comments on secular laws that 'from what he ordained in divine matters ... their character may be inferred'. So he stresses that bishops and abbots, before investiture with ring and staff, had to be 'made the King's men' and then attributed to the fact of the conquest all viciousness and all vices.

King William knew that he would have to reward his followers, and with land, despite all specious promises to the English that their rights would be respected. Consequently, all the lands of those who had fought against him at Hastings (and, one suspects, of those who had died at Stamford Bridge and Fulford) were confiscated on the grounds that these men had committed treason by opposing in arms the rightful heir to the throne! The lands were then distributed among the Norman King's followers, who were deemed in many cases to have become the successors of English 'antecessors' (that is, 'predecessors'), and so inherited all the rights of the previous holders. Domesday Book is by no means consistent about this and in seven shires names no antecessors at all and only a few in another ten shires. One possibility is that the Normans were unable to identify those who were the lords of men who held the land in King Edward's time and simply confiscated the lands of those who had rebelled.

Again Lanfranc's collection of Conciliar Church Canons throws light on the legal basis of this. William of Poitiers implies that all Englishmen were guilty of treason by association. Canon 14 of the Sixth Council of Toledo condemned infidelity to a successor king, who therefore could confiscate land and distribute it to his 'fideles'. Canon 75 of Toledo says that all associates of a tyrant should suffer the same penalty with him. After he became Archbishop, Lanfranc distributed examples of his *Collectio* to cathedrals and abbeys, which made copies of them. Eleven of them have survived. His main aim, it has been suggested, was certainly to bring England into canonical conformity with the rest of the Church. It might not have been specifically intended to justify the Conquest, but it certainly contained the main authorities for doing so.

Those land holders, including bishops and abbots, who were allowed to retain possession of their estates had to pay to redeem them. Abbot Baldwin of Bury St Edmunds, for example, paid eleven marks of gold 'when the English redeemed their lands', as well as two marks for Stoneham, in Norfolk, and five pounds for Ixworth Thorpe, Suffolk. Those who redeemed their lands were well advised to obtain writs of confirmation, as without such evidence a man could be deprived again. It began to dawn on the English from 1067 onwards just how insignificant they were in the scheme of things and in the sight of the rapacious Normans upon whom William now relied.

Before he left England to go back to Normandy, the King laid restrictions on his men, to ensure their good conduct. They were ordered to abstain from violence against the English, especially women, and from plundering them. Judges had to be appointed 'to strike terror into the mass of soldiers'. They were scarcely even allowed to drink in taverns because drunkenness led to quarrels and murders. All brigandage, theft and other 'evil deeds' were forbidden and merchants were given the freedom of harbours and highways. This speaks volumes about the real state of affairs in conquered England. Such restrictions have to have been made necessary by the conduct of the Norman soldiery.

Plenty of English men, especially clergy, had readily submitted to the Norman now he was King and served him faithfully. Orderic Vitalis accuses them of being 'covetous of high office' and says they 'shamelessly pandered to the King' in order to secure it. It did many of them little good in the long run, though only one Bishop, Aethelwine of Durham, eventually joined the ranks of those who rebelled.

13

CONFLICT & CONTRADICTION

Early in the spring of 1067, at the beginning of Lent (21 February), William decided that he could no longer delay his return to Normandy, which he had left on 27 September 1066. He had to return in order to reassert his authority and in order to enjoy a 'triumph'. He set off from Pevensey, where he received more submissions, though no names are recorded. He took with him as part of his entourage a selection of English nobles and clergy: Archbishop Stigand, Aethelnoth Abbot of Glastonbury, Edgar the Aetheling, the three Earls, Edwin, Morcar and Waltheof, and other prominent Englishmen such as Aethelnoth the Kentishman. These men served two purposes. They were hostages for the good behaviour of the English ruling class (what was left of it) who might have fomented rebellion against him in his absence, and they were proof of the extent of his victory. Once in Normandy, he set out on a ducal and quasi-royal progress, going first of all to Caen. It was almost a Roman Triumph. He distributed more rich gifts to supplement those already sent from England, to churches in Normandy and the rest of France. To Pope Alexander II he sent King Harold's richly ornamented banner, the Fighting Man. For other churches throughout France there were rich gifts of land in England and of the spoils of the conquest: gold and silver jewelled crosses, ornate vestments, jewelled books and chalices.

On 8 April William was at Fécamp, where the dukes usually celebrated Easter. On the feast of St James, 1 May, he attended the consecration of the Church of Our Lady and St Peter at Dives, where he issued ordinances 'for the common good', to restore peace to Normandy. On 1 July, he was at Jumièges. Prior Lanfranc of Bec was sent to Rome to obtain a pallium, not for himself but for John of Avranches, who was promoted to be Archbishop of Rouen. Lanfranc profited from his visit, receiving papal recognition, and returned accompanied by two papal legates.

William was congratulated, in Norman sources, for the manner in which he restored and maintained order in Normandy, with praise as a wise lawgiver and firm administrator, although no written evidence of such law-making activity has survived. It was done through ducal ordinances, presumably by word of mouth, at the King-Duke's 'nod' as Eadmer of Canterbury puts it. The charters issued contain boasts such as that he was 'Duke of the Normans who acquired the Kingdom of England by war' (so the mask slips a little) or 'Lord of Normandy and, having been created so by hereditary right, Basileus [King] of the English'. The propaganda does suggest that all had not been quite as peaceful in Normandy as he might have wished. He remained there from April to early December and would not have returned even then had he not been urgently required back in England. It must have been taking him far longer to restore 'peace' in Normandy than he might have expected.

England had been left to the tender mercies of William fitzOsbern, who was responsible for England north of the Thames, and Bishop Odo of Bayeux, who had responsibility for the area south of it. There was a sort of division into two separate zones; the South or occupied zone and the North or unoccupied zone, still ruled to an extent by the Earls Edwin and Morcar. Earl Waltheof still held an earldom centred on Huntingdonshire while William had sent Tostig's former agent, Copsige, to rule in Bernician Northumbria. Cospatric, son of Maldred, still ruled in Bamburgh. A survivor from King Edward's reign, Ralph the Staller, had an earldom in Norfolk.

For this reason, and because Englishmen are found witnessing early writs of the Conqueror, while English sheriffs still held office in their shires and bishops and abbots retained their sees and abbacies, it is conventional to argue that William intended to rule an 'Anglo-Norman Realm'. It is argued that he could call on loyalties previously centred on the Old English Royal House; he called himself specifically 'King of the English'. On the other hand, it is said, and to an extent correctly, that from 1066 to 1087, William's dominions constituted a single realm. Inevitably, the aura of kingship tended to affect the administration and government of Normandy where he was still 'Duke of the Normans'.

The Courts he held on both sides of the Channel contained much the same personnel. He was King of a single aristocracy, which included at first several distinguished Englishmen. In the opinion of some historians England and Normandy exercised reciprocal influence upon each other and there was a political union. But the magnates in England were to become predominantly Norman and allowed to exercise control over the administration of the joint realm. There came about a radical change in the higher ranks of the social order, which was to involve the total destruction of the ancient nobility and the substitution for it of a new aristocracy from overseas. The English earls were soon to disappear and there was widespread destruction of English lives and property. While it can be argued that this was in part a reaction to the rebellions that sprang up repeatedly from the late summer of 1067 onwards until about 1076 it can also be suggested that that itself was a reaction to the systematic imposition of what Orderic Vitalis was to call 'the Norman Yoke'. It is difficult to credit that William had not intended this to happen. Yet there was certainly a convincing display of an intention to maintain continuity with the Old English past.

One manifestation of what might have been a decision by William to maintain continuity was the use which was made of the Old English Ordo for William's coronation, and another was the rapidity with which William moved to secure that coronation. The Ordo was used to make William a King, since he had no claim to be an Aetheling. Old English kings simply did not rush to get themselves anointed. The usual delay was of about one year, as in the cases of Aethelred and Edward the Confessor. King Edgar had actually delayed his coronation until he reached the age of thirty, a delay of many years. He had become King in 959 but his coronation was delayed until 973. Old English coronations proclaimed that a man was King, they did not make him one.

William found it essential to defend his 'Anglo-Norman realm' from many enemies. From late 1067 until 1072 he was to be preoccupied with the necessity of dealing first with the many risings provoked by Norman government and then of removing the Danes and overawing the Scots. Thereafter he devoted most of his time, while making occasional visits to England, to protecting his duchy. These policies were driven by political and military necessity.

Others argue that he had intended to create a genuine system involving both Normans and Englishmen in his government. But this realm neither resembled the Anglo-Danish state created by Cnut the Great nor was it a combination of English, Danish and Norman elements. William retained the framework of Old English government through courts of shire and hundred, employing the 'shire reeves' (sheriffs) and hundredmen, just as the Old English ecclesiastical dioceses were retained. William's system of administration differed little from that prevalent under Edward the Confessor. That was a matter of political common sense. Even his attempt, very quickly given up, to learn English was for his own purposes in order to try to gain access to the English past because he could not afford to disregard the Old English administrative machine. But he allowed his first Norman Chancellor to initiate the issue of writs in Latin.

In a similar vein he retained the system of writs as a means of conveying the royal will to the shires and hundreds and, in the earliest years, English nobles and officials are found acting as witnesses to them alongside Norman lords, thereby making good use of a surprising degree of English support. Enough Englishmen were retained to prevent an immediate revolt. So William gave an appearance of trying to rule with the help of Englishmen. William was certainly well served early in his reign by men well versed in the language and procedures of English law and administration, men like Earl Waltheof, Bishop Wulfstan and Abbot Aethelwig.[1] Hemming, the Worcester cartularist, said that the Abbot was a man who could intimidate even the French because he had studied English law and administration.[2] What is not so clear is how long William's rule with the aid of English magnates might have continued. That remains an unanswerable question because Norman rule provoked resistance even if King William had not intended that it should.

It is common to stress William's ruling that all men were to enjoy 'the law of King Edward', which in practice actually meant the law of Cnut, since King Edward is not known to have issued a code of laws of his own. Edward had, even as late as 1065, agreed at the behest of the Northumbrian rebels to renew the law of Cnut, which he might well have promised to uphold when he returned to England in 1041. In practice William intended to make England his kingdom in a way in which it had never been King Edward's. He made much more use of the full potential of English institutions than Edward ever attempted. It became William's kingdom because of his insistence on continuity in the administration rather than despite it. This might have been one of William's characteristic charades. Every landholder in the kingdom, whether Norman or English, now held his land by William's favour and, by performing homage and rendering service, had to acknowledge that this was so.

William, then, for a time, a very brief time as it turned out, did make use of influential Englishmen in order to achieve a smooth transition from the old to the new order.[3] But they were only retained in an ornamental position, kept at Court to enhance its dignity, rather than being given positions of real authority. In 1067 they were really taken to Normandy as hostages for the good behaviour of their fellow countrymen during William's absence, a measure of distrust that was to contribute to the inevitable result.

The use made of ecclesiastics was of greater value. None are known to have betrayed William's trust other than Bishop Aethelwine of Durham. Such was Stigand's influence over other English magnates that to retain him in office as Archbishop was a necessity. Ealdred was loyal; Aethelwig made himself useful; Wulfstan assisted Norman rule in Mercia. Such assistance may have delayed but did not prevent rebellion. Englishmen had to be appointed to authority in Northumbria, which had not yet submitted, hence the choice of Copsige and Cospatric. So there was active support from the higher clergy and outward loyalty from the surviving nobility. But it was soon made abundantly clear that to survive under Norman rule it was necessary to give active support.

William certainly gave the appearance of tempering justice with mercy and his magnanimous treatment of Exeter was a case in point. But this followed from a pattern of behaviour established in Normandy where clemency was used as a political tool, employed to win hearts and minds. Thus he later repeatedly allowed rebel lords to be reconciled and admitted to his favour, just as he did the same for Count Eustace of Boulogne despite his abortive raid on Dover in 1067.[4]

If the King wanted to form an Anglo-Norman State, he did little positive to accomplish it. The retention of Englishmen in office and the use he made of English governmental institutions do not amount to a settled policy. No attempt was made to place any Englishman in authority in England during his absence in Normandy in 1067, instead William took most of the surviving ruling class with him. He confiscated not only, as he could reasonably be expected to do, the lands of King Harold and his brothers, but also those of all the men who had fought against him, so depriving their heirs of their inheritance. Inevitably they turned against him and it is a wonder he did not realise that they would. Or was this a calculated act intended to drive the English into rebellion so that he could confiscate more and more land with which to reward his Norman followers?

In due course the reform of the Church was undertaken by Lanfranc, who issued copies of his *Collection of Canons*, which George Garnett has called 'an emphatic statement of the imposition of the Conquest',[5] as was the systematic rebuilding of cathedrals and abbey churches. William of Poitiers implies that it had been William's intention to have Lanfranc as his Archbishop of Canterbury from 1066 onwards. During 1066, Lanfranc certainly had shown William how a violent conquest could be defined under Canon Law as an act of piety. Lanfranc was 'the Cheshire cat of the Norman Conquest'.[6]

During William's absence, castle building had proceeded apace. London saw work on the Tower; another castle, called Baynard's Castle, was built near the river, while Montfichet went up north of the city. Another had already been built at Berkhamstead where William had received the submission of London. William fitzOsbern saw to it that castles multiplied, a policy that must have had William's endorsement. After all, as Eadmer commented, everything depended on his nod. Another went up at Winchester, fitzOsbern built one at Norwich and a string of castles was built along the Welsh border at Berkeley, Chepstow, Clifford, Monmouth and Wigmore. These were the 'official' or royal castles rather than those the many Norman lords were busily building for themselves. The *Chronicle* complained that they 'built castles here far and wide throughout this country and distressed the wretched folk, and always afterwards it grew much worse. May the end be good when God wills!' In Odo's area castles spread throughout Sussex and became the centres of castleries known as 'Rapes'.

Most of the arrangements depended, as did so much else, on the verbal instructions of King William. Estates were being distributed but the exact manner by which this was accomplished remains largely undocumented. Few writs have survived and even fewer charters. Domesday Book testifies that many were given 'by the King's writ and seal' but that others were granted by word of mouth through the king's officers. There were also many cases of estates simply being seized without any authorisation at all as the jurors testified that they had never seen writ nor seal nor heard the word of the king's officer.

Odo and fitzOsbern are described as the King's loyal servants being in turn well served by loyal castellans. The sources are full of complaints of oppression and lack of discipline. Orderic talks about the conduct of William's 'haughty deputies who despised his strict orders and tyrannized the people'. William's two commissioners allowed women and property to be attacked by their Norman followers and permitted no redress. Orderic was so dismayed that in fact he suppresses, when using his copy of the work, William of Poitiers' more fulsome panegyrics on William and, in his expanded edition of the work of William of Jumièges, tones down the more laudatory passages.

It is obvious that Odo and fitzOsbern simply held down the areas committed to them by force. Some of their men governed well but most irresponsibly heaped heavy burdens on the people so that the English 'groaned under the Norman yoke'. The Normans are accused of arrogantly abusing their authority and it was said that they 'mercilessly slaughtered the native people like the Scourge of God'. The result was the growth of efforts to find ways of shaking off this intolerable oppression.

In the North, Copsige, who was 'entirely favourable to the king and supported his cause', proceeded to collect the geld levied at the Christmas Court and ignored local efforts to win him over to opposition to Norman rule. Rashly he dispossessed the thegn Osulf of the House of Bamburgh (whom Copsige blamed for the driving out of Earl Tostig). The reaction came swiftly. Five weeks after his appointment by the King, Copsige, while feasting at Newburn on the Tyne, was besieged in his own house by Osulf and his supporters. Copsige managed to escape and took refuge in a nearby church. Osulf simply set fire to it, driving Copsige out and beheading him, while his escort had been cut down mercilessly while trying to escape the flames, 11 March 1067. Worse was to come.

The misgovernment of the King's representatives provoked risings, first in Herefordshire and then in Kent, areas associated directly with fitzOsbern and Odo respectively, and where oppression was perhaps at its worst. The most powerful thegn in Herefordshire and Shropshire, Eadric the Wild, paid only lip-service to Norman dominance, but he made an alliance with the Welsh princes and, in August, advanced into Herefordshire as far as the River Lugg near Leominster, ravaging and plundering estates now in Norman hands. Honour satisfied, he then withdrew. He had driven the Normans to take refuge in their castles until the storm of revolt had passed. No attempt was made to pursue him back into Wales.

Kent was a different matter. There the dissident thegns had called upon Count Eustace of Boulogne and in conjunction with him organised an assault on Dover castle and the surrounding burh. Eustace was at odds with William at the time, feeling he had been inadequately rewarded for his part in the Conquest. Perhaps he had expected to be given custody of Dover, which would have given him control over both ends of the Channel crossing.

He agreed to bring over a fleet and plenty of armed men and make himself master of the castle. The insurgency took advantage of the absence north of the Thames of Bishop Odo and Hugh de Montfort, the castellan of Dover. Eustace made a successful landing and was joined by the Kentishmen. They must have hoped their action would attract support from elsewhere in England. But they failed to occupy the castle, which put up stiffer resistance than had been expected. Even the citizens of Dover (who had no reason to love Eustace) joined in the resistance to them. Perhaps thinking Odo or de Montfort had returned unexpectedly, the Count's nerve failed him and he retreated towards his ships. His men had fled at the very mention of Odo's name, and Eustace escaped rather ignominiously by ship. Bishop Odo and de Montfort then returned at almost the same time and completed the mopping up of the rebellion.

But the Norman administration was severely shaken. They knew that exiled Englishmen and some of those still in England were in touch with each other and seeking help from King Swein of Denmark and even from the German Emperor. But Swein preferred to watch events from afar and await his chance to profit from them. The first stirrings of revolt had been successfully dealt with, or so it seemed, but there were indications of rising trouble in the South West of England. The burgesses of Exeter were showing signs of an intention to defy the King. They were attempting to form a league of West Country towns to oppose the spread of Norman power. Countess Gytha, Earl Godwin's widow was at the centre of the disaffection and residing at Exeter.

King William now chose 6 December to return via Dieppe to Winchelsea, the same day that Christ Church Canterbury burned down.[7] Upon his return he took great pains to appease everyone. He was especially gracious towards various English collaborators who attended the Christmas Court. He granted favours to those who asked for them. Orderic acidly remarks that such favours 'often bring back to the fold persons whose loyalty is doubtful'. The various rebels were tried and condemned in their absence, as was Eustace of Boulogne. William gave the See of Dorchester to Remigius of Fécamp.

The Bishop was to seek consecration at the hands of Archbishop Stigand, despite his uncanonical status.[8]

Action was taken to fill the gap created by the murder of Copsige, the vacancy being filled by the nomination of Cospatric, son of Maldred, a descendant through Earl Uhtred of Bamburgh of the founder of the House, Earl Waltheof I. Cospatric simply bought the earldom from William, no doubt promising that he could collect the geld. He was a frequent visitor to William's Court until he became involved in rebellion.

The English were still desperately seeking the aid of Swein of Denmark, and during 1068 Abbot Aethelsige of St Augustine's, Canterbury, took gifts to him, remaining there for two years before returning to England. Others negotiated with the powerful Archbishop Adalbert of Bremen. It was all to no avail. These appeals had to be made, as it was quite impossible for the English to drive out the Normans without overseas assistance, so heavy had been the losses at Stamford Bridge and Hastings. Aethelsige on his return found he had lost the support of his monks and was driven out again. The monks blamed him for the loss of monastic lands seized by the Normans.

But in the south and west of England no actual submissions had yet been made. Norman penetration had not yet proceeded that far. The citizens of Exeter had continued their efforts to form a league of resistance, strengthened their walls and levied troops from the surrounding area, preparing to resist the Norman King. They urged other towns to 'combine with them and fight with all their strength against the foreign King'.

Early in 1068 William arrived in the area; the thegns of Dorset were quick to submit, an example soon followed by towns further west. Those that did not submit rapidly enough suffered. Dorchester and Bridport were devastated; these towns might have been members of the league formed by the men of Exeter. But Exeter refused to submit, refusing point blank to admit the Norman King within their walls. This could not be tolerated, so the Bastard called up forces and planned the enforcement of Norman rule on Exeter. Garrisons were placed in other surrounding towns. Very shortly the true nature of Norman rule would be laid bare.

William was aware of rumours circulating in England that 'hinted that the Normans were to be massacred by the hostile English' supported by the Danes and other 'barbarous peoples'. There was rumour of a surprise attack to be launched during Lent while the Normans were doing penance in church. William probably intended to strike firmly and make an example of Exeter.

William found that the citizens were by no means unanimous in their opposition to him. There were two parties. One preferred submission over defiance, the other, perhaps encouraged by the presence of Countess Gytha, was all for resistance. The latter party had thrown down the gauntlet to William, closing the gates and preparing resistance, which might well have been provoked by the demand in 1067 for payment of a heavy geld. Domesday Book records that Exeter did not pay geld 'except when London, York and Winchester paid geld and that was half a mark of silver for the use of the thegns'. (A mark was one-third of one pound, 6 shillings and 8 pence, so the city owed 3 shillings and 4 pence or about six times as much as was paid per hide in Berkshire.)

The more rebellious of the Exeter men had declared roundly, 'We will neither swear fealty nor admit [the king] within our walls, but we will pay tribute [gafol] to him according to ancient custom.' William, suffused with rage, replied that he was not accustomed to accept subjects on such terms and took steps to prepare an assault. He had advanced on the city with an escort of (allegedly) 500 knights and some of them now launched over-hasty assaults on the walls, hoping to impress their lord. That resulted in heavy casualties, while one of the defenders, exulting in this, dropping his trousers, bared his buttocks insultingly at the Normans.

William then organised and launched a relentless attack, which drove the citizens from the walls. All was not well within the town as the peace-seeking party had gained the upper hand, fearing confiscation of their houses and property outside the city. They now sued for peace, surrendered hostages and prepared to open the gates. The Bastard accepted the hostages and then exacted revenge for his losses. One of the hostages had his eyes put out and another was hanged, within sight of the walls. This only stiffened the resolve of the insurgents, who resumed hostilities. The King had to make the usual arrangements for a blockade of the town, surrounding it and calling up siege engines.

A siege of eighteen days followed, after which, those who favoured submission again prevailed, terms for surrender were sought and the gates were thrown open to the King. Rather surprisingly, and perhaps a sign of William's craftiness, he decided to win over as much support as possible and put on one of his displays of magnanimity. Despite reports that some of his knights had been ill-treated after taking refuge in the harbour from a storm, he demanded only that the burgesses render to him exactly the same dues and services as they had owed to King Edward. Perhaps he had genuinely decided to grant clemency to the citizens or possibly hoped to encourage the submission of other towns further west by this action.

The real token of Norman supremacy then followed. William ordered the construction of a castle within the town, in the northern angle of the ancient Roman walls. It was called Rougemont and the gateway to it still stands. Baldwin de Meules (brother of Richard fitz Gilbert and a son of Count Gilbert of Brionne) was made the castellan and received one-third of the annual tax of 18 pounds demanded from Exeter. This man Baldwin was thereafter for a time Sheriff of Devon and also ruled the Cornish peninsula. The whole of Devon now submitted, much to William's satisfaction. Within a very short time William's magnanimity paid off. The men of Exeter fought for him against their fellow countrymen when the 'Sons of Harold' (Godwine, Edmund and Magnus, supported by Tostig, son of Swein Godwineson) attacked later in the year.

William marched through Cornwall, meeting no resistance, while the towns of Gloucester and Bristol further north submitted around the same time, no doubt cowed by reports of events in the South West, and it is possible that Oxford also surrendered. Countess Gytha and 'the wives of other good men' escaped (either during the siege or were possibly allowed to do so, thereby removing a difficult prisoner) and took refuge in the Bristol Channel on the island of Flatholme. Countess Gytha's flight serves to confirm her complicity in the resistance. The King now had control of the western region, and his success is demonstrated by the failure of subsequent attempts at rebellion. Exeter had acted virtually alone and too soon, without waiting for assistance from other sources. It is possible that they had been expecting the help of the Sons of Harold. These men (probably known as the 'Sons of Harold' because they were led by Godwine and his brothers) had formed a resistance force based in Ireland, gathering a fleet together and recruiting armed support (just like Harold in 1051–52) from the King of Dublin and Leinster, Diarmid Mac Mael n'Ambo. Their intention was to stir up resistance to the Norman occupation, in the hope of triggering a widespread uprising.

They were to cause further trouble in the South West during the summer of 1068. The Sons of Harold brought a fleet of fifty-two ships and many armed men (perhaps between two and three thousand) to Avonmouth near Bristol. They attacked the city and ravaged the area, the usual method of warfare in this period. The citizens of Bristol resisted fiercely, so the Sons of Harold withdrew with their plunder. From there they descended on Somerset, landing at Porlock (near Minehead) and moving inland. At Bleadon they encountered the local Staller, Eadnoth, who gave battle. There were heavy casualties on both sides, including the Staller himself. The Sons were driven off but that was not to be the last of their efforts.

For the moment William was triumphant and so, satisfied that he had quelled incipient revolt, he now held a court at Winchester, for Easter 23 March 1068 where it was arranged that his wife, the Duchess Matilda, should be brought over to England to be crowned queen. She duly arrived, at Pentecost, 11 May, and was crowned. William himself held a solemn crown-wearing to demonstrate his supremacy. The *Chronicle* alleges that it became his custom 'as often as he was in England' to wear his crown in this manner three times a year, at Christmas, Easter and Pentecost, at Gloucester, Winchester and Westminster. He frequently did so but not, as far as the evidence goes, quite as regularly as the *Chronicle* states. On at least one occasion the ceremony was held at York.

Despite the splendour of the occasion, this demonstration of hubris brought with it its attendant nemesis. William had assumed that it was now safe to bring his wife to England but the coronation was almost immediately followed by, perhaps actually triggered, a series of more serious rebellions, which bade fair to disrupt his control over his kingdom. Had he not reacted decisively, he could have suffered even more serious damage, but react he did and, in the end, it was the remnant of the English nobility that lost all political authority and influence.

Rising discontent surfaced in Mercia and Northumbria; the King was 'informed that the men of the North were gathered together and meant to make a stand against him if he came'. It must have seemed as though all efforts to include Englishmen in the new Anglo-Norman Government had been in vain. Some degree of resistance had coalesced around the ambiguous figure of Earl Edwin of Mercia, who, it seems, absented himself from the Queen's coronation. He felt threatened by the construction of the chain of castles along the Welsh border and into his earldom. He could well have felt slighted by the authority granted to Abbot Aethelwig of Evesham, an arch collaborator. William was making use of this able and intelligent cleric and granted him power of administration and justice over seven shires, three of which were within the boundaries of Mercia.

Orderic Vitalis reports that after the submission at Barking, Edwin had received some authority over part of Northumbria, probably Yorkshire and had even been promised (like Earl Harold) the hand of one of William's many daughters. But it was now 1068 and there was no sign of the fulfilment of that promise. It was further said that William was listening to 'dishonest counsels' from 'envious and greedy followers' and so had 'withheld the maiden'. Edwin was under further pressure from the appointment of Roger of Montgomery as castellan of Shrewsbury. The latter had even been granted the title of 'Comes' in a writ issued at Whitsun 1068. Edwin's patience was about to run out.

Earl Edwin allied himself with the Welsh princes (who feared a Norman incursion into Wales), just as his father Earl Aelfgar had done. Bleddyn, Prince of Gwynedd, had allied with Eadric the Wild, and these two made overtures to Edwin, who called up the forces of his Earldom and awaited events. The King called up his troops and set out northwards from Winchester into Mercia. This was a military rather than a royal progress and the King ordered castles to be built in major towns as he advanced.

The first was at Warwick, where the motte, known locally as 'Aethelfleda's Mound', still stands within the grounds of the great stone castle.[9] Henry of Beaumont was appointed castellan. Another castle went up at Nottingham, castellan William Peverel. Having overawed Mercia, William went on into Yorkshire. As he advanced all signs of resistance melted away. Edwin, and his brother Morcar, had done nothing.

The real centre of disaffection now lay beyond Mercia, in Northumbria. The lords in that region had not yet fully submitted to the Normans nor had any Norman yet set foot there. The Northumbrians perhaps imagined, like the men of Exeter, that they could bargain with the King, as they had done with King Edward. William had no Earl Harold at his side to calm his wrath and advise conciliation. But William perhaps had been caught between his policy of promoting Englishmen and his need to satisfy the ambitions and avarice of his most powerful Norman supporters. The King now took firm military action.

At York the opposition had gathered around a great thegn called Archil, but he and his allies submitted (Archil's son being surrendered as a hostage). William built the first castle at York, known as Clifford's Tower. The Coppergate area was flooded, by damming the River Foss, to create a moat for it. William Malet was appointed Sheriff of Yorkshire and Richard fitzRichard became castellan at York. William gave rich gifts at the shrine of St John of Beverley to appease Yorkshire opinion and in thanksgiving for his rapid success.

A late report[10] says that Archbishop Ealdred of York was commissioned at this time to offer the Yorkshiremen safe conduct if they submitted, with confirmation of their estates, but what the King actually did was to demand hostages and imprison some of the leading thegns, confiscating their lands.

The threat to Mercia as the King advanced north had been far more serious than most sources reveal, as they were more concerned about events in Yorkshire. Edwin and Morcar had not dared offer battle, preferring peace to war. They had sought reconciliation with the King and apparently received it, as they took up permanent residence in the King's household. Perhaps William had required their permanent presence near at hand in a kind of 'house arrest'.

Returning south, William continued building a chain of royal castles, at Lincoln, Cambridge and Huntingdon, which must have both enraged and overawed the Fenmen. Lincoln castle was given to a certain Turold of Lincoln. Hostages were taken from 'all of Lindsey' (north Lincolnshire near the Humber). The castle building did what it was intended to do and deterred further immediate resistance. It was accompanied by a policy of continuous ravaging. This had been William's method ever since Hastings. Ivo Taillebois was appointed Sheriff of Lincolnshire (which effectively deprived Maerleswein of his office). There was little resistance but the borough of Torksey was later reported to have been laid waste. At Cambridge the castle occupied the site of twenty-five houses with the townsfolk forced to move the entire city down hill and across the river, well away from the Norman garrison.

Despite his apparent success, William had not yet destroyed the capacity for resistance in Northumbria. The situation there had most likely been far more of a threat than the bland account given in the *Chronicle* would suggest. Orderic Vitalis says there had been 'a fierce insurrection' caused by the King's failure to keep his promises to provide good government and maintain the law of King Edward.

Orderic reports that large numbers of leading Englishmen (Edwin and Morcar had certainly been involved) had met together to complain of the injustice of Norman rule. Appeals, he says, were sent out 'to all corners of Albion', that is, to the whole island of Britain, inciting men to act, openly or in secret, against the enemy. Prayers were said in the churches for the success of the rising, and men were urged 'to recover their former liberty and bind themselves by weighty oaths against the Normans'. Even William of Jumièges, in a vague passage, talks about a general conspiracy, while giving no date for it. Appeals were again made to Swein of Denmark urging him to 'claim the throne of his ancestors' (the Danish kings). (For this period Orderic made use of the lost ending of William of Poitiers' *Gesta Guillelmi*.)

It could also be that Earl Cospatric of Bamburgh had been behind the opposition developing in Northumbria. He had made no real attempt to govern Northumbria in the Norman interest nor to discourage disaffection. But just as Cospatric might have been contemplating taking action against the King, he had been distracted. King Malcolm III of Scotland was reported as contemplating an incursion down the western side of the Pennines, after harrying Bernicia in revenge for an earlier attack on his men in Cumberland by Cospatric's men. King Malcolm had lost control over his wild Scots, who harried Edenvale.

It looks as though Maerleswein the Sheriff and some of the Yorkshire thegns had fortified sites in the Yorkshire marshes and along the Humber, aiming to hold the line until the Mercians and Welsh arrived. But William had taken pre-emptive and rapid action, overawed Mercia and advanced into Yorkshire so forestalling the plot. Many men chose now to retreat into exile. Others faded away into woods and marshes and bided their time in the traditional Northumbrian manner. They preferred the tactics of guerrilla warfare to open battle and thus kept the Normans constantly on the alert. Cospatric, caught out by the speed of William's response, took refuge in Scotland, which probably contributed to the collapse of the rising.

Among those who returned, temporarily, to William's service, was Aethelwine, Bishop of Durham, who was now sent to Scotland to offer terms for a peace settlement to King Malcolm. William was seeking an end to any Scottish help for English dissidents. Malcolm apparently agreed, possibly because his attention was focused on his forthcoming marriage to Edgar the Aetheling's sister Margaret. The agreement did not extend to any Scottish acknowledgement of

William as Malcolm's feudal overlord and more likely included a vague agreement to some sort of right for William over debatable areas like Cumbria or parts of Lothian. But Bishop Aethelwine, in failing to obtain guarantees from Malcolm that he would not help the English exiles, had done himself little permanent good in William's eyes.

The King did, however, now seem to believe that he had 'completely rid the kingdom of all his enemies' and so proceeded, on his return south, to disband his mercenary soldiers. It was probably the end of their contracted period of service. Some barons remained concerned about continual reports of small-scale risings and sought leave to return to Normandy, alleging that their wives were missing them. Some of these barons later returned to England. The English continued to suffer Norman harassment and Orderic reports daily slaughter and the 'wreaking of destruction and disaster on the wretched people'. The land was devastated wherever the King and his army passed and it was said that 'fiends' stalked the land.

Relative calm descended on England from autumn onwards and William was satisfied. He held a crown-wearing at Christmas, probably at Gloucester and was able to issue some writ-charters confirming men in possession of their lands. Bishop Giso of Wells was one, getting back possession of Barnwell in Somerset, which, he alleged, had been wrongfully taken from him by Harold, who is, notably, still referred to as 'King'. Several English notables witnessed the writ. William was still paying what might have been only lip-service to the idea of an Anglo-Norman kingdom. The Aetheling Edgar had by now taken refuge in Scotland (and perhaps forfeited any estates and honours he might have been given), taking his whole family with him, his mother Agatha and his sisters. He had realised that he had at that point little hope of real authority under King William and might have been listening to siren voices promising future revenge and promotion to kingship.

It may be that the concept of an 'Anglo-Norman Realm' is a construct devised by historians[11] rather than an accurate way of labelling King William's reign. Historians perhaps confuse the reality, Anglo-Norman England, and the idea that England and Normandy somehow became a single realm. This may be because, once the English rebellions had been finally extinguished, William had to spend most of his time defending his hold on Normandy and even the great events of 1086 and the making of Domesday Book arose from fears of the invasion of England by the same enemies who threatened Normandy.

14

REVOLT, REBELLION & REPRESSION

At the Christmas Court of 1068 King William, unconcerned about the activities of various disaffected English magnates, and convinced that he had pacified the North, decided that it was time to put a Norman in charge of Northumbria, especially that part which lay between the River Tees and Bamburgh, known as 'Saint Cuthbert's land'. The King's choice fell on an otherwise unknown Norman named Robert de Commines, probably a soldier of fortune. He became Earl of Bamburgh, as Cospatric had taken refuge in Scotland. Commines went north with an escort of 500 knights and arrived at Durham in late December 1068.

Despite warnings and protests Robert de Commines occupied the Bishop's House, the seat of episcopal authority. He proved to be a man of the same stamp as William fitzOsbern, haughty, arrogant and rapacious. His behaviour soon elicited a savage reaction from the Northumbrians, for he treated his province as a land in need of conquest, and its inhabitants 'as if they had been enemies'. Their homes were looted and the Norman troops plundered at will. Robert was paying his men by 'licensing their ravages and murders'.

Bishop Aethelwine of Durham warned the Norman to expect trouble but was ignored. (Rumours about trouble brewing among the English had begun during Lent and it was alleged that they planned to assassinate Norman soldiers while they were hastening to church to do penance.)

As predicted, the Northumbrians struck. The Bishop's House was set ablaze and the new earl and his companions were trapped and then killed while trying to escape. The rebels, exhilarated by their success, took up arms against the garrison at York. Having made their preparations, they gathered supplies of men, arms and money and proclaimed that they had chosen as their king 'a certain boy, nobly descended from the stock of Edward', that is Edgar the Aetheling. It is not clear whether the Aetheling had been consulted in advance. Their preparations took some time to be effected. In the late spring they descended on York, besieged then took the castle and killed Richard fitzRichard, the castellan. The men of York joined the rebellion and the great thegn Arkill sent word to the Aetheling, summoning him to come and take the leadership of their movement. It was not unlike the rebellion of 1065 when they had chosen their own earl. They probably hoped that Archbishop Ealdred would crown the new pretender, but the Archbishop died before he could be asked. The Earls Edwin and Morcar, confined at William's Court, took no part in the rising. But the attitude of their men, in Yorkshire and Mercia, was a different matter. William's later movements reveal that there was trouble in Cheshire and Staffordshire and that Eadric the Wild and Prince Bleddyn, associates of the Earls Edwin and Morcar, were involved.

William moved rapidly north and put the rebels to flight, killing many and ravaging York. The castle at York was retaken and a second fortress was built on the right bank of the river, the Baile Tower. The Aetheling beat a hasty retreat back to Scotland. The King again only planned his move as a demonstration in force as he had no intention yet of dealing with Durham. Having re-taken and re-fortified York, he returned south. It was by now March 1069 and he intended to hold Court in Winchester at Easter, leaving William fitzOsbern as castellan of York for the time being.

At the Council at Winchester, Easter 1069, Bishop Aethelric, the former Bishop of Durham then living in retirement at Peterborough, was moved to Westminster, where a watch could be maintained on him; his brother and successor at Durham, Aethelwine, was outlawed.

Yet the power of the North remained unbroken, and it was always to prove difficult to make the Northumbrians accept a pitched battle. Despite his apparent success, William nervously took the precaution of sending Queen Matilda back to Normandy. It is probable that she took with her William's son Henry, born in September 1068.

In the summer, further problems arose. Around 24 June, the Sons of Harold again returned, in what was beginning to look like a policy of an annual attack. They came in over sixty ships (between three and four thousand men), entered the River Taw, ravaged and plundered Devon and attacked Exeter. Castle Rougemont, supported by the townsfolk, repelled them. A Norman force under William Gualdi and Count Brian of Brittany drove them off, though it was said to have cost the lives of 1,700 men, and the Sons left never to return again.

But sometime during the year, probably between 15 August and 8 September, a force of Danes commanded by the Jarl Asbjorn, brother of King Swein, accompanied by Jarl Thurkil and three of King Swein's sons, Harald, Cnut and Bjorn, together with a bishop called Christian, raided the South East of England with almost 240 ships, a formidable force. Starting at Dover they harried along the coast from Sandwich to Ipswich, and on to Norwich. At each place they were repelled and at Norwich Ralph de Gael 'fell on them and drove many to their death by drowning'. But they did not leave. Instead they dropped anchor in the Humber and waited for the English to rally to them. It is suggested in one source that more ships joined them and even that a fleet brought the Aetheling south. Orderic Vitalis names such figures as Earl Waltheof, Cospatric, Maerleswein and Yorkshire leaders like the sons of Karli[1] as involved. York was again threatened, and William Malet, now in command, boasted to King William that he could hold out for a year if need be.

The *Chronicle* reports how there now came 'all the people of the land, riding and marching, forming an immense host, greatly rejoicing; and thus all resolutely went to York and broke down and demolished the castle' (possibly the Baile Tower). It was now 19 September 1069 and the Normans in the main castle had taken their own precautions. They had decided to create a 'dead zone' around the castle by burning down a number of houses. Unfortunately, the fire got out of control and destroyed much of the rest of the city, including York Minster. The Danes arrived by 21 September but, in view of the devastation, did not stay. There was no plunder to be had and no means of laying siege to the castle.

Unhappily for the Normans, the fire and smoke had driven them out of the fortification and it was claimed that some 3,000 perished (most likely an exaggerated figure). Meanwhile, news of the rising had spread throughout England, and it was reported that many plots were being hatched. Some rebels took refuge in woods or on islands and among marshes and lived like outlaws. But the *Chronicle* admits that the English, even with Danish support, were unable to meet William in a pitched battle.

William Malet desperately sent word to the King that he might be compelled to surrender, and King William raced north again, bursting in upon his enemies in York a few days after 20 September. He then ravaged the shire. The Danes retreated to the Humber where William could not get at them. The minster was further damaged. Large bodies of men were sent to disperse the rebels, but they had already withdrawn into the hills. One contingent advanced as far as Northallerton and were enveloped in 'a great darkness' (presumably a great fog), which completely disorientated them and in terror they retreated to York. The local people claimed that Saint Cuthbert had struck to defend his own land.

There were ill-organised and uncoordinated risings in many places, by men Orderic Vitalis calls 'silvatici' or wild men of the woods. The South-Western peninsula rose in revolt and there were risings in Cheshire and Shropshire, along the Welsh marches and into Staffordshire. In East Anglia the Isle of Ely became a centre for the activities of the outlawed Hereward. England was becoming difficult to hold down since, as soon as a rising was dealt with in one area, another sprang up elsewhere. William could not be everywhere and focused his attention on the currently most dangerous area, leaving his local commanders like Bishop Geoffrey of Coutances, Count Brian of Brittany and William fitzOsbern to control their own districts. Everywhere the Normans went the same ruthless tactics were employed; men were killed or captured and then mutilated savagely, losing hands or feet, as Geoffrey of Coutances did in relieving Montacute castle. Unfortunately for the English the risings remained uncoordinated and ill-planned. There was no charismatic leader available to pull the resistance together. Risings were only loosely occurring at similar times and were never part of a master plan.

King William left his major lieutenants to deal with scattered risings around the country while he himself was mainly concerned with the danger from the North, where there was a threat of reinforcements provided by the Danes. He sent men to seek out the hiding places of the rebels and made his own move against the Danes. Dealing with the greatest threat first, he drove them out of Lindsey and into Holderness, wiping out their encampments, especially at Axeholme. This drove a wedge between the Danes and the English rebels further inland and allowed William time to show himself in Staffordshire, repel Eadric the Wild and return to Nottingham, where he had earlier built a castle.[2] The rapidity of his attacks was remarkable.

For a time the Norman enterprise had hung in the balance as resistance had threatened to become more coherent. But the centre of resistance remained in Northumbria, in Saint Cuthbert's land where the influence of King Malcolm could make itself felt. His forthcoming marriage to Edgar's sister Margaret would be likely to commit him more firmly to the English cause. The death of Archbishop Ealdred on 11 September had left a vacancy, giving rise to the possibility of the creation of an independent metropolitan Archbishop chosen by the Northumbrians rather than by King William.

Ealdred had last been heard of at York for one of the great feasts earlier in the year. He had protested to King William over the depredations of William Malet, whom he had threatened with excommunication. Legend later claimed that the Archbishop had sought out the King, allegedly in London, seeking compensation. He was said to have refused to give William the kiss of peace until he did justice and to have scolded and cursed the King for his misdeeds. He was alleged to have declared, 'I give thee my curse as thou art a persecutor of God's Church and an oppressor of Her Ministers, breaking oaths you swore to me at St. Peter's altar. As I once blessed you wrongfully, I now curse you rightfully.' The legend goes on to claim that the King, shamed by the Archbishop's outburst, fell at his feet and begged forgiveness. Ealdred raised him to his feet and forgave him on condition that he was given a writ ordering Malet to make good the damage he had caused.

It's a nice story though the emotive details are unlikely to be true. It does, however, illustrate the change in later English attitudes to William and raises the possibility that there had been disputes between the Archbishop and the King. Ealdred might well have resented Lanfranc's growing influence with William. William of Malmesbury confirms that there were complaints by Ealdred over the high level of William's taxes. He remarks that Ealdred honoured William only so long as he ruled with moderation.

From Nottingham, then, hearing that the Danes hoped to reoccupy York, William returned to the city. He found York a burnt-out scene of desolation but nonetheless decided to spend Christmas there and sent for the regalia in order to hold a crown-wearing, to demonstrate that Yorkshire was part of his dominions. It was at York also 'in the fourth year of his reign',[3] that is, 1070, that William followed the example of King Edward by confirming 'the Law of King Edward' just as Edward himself had confirmed that of

Cnut in 1065. Having dealt forcefully with rebellion he was always ready to offer justice.

He demanded and received hostages, including Thorgautr (Bishop of St Andrews), who was to be a hostage for the whole of Lindsey. It is likely that this was when Count Alan of Brittany was given the castlery that formed the centre of his great fief of 'Richmondshire'. Other lordships were created for the defence of York in the hands of Ilbert de Lacey, William de Percy and Hugh fitz Baldric.

After Christmas, William set in train events that led to the systematic harrying of the North. The rebels had retired from the field, believing that there would be no warfare in the depths of winter. They could also have been hoping for the arrival of King Swein himself. William's crossing of the Aire (probably in the vicinity of Castleford) had driven the Danes back to their ships, and he now allowed them to forage for supplies on condition that they agreed to leave England in the spring of 1070. It was a hard winter and many Danes starved to death.

At that Christmas Court it also seems to have been decided, possibly on the urging of William fitzOsbern, to recoup the expenses of these campaigns and the losses that had been suffered, by confiscating the remaining wealth of the rebels. They had, it seems, deposited large sums of money in the monasteries of England for safe-keeping, believing that the sanctity of these places would be protection enough. But 'in the Lent of this year' (1070), says the *Chronicle*, 'the King caused to be plundered all the monasteries which were in England'.

A twelfth-century source, Gervase of Canterbury, recorded the tradition that the King seized all the charters and moveable wealth of the monasteries, not just what the thegns had left with them. The *Abingdon Chronicle* confirms this. It reports that 'officers of the Court ... obtained knowledge through informers ... and everything that was found stored was taken away'. No respect was paid to the sanctity of the monasteries. Even the surrounding villages were searched and devastated. Queen Matilda is said to have taken the opportunity to demand that Abingdon send her its most precious ornaments so that she could take her pick of them.

William had been in Northumbria. The Northerners had doubtless expected him to return south for Christmas, but he had not done so. Instead, in the New Year, he set about accomplishing his final solution to the Northumbrian problem. He first resolved the Danish threat, by resorting to the time-honoured method of bribery. In effect he proposed to pay 'Danegeld', since he had no fleet with which to compel the Danes to leave. He could also have meant the money as ransom for William Malet and his family and Gilbert of Ghent, who had been taken prisoner by the rebels before the King's arrival.

Of no action of William was the dictum of Machiavelli that any Prince seeking to maintain his rule would have to 'work against what is merciful, loyal, humane, upright and scrupulous' more accurate than of the King's pacification of England north of the Humber. The Northerners had taken refuge in the hills and dales, expecting the Danes to launch an all-out attack in the spring, but William was determined to forestall any such attack.

In seeking to pacify the North, William is said to have succumbed to the urge for cruelty, making no attempt to restrain the brutality of his men. They were allowed to harry the land, turning homes and farms to ashes and a desolate wasteland. William of Poitiers appears, like William of Jumièges, to have decided to end his account of William's actions without referring to the campaign in the North. Both would have been ashamed of what happened. Crops, herds, chattels and foods of every kind were destroyed. This campaign was launched in mid-winter with devastating ferocity. Orderic Vitalis puts the death toll at 100,000 people[4] (out of an estimated English population of two and a half million at most). The Chronicles all lament the ravaging and wasting of the North, and Domesday Book reveals, with its repeated entries of estates rendered 'waste', the extent of the damage still visible in 1086. Orderic records his own verdict: 'I dare not commend him. He levelled both the bad and the good in one common ruin by a consuming famine ... he was ... guilty of wholesale massacre ... and barbarous homicide.' Modern opinion might well call it genocide.

The King began the campaign in person, marching into the far North to Jarrow and Wearmouth on the Tyne. Jarrow church was burnt. William remained there for some fifteen days, possibly until Earls Waltheof (in person) and Cospatric (by proxy from the safety of Scotland) had submitted. William had heard that a nest of his enemies had taken refuge in a narrow neck of land sheltered by the sea and marshland. One suggestion is that this was Tod Point near Coatham at the mouth of the Tyne, reachable only along a narrow causeway. The enemy fled at William's approach. Parties were sent out over an area of one hundred square miles to hunt down every Englishman they could find. Some of the Normans, if Orderic is correct, reached Hexham, on Hadrian's Wall, before turning back. William then returned south, probably via Helmsley to York. The area north of Yorkshire, totalling 1,000 square miles, was so completely devastated that no attempt was made to survey it when Domesday Book was compiled. It had become a wilderness. No Norman seems to have laid claim to a fief that far north. In the harsh winter, William's return march was arduous in the extreme, his men suffered from the cold and many horses were lost. William himself is said to have lost contact with the main body of his army for a time, accompanied by only six knights.

On the journey south, he had passed through Durham, where his men pulled down the great jewelled cross (erected by Earl Tostig and his wife) and stripped it of its jewels. William, hearing of this, had been enraged but chose not to punish them himself. He sent messages to Bishop Aethelwine, then in exile at Lindisfarne, demanding that he excommunicate them, but there was no response. The Bishop had apparently decided to set out for Cologne but a storm had frustrated that and he had taken refuge in Scotland. He returned to Durham after the Normans left and discovered the damage.

When he reached York the King received reports of more trouble in Chester. He decided to cross the Pennines and deal with it. It was still winter and the area was a wilderness. He nonetheless led his men south-west, probably through Wharfedale, then across the moors to the Lancashire plain. The harsh conditions caused resentment among the Bretons in his force: 'We cannot obey a lord who commands us to do the impossible!' they said. But by sheer force of character and ferocious demeanour William quelled any revolt. The march continued to Chester. The area around the city was ravaged and Chester hastily submitted. William then went on to devastate parts of Shropshire, Staffordshire and even Derbyshire, which had been the scene of the western rising involving Eadric the Wild and the Welsh.

Conditions had become so appalling in the North that many people fled south, some reaching as far as Evesham in Worcestershire. Those who got there were so starved that little could be done for them; they could not even swallow the food offered and five or six people died every day. Prior Aelfric of Evesham had the unpleasant task of having them buried. William had certainly earned the judgement passed upon him by the *Chronicle* when he died: 'A stark man he was who thought nothing either of men's sufferings nor their hatred.'

The King now returned south. He spent Easter, 4 April, at Winchester, moving to Windsor on 23 May and then to Salisbury, where he reviewed his troops. Those who had been loyal were rewarded and allowed to stand down from active service, but the Breton mutineers were punished by having their terms of service extended.

William still faced the problem of the Danes. Jarl Asbjorn had kept his men on the Humber, as agreed, though many starved and others were reduced to eating rancid meat. But King Swein brought a fleet and joined up with Asbjorn and his men. They moved on from the Humber into the Wash and set up a base at Ely. From there, in collusion with the outlaw Hereward, they had attacked and robbed Peterborough Abbey.[5]

There was no current abbot because Brand had died, 27 November 1069. Turold was unpopular at Malmesbury, where he 'ruled his subjects like a tyrant', says William of Malmesbury. King William decided that this was just the man to cope with Hereward. In a typical jest he remarked that 'as Turold is behaving more like a soldier than an Abbot, by the Splendour of God! I shall find him a foe who is a good match for his attacks![6] He can have Peterborough as a field for his courage and generalship and there he can practise his fighting!' Hereward, before his exile, had been a tenant of the abbey and was a member of Brand's own family, son of the Abbot's brother Asketil, the King's thegn. This man Hereward decided to seize the Peterborough treasure, to prevent it falling into Norman hands, or so the chronicler Hugh Candidus alleges, and he acted after William, at the Easter Council, had appointed Turold of Malmesbury to be Abbot of Peterborough.

Much to their surprise, therefore, the Danes found themselves welcomed by the Fenmen who expected them to help reconquer the whole of England, a wildly optimistic idea. But the only thing they did was to join Hereward in the attack on Peterborough. While this was going on, King William had opened negotiations with Swein of Denmark, whose sole aim was to make a quick profit from the situation. The two monarchs soon reached an agreement, with the help of William's offer of a bribe, and Swein ordered his men to return home. Those at Ely held on to the treasures taken from Peterborough, much to the chagrin of Hereward. After moving for a while to the Thames Estuary, the fleet set out for Denmark. It took with it the plunder from Peterborough. It encountered a North Sea storm. The fleet was scattered, some vessels sank, others ended up in Norway or were driven around Scotland to Ireland, and a few staggered back to Denmark.

Hereward and his men, deserted by their Danish allies, remained throughout the following winter at Ely, harassing the local Norman settlers. Their depredations were contained by the King's local agents, especially the Norman Abbot of Peterborough, Turold (whose appointment in succession to Hereward's uncle Abbot Brand had triggered his attack), and the lord of Castle Acre, William of Warenne.

King William had now, it would seem, successfully imposed his will on the kingdom, from Northumbria to the Channel and from the North Sea to Wales. It is cogently observed that he never again had to face the kind of dangers he had faced from 1069 to 1070. Nonetheless, there was trouble brewing overseas. During 1069, while William's attention was fixed on Northern England, the city of Le Mans had rebelled against Norman rule. Arnold, the Bishop, had been a nominee and partisan of William but was now opposed by a party that wanted Azzo, Lord of Este in Liguria, husband of Gersendis, sister of Count Hugh IV of Maine, as their ruler. Geoffrey of Mayenne had been attracted to the cause. William's seneschal, Humphrey, was killed, the Norman garrison expelled, including Bishop Odo's brother-in-law, William of La Ferté-Macé. Azzo, satisfied, returned to Este, leaving his wife Gersendis and their son Hugh, who was recognised as Count, in charge. Geoffrey of Mayenne made Gersendis his mistress and became the dominant figure.

His government remained unstable and the citizens of Le Mans in turn again rebelled and formed a 'commune'. An attempt by them, led by Bishop Arnold, to take the castle of Sillé was repelled. They had been betrayed by Geoffrey, who found it wise not to try to re-enter the city. Hugh was sent to safety, to his father in Italy. But by the end of the year the revolt was crushed and Geoffrey had re-established control.

These events must have disturbed King William but he had other, graver, matters to attend to and he is thought to have returned to Normandy before May 1070. A charter dated 2 April 1069 grants land in Harmondsworth, Middlesex, to Rouen Abbey, which implies that he was in Normandy.[7] During 1070 yet another great change came about. On 16 July Baldwin VI of Flanders, William's brother-in-law, died and a succession dispute arose that was of concern to Normandy. Baldwin had two sons, Arnulf (who received Flanders) and Baldwin (who was given Hainault). As they were both too young to rule, their mother Richildis became regent. This was resisted in

Flanders, especially by Robert the Frisian, brother of Baldwin VI. Richildis appealed to Earl William fitzOsbern for aid (the King having sent Earl William to Normandy, early in 1071, no doubt to keep watch on events in Maine).

Richildis having offered to marry the Earl in return for his assistance, he accepted and off he went to Flanders, 'as if to a game'. A decisive battle followed between the two sides, at Cassel, 22 February 1071. William fitzOsbern was killed, Richildis was deposed and Robert the Frisian became Count of Flanders. William had lost the Count of Flanders, his most powerful supporter, Maine was slipping out of his control, and a hostile prince now ruled Flanders.

All this must have upset William's peace of mind far more than the mere activities of Hereward. William had concerns on the Welsh borders where the great palatine earldoms were being established: Hereford, Shrewsbury and Chester. Scotland in 1070–71 was a refuge for disaffected Englishmen, especially the Aetheling, now about nineteen or twenty years old, whose sister was now Queen of Scotland. William's campaign in the North must have been taken as a threat by King Malcolm. The frontier between England and Scotland was still very ill-defined, and Malcolm had interests in both Lothian and Cumbria. The question was whether these two areas would in future be English or Scottish. The devastation of the North had created a power vacuum on the border.

Even before William had reached Winchester (in spring 1070), Malcolm had carried out a devastating raid into Durham and Cleveland, making the situation there much worse. Earl Cospatric fell out with Malcolm and took reprisals against him by ravaging Cumbria. But King William had been in no position to act against Scotland. With Malcolm's support now looking rather suspect, the remaining English magnates in Scotland decided, during 1071, to return to England, probably travelling by sea to the Wash, with the intention, it is thought, of seeking refuge on the Continent.

Furthermore, during the spring of 1071 the Earls Edwin and Morcar had begun to fear for their lives. They had been under virtual house arrest for some time and now heard rumours that William intended to imprison them. Various Norman lords had cast greedy eyes on the estates of the two earls, as yet not in Norman hands, whispering against them to the King. Accordingly they fled secretly from the Court and travelled 'here through woods and there over open countryside', just like Orderic's 'silvatici'. They were on the run for about six months until they eventually met and joined up with the party from Scotland, somewhere south of the Wash. That consisted of Bishop Aethelwine of Durham and a Danelaw thegn, formerly of great wealth, called Siward Barn, together with many of their thegns and commended men. The earls also had many men with them.

Others had preferred to take ship from Wearmouth and escape to Cologne or had joined the Aetheling in Scotland. Storms had prevented both groups from crossing the North Sea and Aethelwine's party had ended up at first on the Humber and then came down to the Wash. It was now probably September 1071, and the period of equinoctial gales. Entering the Ouse from the Wash, they reached a place called 'Welle', probably in the vicinity of Upwell and Outwell near Wisbech, on the 'Wellstream'.

The whole party was met by Hereward and joined him at Ely, intending to spend the winter there. Earl Edwin stayed only briefly, preferring to try for Scotland. On his way north he was betrayed by three of his own servants to a party of Normans and slain. The location was somewhere near the Wash, a spot 'between a rising high tide and a tidal estuary'. His head was cut off and taken to King William, in the expectation by the three traitors of a reward. To their horror William, in disgust at their treachery, banished them from England.

Earl Morcar and the others took up residence at Ely. King William saw that as a threat and decided that enough was enough. He gathered an army and even sent ships into the Ouse, to besiege the Isle of Ely. The isle was at that time surrounded on all sides by fens and rivers and was seen as impregnable to direct assault. William feared that the English leadership could be reinforced by men from the Continent, especially exiled thegns with Danish support. He might even have feared the intervention of Robert the Frisian.

The story of the siege at Ely was recorded in the *Liber Eliensis* and in a document called the *Gesta Herewardi*.[8] The *Peterborough Chronicle* sums up the campaign thus: 'When King William heard of this, he ordered out naval and land levies and surrounded the district, building a causeway as he advanced deeper into the fens, while the naval force remained to seaward.'

Rather than 'build' a causeway, he actually seems to have widened and strengthened an existing winding track through the Fens so that his men could assault the isle. The causeway is mentioned in a writ issued in 1082 and it says that 'those men are to maintain the causeway at Ely who, by the King's command, have done so hitherto'. In fact he was unable to cross the Old West River (now part of the Great Ouse) because of the ferocity of the defence. A first attempt at a crude bridge collapsed and killed many men who had tried to rush across it. A second was burned down by Hereward's men and many Normans died in the fire that spread through the Fen, often in the peat below the surface. But the Abbot of Ely, Thurstan, fearful of the loss of abbey lands confiscated by the King, betrayed the defenders.

He sent word telling William of another Fen track that would bring him to a place much nearer the abbey, where the river could more easily be crossed. William seized his chance and led his men to the designated location, probably in the vicinity of the hamlet of Little Thetford where a stretch of the river was later called 'Hereward's Reach'. There he constructed a pontoon bridge out of flat-bottomed fen boats (forerunners of the punt) and crossed onto dry land. From there, he attacked the defences of the abbey, in a pincer movement through Witchford and along Akerman Street (roughly along the present A10). Through secret envoys he had gulled Morcar and the other leading men into surrender, promising them his peace, so that resistance was minimal. Hereward was not there at the time, as he had been out foraging. He and his closest supporters escaped, hid for a while in the forest called 'Bruneswald' and then most likely fled again, like so many others, into exile.

The King fined the monks over 1,000 silver marks for their part in the resistance. They had to surrender everything of value in the abbey in order to find such a vast sum, including a gold and silver image of the Virgin Mary, enthroned, holding the Infant Jesus. William paid a brief visit to the church but, typically, dared not approach too close to the tomb of St Aethelthryth (Etheldreda), lest he incur the saint's wrath. He threw a gold mark onto the High Altar and hurriedly left.

He spurned Thurstan's efforts to appease him and ordered a garrison of knights to be placed at Ely, with duty to do castle guard at Norwich. (There was no castle at Ely until the early twelfth century.) Having ordered a castle to be built at Wisbech, and having stamped out the last remnants of English resistance, King William withdrew, via Cambridge to London.

15

LORDSHIP IN CHURCH & STATE

From the very beginning of his reign, and especially after his coronation, William assumed that he was now sole Lord of all the land in his kingdom as the heir of King Edward. Under the Old English Kings, landowning men had held their land freely, owing to the King only the three services: service in the fyrd, work on bridges and work on the construction of fortifications (the burhs). They might commend themselves to the protection of a lord but that did not mean that their land was held from or under him. As Domesday Book recorded, many men might 'go with their land to whatsoever lord they wished'. Some held their land as 'bookland', which meant that their possession of the land was guaranteed by their possession of a charter from the King recording the grant of the estate or the confirmation of a previous grant. They were free to exchange, give, sell or bequeath the land to any heir of their choice, or give it to the Church.

The consequence of William's claim was that all landholders in England were now his dependants, directly or indirectly, could forfeit the land by rebellion, and owed the King service, which might be military or take the form of less 'honourable' service. This is most obvious in the case of the Church, largely perhaps because Church records, in the form of charters, writs, chronicles and cartularies, have survived, because the Church kept its own records whereas lay lords have left little written evidence of the terms on which they held their lands since most of them were illiterate. Many of the Norman land-grabs were certainly illegal, that is, made without the endorsement of king's officer or a writ, but Englishmen found it impossible to challenge them without proof acceptable to a Norman court. For example, Domesday Book records that Azor the Dispensator (Steward) ought to have retained one hide of land in Ardington (Berkshire) because the men of the hundred testified that King William had restored it to him when at Windsor and gave him a writ. But Robert d'Oilly held it 'unjustly' though no one had seen the King's writ which granted it to him nor a king's officer.[1] One modern historian has called the Norman lords a 'kleptocracy', an aristocracy of thieves.[2]

The results of this were the introduction into England of tenure by knight service and the imposition of quotas of knights owed by tenants-in-chief to the Crown. The imposition of quotas, called 'Servicia debita' by historians, is most obvious in the case of the Church since chronicles specifically report that they were imposed and writs survive which refer to knight service. A good example comes from a charter of Abbot Baldwin of Bury St Edmunds, issued probably quite early on in the reign. It records that 'Peter, a knight of King William' is to be the 'feudal man', by homage, of Abbot Baldwin. He is to serve the abbot within England 'with three or four knights at his own expense' and must also provide one knight to serve the abbot wherever and whenever the abbot needs him as part of his retinue.[3] Tenure by knight service, and the imposition of quotas, can thus be shown to have begun under King William, a common assumption in the twelfth century being that both institutions were first introduced by him.

Another aspect of the assumption that William was now lord of all England becomes manifest in his treatment of the Church. With the cooperation of a papal delegation, he proceeded to remove from office as many English bishops and abbots as he could. Eventually Bishop Wulfstan of Worcester became the sole survivor and all bishoprics and abbacies fell into Norman hands. Also, through the agency of Archbishop Lanfranc, William permitted and encouraged the 'reform' of the English Church to bring it into canonical conformity with the rest of the Church. This 'reform' was not undertaken in order to justify the Conquest, though William had allowed Pope Alexander II to assume that one of the King's purposes in enforcing his claim to the English throne had been to allow him to reform the English Church. William's real purpose was rather different. He intended to establish and manifest firm royal control over the Church, as a way of consolidating his hold on the country.

But reform also went some way in fact to justify the Conquest in the eyes of the Church, and won for William both ecclesiastical and papal support. Lanfranc produced the necessary ecclesiastical authorities, in the form of canons and decretals, when required to do so.[4] The result was, as Eadmer of Canterbury wrote, that 'Everything, divine and human alike, waited on his [William's] nod'. Eadmer records the advent of new institutions, such as archdeaconries, calling his work, a 'History of Novelties'.⁵ Unfortunately he did not include much about William's secular novelties, as he wished to write about 'what he ordained in divine matters', while commenting that from them the character of William's secular laws could be deduced.

He then claims to uncover 'the roots of all viciousness ... all vices' in the fact of the Conquest and in the powers acquired by William in the process. He tells his readers that all clerics had to do homage, and that bishops and abbots, as in Normandy, had to accept their staff of office from the hand of the King, which denoted the conferral on them of the temporalities (that is, the lands and properties) of their sees or abbacies. There is no sign that this was done in pre-Conquest England.

It is probable that Eadmer knew that the fiefs of lay tenants-in-chief were also bestowed by the hand of the Conqueror but deliberately chose not to record that he had done so. Instead, he records the bestowal of the staff on clerics and implies that, like lay lords, they first had to become the King's men before they could have their estates.

One of the ways in which William of Poitiers had sought to prove that Harold had been a usurper and a faithless vassal had been by insisting that William 'received him as his follower through his hands' and that he then 'gave him all his lands and powers' at his own request! Harold was then said to have sworn 'fidelitas' (loyalty) to William. This is absurd since Harold held all his lands in England either as part of his inheritance from his father, Earl Godwin, or as a consequence of his status as Earl of Wessex. He did not hold them from King Edward precariously, like some kind of benefice, and would have regarded such a ceremony as Poitiers describes, if it occurred, as a charade.

William of Poitiers is using the same format as he attributes to the submission of Count Herbert of Maine to the Duke, who, he says, had 'given himself to him with his hands and received back from him everything of his, like a knight from a lord'. The duplication is plain. He is attributing to both the gift to them by William of the land which they already owned! Maine, of course, already stood in a feudal relationship to Normandy. It is not clear how far William of Poitiers was influenced by post-Conquest events, but that he was influenced seems unmistakeable. After 1066, in England, it does look as though a link had been formed between the act of placing one's hands between those of a lord and that of being granted some sort of tenure of land by that lord.

He also asserted that Archbishop Stigand had given himself with his hands to the Duke and confirmed his loyalty (*fides*) with an oath. If so, the Conqueror did not allow the ritual to oblige him to protect Stigand from deposition by the legates. A similar rite was probably performed by all those who submitted to William. Even Edwin and Morcar 'surrendered themselves and all their possessions' to William, swore oaths and he then 'restored to them all that they possessed'. This, as probably also in the case of Harold, was obviously under duress. The English were being required to do homage, in effect, though they might well have seen it as becoming William's commended men. Most Normans, and those from elsewhere who took service with him, would have already done homage to William in Normandy.

In Normandy William had been the protector and ruler of the Church ever since he had obtained real power. He inherited the tradition of a ruler's responsibility for its protection and organisation. As 'heir' to King Edward, he now assumed the same role in England. He would have known that dominion over the Church on the part of local princes had long been accepted by the papacy, which exerted its power through kings and princes. As a committed Christian, William also knew that he was responsible to God for his conduct and the salvation of his own soul. That was why those who could do so, including William, made gifts of money and land to churches as some sort of compensation, or penance, for their sins.

When in Normandy, William had participated in ecclesiastical councils and he now did the same in England whenever he was present. He was fond of participating in religious rites intended to secure for him God's blessing on his enterprises and secured a papal banner and blessing on his invasion. In 1066, he had organised a procession with the relics of St Valery to secure a favourable crossing of the Channel. He had bishops and a number of monks with him at Hastings. The bishops were Odo of Bayeux and Geoffrey of Coutances.[6]

After Hastings William had allowed the imposition of penances on those who had taken part in the battle and on those who had inflicted death or injury between then and the coronation. It was also applied to those who had killed men since then up to the time

of the imposition of the penance. The penances had been the work of
Norman Bishops and confirmed by the authority of the papal legate,
Ermenfrid, issued during a visit to Normandy in 1067 (while William
was there) and again in 1070 during the Council of Winchester.

For killing or injuring men in battle a penance of one year for each
victim was imposed, or of one day a week for life and the building
of a church if the numbers were unknown. So there was a symbolic
cleansing after the Conquest. Penances were also imposed for the
same offences committed after the battle and after the coronation.
In the latter case a distinction was made between killing or injuring
as an act of wilful murder and the killing or injuring of rebels.
The killing or injuring of Englishmen who offered resistance after
Hastings was thus being treated as an act of public war and implies
that they too were regarded as rebels.

The last step in this process was the visit of the legates in 1070
and a solemn crowning of the King by them at Winchester at Easter.
William constantly sought to give his actions the colour of legitimacy,
just as he sought to give his government an air of continuity with
legality. Following a period of coexistence from 1066 to 1070 came
the deposition of bishops and abbots, which William took care to
have endorsed by the legates. The aim was the restaffing of the entire
hierarchy with Normans, and he made sure that the highest spiritual
authority on earth, the papacy as represented by the legate Ermenfrid,
was on his side before he set about it. The replacement of the higher
clergy was carried out with punctilious regard for legal forms. But
the political implications are revealed by the care taken to install a
Norman as Archbishop of York.

William then revived the practice, which had long been abandoned
in England, of holding councils of the English Church. Such synods
were in the eleventh century an essential tool used by the reform
movement then at work in the Western Church. Eight councils
are known to have been held between 1070 and 1085; three at
Winchester, one at Windsor, two in London and one at Gloucester.
William attended most of them and Eadmer asserts that nothing they
did was done without his consent, though the details of ecclesiastical
legislation were the work of Archbishop Lanfranc. The King was
always ready to reinforce the Archbishop's authority with his own,
as the famous writ, issued in English and in Latin between 1070 and
1076,[7] regarding spiritual pleas (episcopal jurisdiction over offences
committed by clergy), shows. In future no such cases would be heard

in the hundred courts (by bishops sitting with the sheriff) but in the episcopal courts. The authority of the King himself or of the local sheriff was to enforce decisions of the episcopal court.

The weight of ecclesiastical censure was brought to bear on the English. The Winchester Synod (1072) required every parish priest to say three Masses for the King's health, and ruled that anyone who spoke treason against William or his rule was to be excommunicated, that is, cut off from the services and sacraments of the Church.

One story suggests that not all Normans were enamoured of William's new-found status, based as it was on the fact that he had 'subdued this land to himself by warfare', as Eadmer puts it. The King summoned Guitmund of La-Croix-Saint-Leuffroy to England and offered him a bishopric. He refused point blank and had the temerity to tell William that the Conquest represented the spoils of robbery and that there was no authority in the Bible for imposing on Christians a bishop chosen from among their enemies. He said that Edgar the Aetheling had a better right to the throne than William and told him to watch out for the safety of his soul. The tale comes from Orderic some fifty years after the event and may not be true but is plausible since Guitmund was a well-respected theologian who left Normandy to join the entourage of Pope Gregory VII. Guitmund was a man of great moral fibre and commitment, just the sort of man William might have hoped to recruit to improve the quality of the episcopate. By Orderic's time it was possible to describe the Conquest in terms of what it was – daylight robbery. Eadmer says that William chose as bishops men 'who would have been deemed unworthy, if they had not obeyed his laws in every respect'. Perhaps William had been getting tired of too many yes men.

The final aspect of William's relations with the Church concerns his relationship with the papacy. Up until 1072 all had gone quite well. William had successfully enlisted the support of Pope Alexander II, with the help of Lanfranc whose pupil the Pope had once been, and of Hildebrand, Archdeacon of Rome and the real power in the Curia. But Alexander died and his successor, as Gregory VII, was that same Hildebrand. From 1073 onwards, Gregory was careful to respect William and never took extreme measures against him, since he needed William's support against the German Emperor, Henry IV. Relations between the Pope and King William were nonetheless not always cordial.

Lanfranc was censured by Pope Gregory for neglecting his duty to pay 'ad limina' visits to Rome, which he did not do on grounds of age and infirmity. The Pope also examined very thoroughly the credentials of William of Bonne-Âme, King William's choice for the archbishopric of Rouen, as he was thought to be the son of a priest and therefore possibly illegitimate. Gregory's general stance towards lay rulers was that they were expected to be obedient to papal wishes. To that end he had improved the moral tone of the papacy and the Church and instituted the custom of using permanent legates to enforce papal decisions, while insisting on regular visits to Rome by bishops.

William, on the other hand, took his stand on the ancestral customs of the Old English Church. He was quite prepared to continue to pay 'Romescot' or Peter's Pence, a regular contribution to the needs of the papacy, even apologising when payments were late because of his absence in Normandy. But in 1080 he utterly rejected a demand on Gregory's part for an acknowledgement that he was some sort of papal vassal[8] (one of the implications of his status Gregory drew from the bestowal on William of a papal banner in 1066). William insisted that there was no precedent for that assumption and that it was contrary to English custom. The Pope argued that William owed him a debt of gratitude and put forward the thesis that all secular rulers were inferior to the Pope as the moon is to the sun. William, however, was always ready to adhere to English custom when it suited his purposes. His voice is clearly to be heard in his letter, in 1080, in response to the demand. 'I have never desired to do fealty, nor do I desire it now. For I neither promised on my own behalf nor can I discover that my predecessors ever performed it to yours.'[9]

Gregory had, of course, reminded William of the great debt he owed to him when, as Archdeacon Hildebrand, he had 'suffered great infamy through the mutterings of certain brethren, that by my exertions on your behalf I encouraged great slaughter'. He also pointed out that he had 'laboured that you might rise to the dignity of kingship'. He was clearly trying to call in an obligation earned by favours done. It failed.[10] William went on to refuse to allow papal letters to be published in England without his consent, or legates to enter the country without his express permission. He was adopting the traditional practice of English kings. But he always acknowledged that Gregory was the 'most exalted pastor of Holy Church' and said he desired to 'show to you above all men unfeigned respect and obedient attention'.

Lordship over the Church was one side of the coin. William was also lord over men in their secular capacity. In his collection of the 'common geld' or 'king's geld', as Domesday Book terms it, he exacted to the full the rights of an Old English king.[11] Justice continued to be administered through courts of shire and hundred. Royal instructions were issued through the writ; a brief unvarnished statement of the royal will. That administrative instrument was developed into the 'writ-charter' by which lands might be granted or the possession of them confirmed.

Although no genuine law codes of King William have survived, it is generally accepted that some of his enactments (which in many cases could have been made by word of mouth) are to be found in twelfth-century compilations of laws attributed to him. One of the most significant, found in (amongst other sources) the 'Ten Articles of William I', is the imposition of the 'Murdrum Fine' (from which comes the modern usage 'murder' for homicide). It provides evidence of the impact of a new and alien ruling class on the native English population and their reaction to it.

It seems that so many Normans were being slain, often covertly and probably by rebel Englishmen like Orderic's 'silvatici', that action had to be taken to deal with it. A document written in the time of King Henry II records the traditional account of the events which gave rise to the murdrum fine.[12] It alleges that 'the remnant of the conquered English secretly laid ambushes for the Normans ... and slew them in secret'. It claims that, in order to avenge these deaths, a plan was devised to impose on the hundred in which a Norman was found slain a financial penalty (variously put at 36 or 44 pounds sterling, 8,640 or 10,560 silver pennies). The idea was that men would quickly seek out and hand over the guilty party. The murdrum fine illustrates William's approach to the issue of law and order. He sought to make money out of it.

The Ten Articles version confirms much of this. The king issues the instruction for the maintenance of peace and security. The local lord is ordered to arrest the slayer within five days, if he can, or pay 46 marks of silver (7,460 silver pennies) while his money lasts out and then make the whole hundred pay the fine remaining. These were enormous sums of money and must have had a considerable effect. The decree was issued at Gloucester and William is known to have been there in 1072, which is therefore the probable date of the decree.

The same source also says that if in cases of perjury, murder, or theft a Frenchman summons an Englishman to defend himself in court, the case can be tried by ordeal of (red hot) iron, the English procedure, or trial by battle, which was the French custom, at the Englishman's choice. Trial by battle was regulated in a writ[13] and an Englishman could opt for the case to be tried by the English procedure of 'compurgation' where sworn testimony was supported by the oaths of supporters. It was also ordered that those desiring to retain the status of a freeman had to belong to a 'frankpledge' (the Norman word for a tithing), that is, a group of ten men each of whom gave security, individually and collectively, for the good behaviour of the others. The Normans applied the system more rigorously and systematically. Frankpledge developed into a system for reporting to the hundred court all crime within its boundaries and a requirement, like the murdrum fine, for the members to produce a criminal for judgement.

The Conqueror also distributed to his leading barons the estates of fallen or exiled thegns (which became known collectively as a baron's 'fief'), reserving to himself the royal demesne of King Edward and all the estates of the Godwineson family. The new landholders, now referred to as tenants-in-chief (that is, holding directly from the King), then in due course granted out estates (or fiefs) to be held by their men in return for military service. There was no preconceived plan drawn up by King William and the process of subinfeudation was neither rapid nor systematic. Many barons, and the bishops and abbots, at first simply retained their men as part of their household without granting out fiefs.

Many estates were granted in a wholesale fashion, that is a prominent baron would be granted all or most of the estates of an English earl or thegn, especially the estates of king's thegns. Some of the estates of these landowning men were to be found in a relatively restricted area, and to them would be added in many cases the lands of men who were commended to the English landholder. Other lands added to the fief might be those of men who had been under his predecessor's jurisdiction. Yet these men did not necessarily hold their lands from their lord. Blocks of land could also be formed within a particular hundred (or *wapentake* in the Danelaw) by lumping together the estates of several pre-1066 owners. Thus some barons acquired quite a compact fief, which could be made tidier or have gaps filled in either by the addition of estates belonging to lesser thegns or by exchange of lands with another tenant-in-chief. Domesday Book notes many of these exchanges.

After the larger estates had been granted out, other fiefs were created by lumping together estates belonging to several thegns, again along with the lands of commended men and of 'sokemen', and so on until all the land had been distributed. This process must have gone on for years. More land became available after the rebellions and after the conquered area was extended into Northern England. Disputes often arose over exactly which estates were to be included in a particular fief, especially as some men, William Malet being a prime example, had simply seized estates for themselves without waiting to receive a royal writ or being enfeoffed by a king's officer. There were a large number of these disputes still awaiting a judgement on the part of King William (as Domesday records) when he died in 1087.

Gradually the major baronial fiefs were also reduced in size. The amount of land reserved for the lord, his demesne land, was reduced, as subinfeudation took place and fiefs were granted out in return for knight service, so creating 'knights' fees' (parcels of land held by the service of one knight). On some great fiefs a class of middle ranking landholders arose who held quite large fiefs from a lord (who held of the King as a tenant-in-chief). These middle-ranking men were to become known as 'honorial barons', barons of the 'honour' (as the fief of a great tenant-in-chief was often called). These honorial barons in their turn granted out knights' fees to their tenants, again to secure men to do the military service owed to the tenant-in-chief. Not all fiefs went to knights, some went to a class of men called sergeants who held in return for other services, some military, some agricultural and some very miscellaneous in nature, such as the rendering of a token pair of white gloves to the lord once a year.

The number of knights a tenant-in-chief might owe to King William, the 'servitium debitum', was at first quite ill-defined, resulting from bargains struck between the King and his warrior followers. It could range from a single fighting man to as many as a hundred. Thus a writ issued around 1072, to Abbot Aethelwig of Evesham, commands the Abbot to attend the King after summoning 'all those who are in your bailiwick and jurisdiction' (who were to bring with them 'all the knights which they owe me duly equipped'). Aethelwig was especially commanded to attend with 'those five knights which you owe me from your abbey'.

The king made agreements with his tenants-in-chief, such agreements becoming more precise as time went on as shown by the grant of a fief to William Baynard, with a farm in 'Totenhala', by the Abbot of Westminster in or shortly after 1083. The Abbot, following the example given by King William himself, agrees that William Baynard is to hold his land 'for the whole of his life by the service of one knight'. In this case the fief is to return to the Church when Baynard dies.

This whole process of distribution of estates was overseen by the King himself, through the issue of writs or by sending out his own agents who announced the grant of a fief in the shire or hundred courts. Domesday Book implies that the estates were often granted out county by county rather than by regions, using the hundred (or in Danelaw areas *wapentake*) courts to effect the grants. As the *Chronicle* remarks sadly in 1067, William, on his return from Normandy, 'gave away every man's land'.[14] This was finally decided upon at the Christmas Court and took effect early in 1068. So the system was developed thereafter by King William pragmatically, in piecemeal fashion. His purpose was to ensure a ready supply of troops, especially trained and well-equipped knights, to deal with the recurrent military crises which came as he struggled to retain control of a kingdom he himself had thrown into chaos.

One last aspect of lordship after the Conquest was the position of a lord as owner of a 'manor' (a word borrowed from Norman French for an estate farmed for the lord's profit). Such farming had certainly existed in England before the Conquest and much of the way an estate was run after 1066 remained just as it was before that date, but as a result of the upheaval of the Conquest, many classes of persons were economically depressed.

Men who had lost much land found themselves more dependent upon a lord than previously. Many lesser thegns, sokemen and ceorls, all of whom had been free men owning their own land, lost it and became members of a large variegated class, which Domesday Book and other documents call 'villani' (from 'villa', a village or township). They now owed agricultural and other services to a lord, working on his demesne, and held a small quantity of land in return. In the fullness of time and with further economic and social pressure, these people evolved into 'villeins', a class of servile, unfree peasants owing services, defined by custom, to a lord and utterly dependent upon him and his good will. Without the lord's consent they could not leave the manor, nor marry, nor become a priest or monk. Their wholesale and long-term economic decline into servitude began with the Conquest.

A major aspect of Norman government was the holding of hearings, called 'land pleas', to deal with disputes over the estates which had been granted out. Most were concerned with the attempts of the Church, especially the abbeys, to recover lands lost to lay holders. They were great show pieces designed to display the effectiveness of Norman justice. At Penenden Heath in 1072, Archbishop Lanfranc claimed the rights of his see and the Abbey of Canterbury against Bishop Odo. He was able to recover much land where he could show evidence from English sources. There was a series of hearings, begun seriously in 1080, into disputes over lands lost by the Abbey of Ely. They were only partly successful and the dispute rumbled on for fourteen years. Domesday Book gives evidence of a number of smaller pleas and eventually King William issued a writ compelling sheriffs who had received or simply seized Church land to return it. These pleas reveal exactly what William had to do to curb the excesses of his men.

Many other changes were effected simply by the exercise of royal authority. The creation of great fiefs led to the formation of baronies held by those who owed King William a substantial quota of knights. He created about 170 baronies, which soon came to be called Honours. He fixed the quotas levied on these barons quite arbitrarily. But the other feudal customs such as relief (payment for investiture with a fief, especially by an heir), wardship (when the heir to a fief was under age) and marriage (the right of a lord to control the marital alliances of his vassals) took a long time to be settled.

16

THE NORMAN SETTLEMENT

Having settled the problem of Ely (1071), the King turned his attention to the Welsh border. There, fitzOsbern, until his decision to go off like a knight errant to Flanders, had been keeping his eye on the activities of the Welsh. He had taken action in South Wales, in conjunction with Caradoc ap Gryffydd ap Rhydderch, against the troublesome princes of North Wales. There had been at least one skirmish, on the River Rumney. After that the Normans began their penetration of South Wales. There are reports of 'French' harrying in Ceredigion, Menevia and Bangor. Further north, on the Mercian border, Roger of Montgomery made incursions into Dyfed and Ceredigion, while further south, fitzOsbern saw off the Welsh princes Rhys Cadwgan and Meredydd.

William's policy in response was to establish fiefdoms at Chester and Shrewsbury and set men to defend Offa's Dyke. These fiefs did not immediately become earldoms. Chester was assigned to Gerbod, brother of Frederick Oosterzele-Scheldewindeke, who was the brother-in-law of William of Warenne. However, Gerbod grew tired of the attentions of the Welsh and returned to Flanders in 1071. He might also have been disappointed not to be given the title of earl.

He was replaced by Hugh of Avranches, who was certainly in North Wales from 1073 onwards. Shrewsbury became an earldom for Roger of Montgomery by 1073 (though he was termed 'Comes' much earlier) so earldoms were being created between 1071 and 1074. On the death of his father William fitzOsbern, Roger (his younger son) inherited his earldom of Hereford but was not given any of the other responsibilities fitzOsbern had so willingly accepted.

It was Scotland that posed the greatest immediate threat. There the exiled English magnates had gathered around the Aetheling and were sustained in their hopes by King Malcolm, solely in order to cause difficulties for William. The forays by Malcolm or by other parties of Scots now provoked action. William of Malmesbury, in a confused account of events in the North, even asserts that one of William's aims in ravaging Northumbria had been to discourage the Scots by depriving them of supplies and sustenance gathered locally when they raided England. King William had also intended to deprive the Danes of supplies, aiming to 'leave nothing near the seashore which a raiding pirate could find and carry off ... or use for food'.

When bestowing fiefs on his supporters in Yorkshire (in order to strengthen the area against Scottish attacks), William had also, in March 1071, appointed a Lotharingian cleric, from Liège, called Walcher, to be Bishop of Durham. Queen Edith is said to have remarked on seeing the Bishop, 'A pretty martyr we have here.' Malmesbury remarks that it was a shrewd guess based on her knowledge of the ferocity of the Northumbrians, as Bishop Walcher was murdered by rebels in 1080.

William of Malmesbury implies that some of the ravaging in the North was repeated in 1072 when William's army passed through Northumbria on the way to Scotland. The harrying in 1070 had left the North even more uncontrollable and the lack of population and absence of Norman settlement had made it impossible to prevent the Scots from raiding deep into England. But the Conqueror was undoubtedly satisfied that he had ended all meaningful opposition in England, having, in Roman style, 'made a desert and called it peace'.

In Yorkshire and further south the process of distribution to William's followers of the estates of fallen and exiled thegns was well underway and William could undertake to resume regular government. Yorkshire was brought within the English shire system. It was placed under the control of a sheriff assisted by a shire court and the geld was more consistently collected.

At Easter 1070 King William had welcomed the arrival of papal legates, the Cardinal Bishop of Sitten, Ermenfrid, a Cardinal Deacon called John Minutus and a Cardinal Priest, Peter Bibliothecarius. It was quite a prestigious delegation. Pope Alexander obviously intended them to 'cleanse' the English Church. At a synod held at Winchester, the legates carried out a solemn crowning of the King, conferring papal approval on his monarchy and intending it to signify that William was a papal vassal. It was not viewed in that light by the King himself, who certainly did not in any sense perform homage to the Pope. The real impact of the repeated crowning was to emphasise the quasi-sacramental status of the anointing and crowning of a king who thereby became king 'dei gratia' and, as it was a matter of grace, ultimately subject to papal jurisdiction.

The main business of the synod had been the deposition process, from 7 to 11 April, for the removal of Archbishop Stigand. William was at last prepared to dispense with his services. Not only was he deposed for having 'usurped' the See of Canterbury (and thereby indirectly accused of irreligiously conducting an uncanonical coronation), but he was also accused of pluralism because he had continued to hold the bishopric of Winchester as well as the See of Canterbury along with several other Church offices including some abbacies. William of Malmesbury adds the charge of simony, and thus of buying and selling offices in the Church, but no evidence of this has been found. It was all too easy for the reform-minded to interpret any payments made when Church offices changed hands as simony, an offence whose moral taint was as deep as its definition was loose.

Stigand was also censured for accepting a pallium from the anti-pope, Benedict X. The Archbishop protested against all these charges and tried to call King William to testify on his behalf. Finally he simply rejected the authority of his judges, no doubt taking his stand on the premise that he had been appointed Archbishop by the saintly King Edward in the traditional English manner in use since the time of at least King Edgar. Nonetheless he was found guilty, deposed and sentenced to life imprisonment in a monastery.

The legates went on to depose a number of other bishops and abbots. Stigand's brother Aethelmaer, Bishop of Elmham, fell with him, as did the Bishops of Lichfield and Selsey. The abbots fared no better. Those of St Augustine's, Canterbury, Glastonbury, Winchcombe, Tavistock (where Sihtric fled into exile and became a 'pirate') and New Minster, Winchester, were all removed as well as Bishop Aethelwine's brother, Bishop Aethelric, who was in retirement as a monk. All were condemned and deposed. It is noticeable that none of the Lotharingian bishops were removed, men like Bishop Giso of Wells. They were all loyal to the Norman King. Only one Englishman survived the cull of the episcopate, the saintly Wulfstan of Worcester, as all the others were removed in the following years. Any who died were replaced, like those deposed, mainly by Normans. Normans also gradually replaced all the English abbots.

Bishop Aethelric of Selsey had the audacity to appeal to Pope Alexander, arguing that his removal was contrary to Canon Law. The

Pope responded favourably. He wrote to King William, ordering the newly appointed Archbishop of Canterbury, Lanfranc, to hear the appeal. The Archbishop did so and then himself upheld the original sentence! On what grounds Aethelric based his appeal remains unknown. It was enough, perhaps, that the Bishop was an Englishman and a kinsman of Earl Godwin, and thus of King Harold. Aethelric was imprisoned at Marlborough and his see went to another cleric called Stigand.

The Church had clearly been 'Normanised', though it was no doubt proclaimed that it had been reformed. Archbishop Stigand was replaced at Winchester by Walkelin of Rouen, a royal clerk, and Elmham, now termed East Anglia, went to Herfast, William's Chancellor. Lanfranc, of course, was promoted to Canterbury. It seems that William now introduced the practice, for which there is no pre-Conquest evidence in England, of investiture of bishops and abbots with their ring and staff by the King. To William, bishops and abbots were ecclesiastical vassals, just as they were in Normandy. Their vast estates made it essential, in his eyes, that they be bound to him by oaths of fidelity and homage.

The increased hierarchical nature of the Anglo-Norman Church was demonstrated after Lanfranc took the See of Canterbury, for he insisted that all bishops in future make a canonical submission to him as Archbishop. That caused some immediate problems. English reaction to it is best summed up in the legend about Bishop Wulfstan. He, it was said, refused to submit, saying that his predecessors had never done so. Lanfranc demanded that he surrender his ring and staff. Wulfstan refused, crying out dramatically that he could return his staff only to him who gave it. Advancing to the tomb of King Edward, he thrust his staff into the stone over the King's body whereupon it stuck fast and no man could remove it! Lanfranc was moved to relent and confirmed Wulfstan in the possession of his see.

Lanfranc had been consecrated as a bishop on 24 June and was installed as Archbishop on the Feast of the Assumption, 15 August, so the demands for submission had come in the autumn. King William had to find a new Archbishop of York as Ealdred had died a year earlier. William's choice fell on Thomas of Bayeux (perhaps recommended by Bishop Odo), and the new Archbishop-Elect went to Lanfranc for consecration. He was appalled to be met with Lanfranc's demand that he acknowledge the superiority of Canterbury over York. He refused and deadlock ensued. Hitherto the two archdioceses had cooperated well, though the arrangements made in the seventh century had left the matter of the primacy in a confused state.

Lanfranc and Thomas quarrelled heatedly, and King William decided that the two would have to go to Rome (they both needed a pallium anyway) in the hope that Pope Alexander would settle the matter. Off they went. But Alexander, although he received them graciously, was not prepared to intervene. He commanded that the dispute be referred to an ecclesiastical court in England.

On their return, by Easter 1072, a 'general council' of the Church in England was held and Lanfranc, in the presence of a papal legate, Hubert, set out the grounds for Canterbury's claim. He based them on the text of Bede's *Ecclesiastical History*, on acts of early English synods, on the testimony of living witnesses and most of all on papal letters (some of which were undoubtedly forgeries though this was not known at the time). The synod found in Lanfranc's favour (what else?). It held that he had established the primacy of Canterbury. It only remained for him to obtain papal confirmation of it, but that he never got. The matter was not settled until well into the twelfth century. The actual outcome of the English synod was more of a compromise: Archbishop Thomas made only a personal submission to Lanfranc, and avoided binding his successors to do likewise. The facts are recorded in a charter[1] drawn up at Winchester, in 'the King's Chapel in the castle', between 8 April and 27 May 1072.

The significant point was that basing himself on English tradition, with the firm support of King William, whose interest in the case soon became manifest, Lanfranc had presented and sustained his case. It would seem that William's real concern was due to his apprehension that an independent Archbishop of York, in an area not yet fully under Norman control, might seek to enhance his own position and authority by crowning a rival king. As Hugh the Chanter[2] puts it, 'It was expedient for the unity and solidarity of the kingdom that all Britain should be subject to one primate; it might otherwise happen, in the King's time, or in that of one of his successors, that someone from among the Danes, Norwegians or Scots, who sail up to York in their attacks, might be made king by the Archbishop of York and the fickle and treacherous Yorkshiremen, and so the kingdom might be disturbed and divided.' The decision was clearly a political rather than an ecclesiastical one. Lanfranc was linking himself to William's 'imperial pretensions', asserting Canterbury's authority over all

England and beyond. As for William, Eadmer insists that his policy was to 'sustain in England the same usages and laws which he and his ancestors had been wont to observe in Normandy'; a clear testimony to the importation into England of Norman law and jurisprudence.

William also, from about 1070 onwards, subjected the bishoprics and abbacies of England to tenure by knight service, imposing quotas of knights on them which varied from sixty, for Canterbury and Peterborough Abbey, down to the Abbey of Ramsey at four and the See of Chichester at only two. It remains a moot point whether he tried as consistently to impose such service on the holders of lay fiefs, though their descendants were certainly rendering such service according to twelfth-century records. The lack of specific evidence may result only from the scarcity of secular as opposed to ecclesiastical records. Lay barons did not require their servants to write chronicles or compose cartularies.

William was also free to make use of many valuable churches as endowments for his household clerks, exploiting for the purpose the English Old Minsters, now annexed to the cathedrals. He used their lands to provide for the canons. The new bishops proceeded to imprint the stamp of Norman culture on England, destroying the existing cathedral churches and replacing them with Norman buildings in the new Romanesque style. Many of these buildings were almost fortress-like in appearance, some with turrets, crenellations and even windows like arrow slits. The Norman Church in England was in every sense a Church Militant.

In the winter of 1071/72 William departed once more for Normandy. The record of his doings there is sparse but the Court he held there was undoubtedly concerned with the situation in Maine. His half-brother, Bishop Odo, was with him. William could not afford to stay long as he was still more worried about Scotland than Maine and so by 8 April 1072 he was at Winchester. There he began extensive preparations for an expedition into Scotland. That prompted his decision to impose the burden of military service on his vassals in England, both ecclesiastical and lay. Much of the military obligation was at that time discharged by the employment of stipendiary soldiers, as subinfeudation could only have been in its early stages and tenure by knight service was only gradually being introduced.

It could have been in relation to the gathering of his army that the writ sent to Abbot Aethelwig of Evesham relates. Some question this because it called on the Abbot to meet the King at Clarendon (Wiltshire), but William loved hunting so he could well have been calling men in to see him while enjoying himself in his customary manner. The writ commands the Abbot to attend the King after summoning 'all those who are in your bailiwick and jurisdiction' who were to bring with them 'all the knights which they owe me duly equipped'. This was to occur before the Octave of Whitsun and Aethelwig was especially commanded to attend with 'those five knights which you owe me from your Abbey'. The writ thus seems to confirm that the obligation applied to lay vassals as well, since it gives the Abbot leadership of other lay vassals and their tenants. Aethelwig is to issue a summons to all those under his jurisdiction.

It is logical to suggest that if the writ was issued in 1072 then these men were required for service in Scotland, as it was exactly at this time that William was preparing to invade and would have been summoning men from all over the kingdom.

Other sources support the idea that it was from then on that William really sought to insist on the service of contingents of knights. The *Liber Eliensis* records his demand as does the *Abingdon Chronicle*. The gathering of the host, in the form of a land army and a fleet, was carried out remarkably quickly, probably by 15 August, including English as well as Norman levies.

The land force travelled by way of Durham, through Lothian to Perth, crossed the Firth of Forth by a ford near Stirling and then turned eastwards towards the upper reaches of the Tay to rendezvous with the fleet. It was a bold and hazardous movement. Much could have gone wrong had the two prongs of his force not made contact. But the whole attempt to bring King Malcolm to battle failed. The wily Scot simply would not play the Norman game. He had no wish to suffer the fate of Harold Godwineson.

But the Scottish King was intimidated by this display of Anglo-Norman power and agreed to negotiate. The two kings met at Abernethy, close to the Norman ships. Malcolm gave hostages to William, the usual diplomatic protocol, and swore to become William's 'man', just as his predecessors had to Kings Aethelstan and Edgar. It remains uncertain whether he saw this as doing homage for the Kingdom of Alba itself or merely for territory in Cumbria and Lothian. It does not seem to have applied to the 'principality of Scotland' because in 1079 William had to send another army commanded by his son Robert, which achieved more or less the same result, but it was then said to give 'surety that the principality of Scotland should be subjected to the Kingdom of England'.

The practical point was that Malcolm had now, in 1072, recognised the reality of the new regime in England. An indication of this was that the Aetheling was, as part of the agreement, expelled from Scotland with all his English supporters. Malcolm remained a greater threat to northern England than any of his predecessors and his raids did not cease, recurring in 1079, 1091 and 1093. However, after Abernethy, William was able to remove Cospatric, the former Earl of Northumbria, from all power in England where he held Bamburgh, without fear of reprisals from Scotland. The King could no longer remain in the North; his supply lines were greatly over-extended, so he decided to strengthen the position of Bishop Walcher and return south.

King Malcolm had now affected to be overawed and had made his formal submission and William had been glad to accept, as he was now 250 miles north of his nearest base at York and there was little food available for his army. He returned by way of Monkchester and came south to Durham, where he ordered a castle to be built for Bishop Walcher (who also bought the earldom of Northumbria from him). Waltheof was confirmed as an earl, holding Huntingdonshire and Northamptonshire and ruling Northumbria in cooperation with Walcher.

The Church of Durham later had a miracle story that explained William's sudden decision to withdraw to the South. The story was intended to explain why the King had confirmed the privileges of Saint Cuthbert with his lands and the saint's jurisdiction over them, and restored to the Church the manor of Billingham. William was said to have been overcome with fear for the safety of his immortal soul because of the guilt he felt for the harrying of the North. He asked to view Saint Cuthbert's body, but when it was unveiled, it was said, he was overcome by a great fever, avoided looking at the relic, and fled south in panic. The situation remained perilous for those ruling in the North and the story was helpful to Bishop Walcher, who still needed protection against insurgents. These were the thieves and robbers, as the Normans saw them, of the type Earl Tostig had dealt with in King Edward's time.

In another version of the miracle story, William sent an agent called Rannulph to collect taxes from the Church of Saint Cuthbert but he failed in his task, because he dreamt that the saint had appeared to him, struck him with his staff and ordered him to leave Saint Cuthbert's land. He awoke to find himself paralysed and remained so until he had promised to do no more wrong to the saint, imploring his forgiveness and offering gifts at his shrine. He recovered only after he had been carried some distance south away from the saint's influence. William, on being informed of this, duly confirmed the saint's privileges. (In all likelihood he had in fact allowed the Bishop to retain the royal revenues to defray the costs of administering the province.) Such stories illustrate the depth of local feelings of hostility towards the Norman regime. Yet they also promote reconciliation. William makes peace with Saint Cuthbert, who was the focus of Northern loyalty. Thus the tales help to embed the new regime by attempting to align it with popular religion.

Durham sources reveal that the situation in Northumbria was far worse than military and political events can explain. Walcher himself needed protection from insurgents and there were continuous low-level Scottish raids. The area was a hotbed of brigandage, as Earl Tostig had discovered to his cost. This lawlessness, the absence of settlement by Normans, the effects of the harrying, all go to explain why the area was not included in the great survey that produced Domesday Book. Even Earl Waltheof involved himself in a feud, attacking the family of Karli Thorbrandson. Thorbrand, known as the Hold, had been slain by Ealdred of Bamburgh, Waltheof's maternal grandfather, because he had slain Earl Uhtred, Ealdred's father. Karli had then killed Earl Ealdred. Waltheof now seized his chance to get revenge, though no one can explain why he chose to do so at this particular moment. Possibly he was currying favour with the King since the sons of Karli had been major figures in the revolt of 1069–71.

Waltheof sent a party of men to kill the sons of Karli while they were gathered at Settrington in the North Riding, most probably during the Christmas period of 1073–74. All present were killed including Thorbrand Karlison, and his brother Gamal. They spared the youngest, Cnut, because of his age. The fourth brother, Sumerled, escaped death only because he was still travelling.

King William, having dealt with Scotland, at least to his own satisfaction, was now free to turn his attention to Maine. He returned to Normandy and in a three-month campaign reaffirmed Norman control. He was back at Bonneville-sur-Touques by 30 March 1073. He had entered the area by way of the Sarthe valley and attacked

Fresnay, striking at a time when he knew that Fulk of Anjou was away. Fulk had been invited by the citizens of Le Mans to help them expel Geoffrey of Mayenne and he had gladly done so in order to establish himself on the frontiers of Normandy.

Fresnay and Beaumont both surrendered to William and he attacked and took Sillé, opening the way to Le Mans. The whole of the Comté duly submitted. Norman ascendancy had been re-established.

But more trouble was brewing. Since 1067 when Baldwin VI of Flanders, Regent of France, died, King Philip had begun to develop his own foreign policy. For that he needed allies, and at first he turned to Flanders, assuming that its Count Robert would share his views, which he did. The agreement was symbolised by the marriage of Philip to Bertha of Hainault, Robert's half-sister. The King also made approaches to Anjou. He had made a pact with Fulk (who was engaged in a struggle against his own brother, Geoffrey), and the two princes had become friends. Philip must have therefore approved of Fulk's move against Maine in 1072, which had disturbed King William. The basis of Philip's policy is clear to see. For the next twenty years he ceaselessly worked in opposition to Normandy by means of alliances with Anjou and Flanders. That policy so hampered King William that he had to spend most of his time in Normandy, centring defence of his kingdom there. In 1074 all of William's opponents across the Channel began to act in concert.

The Aetheling Edgar had returned to Scotland in 1074 (despite the Treaty of Abernethy) and had been received there with honour. He was, after all, the Scottish King's brother-in-law. But Philip of France now realised that he might be a useful pawn in his great game against King William. An offer was sent to the Aetheling which would give him a strategic advantage. Philip proposed to grant him the important castle of Montreuil-sur-Mer, the chief French outlet on to the Channel. That would have enabled the Aetheling to become the focus of and rallying point for all the English exiles. But William was alerted to this and himself made overtures to the Aetheling, offering him an honoured place at his court, which the Aetheling, curiously enough, accepted. Exactly why remains unknown but it reflects badly on the young man's character, as he could so easily be persuaded to change his mind.

He had been in Scotland in July 1074, visiting his sister Margaret. Malcolm 'received' him at court (the word employed, 'underfon',

implies recognition of a vassal by a lord) and while there he had
accepted the offer from King Philip. He was to control the castle
and its garrison and could use it as a base for operations against
the Norman King. So he set out for France to take up the offer,
accompanied by other exiles, but a storm arose, which wrecked his
ship and his chances. His vessel was driven ashore, on the North-
East Coast of England (some of his companions were captured by
local Frenchmen, that is, Normans living in England). The Aetheling
managed to make his way back to Scotland but seems to have
decided that God did not intend him to accept Philip's offer.

William then seized the opportunity to neutralise the threat
presented by the Aetheling. He offered him his peace and friendship
and an honoured place at Court. As the *Peterborough Chronicle* put
it, 'The King revoked the sentence of outlawry on him and all his
men and he was in the King's court and took such rights as the King
granted him.' These rights were not over generous. Domesday Book
records only a meagre amount of land held by Edgar.[3] But there was
a little more to it than that. The *Worcester Chronicle* insists that
the Aetheling, prompted by King Malcolm (possibly aware of his
obligations under the Treaty of Abernethy), wrote first to William
(perhaps suspicious of the King's intentions) seeking guarantees for
his protection, which William agreed to provide and summoned him
to England.

In 1074 King William had, in May, visited Lillebonne and was in
Rouen in November. It was about then that he was made a member
of the Confraternity of Cluny, the great reformed Abbey in Burgundy.
He is also said to have refused an invitation to intervene in German
affairs, though it was rumoured that he intended to attack Aachen
on behalf of the Archbishop of Cologne. Even the Emperor Henry
IV was alleged to have sought his aid against the rebellious German
baronage, though there is no evidence that it was forthcoming. These
stories are evidence more of William's growing power and reputation
on the Continent than of any actual intentions on his part.

As for King Philip, after the Aetheling's defection, he had to find a new
centre of opposition to William and looked for it in Brittany. There, a
number of members of the cadet branch of the ruling family, led by Eudo
of Penthièvre and his sons, held lands in northern and eastern Brittany
facing Normandy. Several members of this clan were also established in
England, where Ralph de Gael, son of Ralph the Staller, was the natural
leader of the Bretons who had received lands from the Conqueror.

There is no evidence of any involvement on King Philip's part in what followed, but he and his allies must have watched what happened intently. Ralph, Earl of East Anglia, now formed an alliance with Roger 'of Breteuil', Earl of Hereford and son of William fitzOsbern. The alliance was sealed by the marriage of Ralph to Roger's daughter in 1075. The marriage took place at Exning, near Newmarket in Suffolk. It is not clear whether William had given his consent for the marriage, as the sources contradict each other. William was in Normandy at this time, as charter evidence confirms, dealing with the affairs of the duchy, and might not have been aware of what was happening.

It is possible that the two earls had allowed their guests to assume that they had the King's consent. The marriage was a splendid affair by all accounts, attended by adherents of the earls, some bishops and abbots, and especially by East Anglian Bretons. But as the *Chronicle* sadly comments, 'Then was that bridale to many men's bale,' reflecting on the disastrous events which followed.

The earls commiserated with each other, each complaining of having been under-appreciated by the King. A conspiracy was formed to the effect that 'they would drive their royal lord from his kingdom'. The exact reason why they sought to do so remains unclear. Maybe their action was simply a product of the boastfulness and arrogance of two powerful young men, their vanity fed by the flattery of their followers. Orderic Vitalis, in his usual manner, provides set piece speeches, which sum up the arguments put forward. William's bastardy was raked up and held against him, and it was said that it would please God to get rid of him! He was called a 'degenerate' who had robbed William of Mortain, and poisoned Count Walter of Mantes and his wife Biota as well as Count Conan of Brittany. He had unjustly seized the Kingdom of England, killed or cruelly exiled the genuine heirs of estates and, above all, had insufficiently honoured his companions in victory, giving wounded men barren and unprofitable lands. So, said the earls, 'All men hate him and will rejoice at his death!' These motives ascribed to them at the time strike modern historians as an inadequate explanation for acting at that particular moment.

However, they concluded that there was no time to strike like the present, since William was absent in Normandy. They fully expected the English to rise up in support of their rebellion, and turned to Earl Waltheof to enlist his aid. To Waltheof they explained that the three of them would rule England, while one of them (unspecified) would wear the crown. Perhaps they allowed Waltheof to think they meant him as they said that the English would not want another Norman King. Earl Waltheof seems to have been careful to conceal his part in all this and even the extent to which he agreed with them. He was, after all, husband of William's niece Judith.

The two earls returned to their castles to prepare the rising and word was sent to Denmark, possibly in Waltheof's name, to canvass support from there. Earl Roger took control of several castles on the Welsh border and prepared to set out to link up with Ralph, who was advancing through Norfolk into Cambridgeshire, as far as Whaddon. The local justiciars fell back before Earl Ralph, leading him on. Lanfranc wrote to William in Normandy, informing him of the rebellion but insisting that it was unnecessary for him to return to England, as the King's men were well able to contain the rising.

Earl Roger advanced from Hereford and was confronted by the King's agents in the West Country, who prevented him from even crossing the Severn. In Cambridgeshire, Ralph was attacked at Fawdon (not far from Duxford) but after a brief skirmish he bolted back to Norwich, shutting himself up in the castle. He was unable to face maintaining a siege and escaped by sea, fleeing to his estates in Brittany. Lanfranc gleefully reported all this to his master.

Norwich held out under the command of Ralph's wife, Emma, a redoubtable lady by all accounts. She held out for three months, then was granted terms for her surrender giving her husband time to reach Dol. Again Lanfranc wrote rejoicing to the King. 'Glory be to God on High!' he said, 'whose mercy has cleansed your kingdom of the filth of the Bretons!' But he still kept watch for a possible incursion by the Danes. They arrived but far too late to be of any use to the rebels. They raided and plundered York, then returned home.

Meanwhile, Earl Waltheof had become a turncoat. He had gone to Lanfranc and made a clean breast of his involvement (which in part explains the success of the countermeasures), making an impressive display of repentance. Lanfranc gave him absolution and, as a penance, told Waltheof to go to William in Normandy. There he was immediately arrested and held prisoner. Earl Roger also had been captured and imprisoned in England.

William was at Westminster for the funeral of Queen Edith, who had died on 18 December 1075. Her body had been brought to Westminster from Winchester so that she could lie beside her husband. William delayed dealing with the earls until his Christmas Court, which followed the funeral. Earl Roger was put on trial, with, in absentia, Earl Ralph, and both were charged with treason. Roger was sentenced to the loss of his earldom and forfeiture of his estates and imprisoned for life. No new earl of Hereford was created to replace him. Ralph too was condemned and forfeited his earldom and his English lands.

Earl Waltheof presented a more difficult problem. He had tried to atone for his actions by a speedy confession and the King's apparent leniency towards him had raised his hopes of acquittal. He had not taken account of the spite of his wife. Judith turned on her husband, denouncing him as a traitor and accusing him of favouring and being an accomplice of the rebel earls. The Council was unable to reach a final verdict immediately so he was remanded in custody to a prison at Winchester.[4]

William was now free to dispose of the lands of the two earls and did so. He also had Queen Edith's lands available. Not only that, but the Council had acted against all those, especially Bretons, involved in the rising. They suffered dreadful punishments. Not content with confiscating lands (as Domesday Book testifies), William proceeded harshly against them.

> Some were blinded, Some driven from the land. Some were brought to shame. Thus were the traitors to King William laid low.

Earl Roger remained a prisoner and died as one, remaining defiant to the end. One year, William, moved to make one of his periodic gestures of magnanimity, and aware that there was a particularly hard winter that year, sent the imprisoned Earl a rich Christmas gift of silk garments and furs. Roger contemptuously made a heap of them in the middle of his chamber and burned them! 'By the Splendour of God!' said William when told of this. 'He shall never leave prison while I live!' The King did order the Earl's release when on his deathbed, only for his son William Rufus to rearrest him, so that he died a prisoner still.

William remained in England until Easter 1076, attending a Council held by Lanfranc at Winchester, so he would still have been in England when Waltheof's fate was decided. The Earl spent the time in prayer, reciting the Psalms, which he had learned by heart. His case was reviewed at Pentecost, 15 May, and he was now sentenced to death for treason under English law (Roger had been tried as a Norman) though he had not been permitted to clear himself under oath, assisted by 'oath-helpers' as English law also allowed. On 31 May, he was taken out to a place of execution on a hill outside the walls of Winchester and beheaded.

He had dressed in full as an English earl and distributed gifts to the poor. Kneeling, he prayed, seeking forgiveness for his sins until the executioner, growing impatient, intervened. 'Rise, we must do the bidding of our master,' he said. Waltheof asked for time for one last prayer and began the Our Father. He had just said, 'Lead us not into temptation' when the headsman's sword flashed. Bystanders swore they heard the severed head complete the prayer, 'But deliver us from evil.' His body was eventually buried at Crowland in Lincolnshire and many of the English regarded him as a martyr. Countess Judith, perhaps dismayed at the result of her testimony, or merely complying with the expected proprieties, had obtained leave from William for the removal of the body to Crowland on 15 June.

Earl Ralph had taken up residence at Dol and allied himself to Geoffrey Granon, a bastard son of Alan III of Brittany. Ralph led an uprising against William. After his return to Normandy, King William besieged him there, with the assistance of Hoel of Brittany, early in the autumn of 1076. The campaign followed on logically from the crushing of the earls' revolt, and King Philip's subsequent manoeuvres suggest that the French King might have had a greater part in this than the record shows. King Philip came to Ralph's aid and drove William back into Normandy, the first of several reversals William was to suffer over the next ten years. The Normans lost many men and horses and much treasure. Ralph still remained a power in Brittany and William was unable to prevent King Philip from occupying the Vexin on the eastern Norman border. The situation was to remain fluid until a truce was negotiated by local bishops between William and Philip at 'Blancheland' (or Brueria).[5]

This agreement (which should probably be placed in 1081) appears to have followed on from a truce between the two Kings in 1077. Fulk le Rechin had unsuccessfully attacked La Flèche, in Maine, around 1077 (and was to do so again, successfully, in 1081 when he burnt the castle). So a temporary uneasy truce[6] with King William followed Fulk's earlier failure. But by 1081 King Philip had attained his primary objective, to force William to negotiate. From the Vexin the French King was in a position to threaten Normandy itself. William had not yet suffered any real loss of territory and Norman administration continued in Maine, under Robert Curthose. The peace could not be expected to last long but the occupation of the Vexin had imposed a limit on the growth of Normandy. The impression is that the initiative in the struggle had passed to King Philip.

Also, of course, these difficulties were to place a strain on the relations between William and his eldest son.

17

DYNASTIC QUARRELS & FOREIGN PERILS & THE DEATH OF WILLIAM

Philip of France used all the means in his power to weaken the position of King William. He failed in his offer in 1074 to establish Edgar the Aetheling in the castle of Montreuil-sur-Mer, he relieved Dol in the autumn of 1076, routing William's army, which had been attempting to punish the Bretons for the aid they had given to Earl Ralph of East Anglia during his revolt. But the quarrels between William and his heir, Robert Curthose, presented Philip with plentiful opportunities for mischief-making and increased the perils that faced King William after 1077.

Robert Curthose first quarrelled bitterly with his father in 1074. He had been growing increasingly dissatisfied with the way in which William treated him, feeling himself scorned. His father's nickname for him did little to assuage his wounded pride. 'By God's resurrection!' William had been heard to bellow, 'He'll be a hero will our Robin Shorty-Pants!' (*Curta Ocrea*). Like his mother, Duchess Matilda, Robert was of shorter than average stature. William of Malmesbury suggests that this nickname was an attempt to puncture Robert's increasingly self-important behaviour.

Although Robert had been given the title of Count of Maine as early as 1063 and had been formally invested as Duke of Normandy (in waiting) in 1066 prior to the invasion of England (an insurance against the risk that William might never return), he had never been allowed to exercise independent authority in either role. William had continued to use the title of Count of Maine himself (it appears in his charters), and of course he retained the Dukedom.

William and his family were in residence at Laigle, in late 1077 or early 1078, where the King-Duke was planning an attack against

Rotrou of Perche, when the breach between father and son occurred. Robert's brothers, William and Henry, were playing a game of dice in an upper room of the house when Robert and a group of his boon companions appeared in the yard below their window. Gleefully the two boys proceeded to drench Robert with a bucket of water (if that is all it actually was), much to his discomfiture and embarrassment before his companions. Mortification gave way to rage. Robert mounted the stairs to remonstrate with his brothers and a scuffle broke out between them, which was only quelled when King William himself intervened to restore order. For Robert it seems to have been the last straw.

The young man confronted his father and clamorously demanded his 'rights'. Orderic Vitalis, in his customary manner, provides his own version of the conversation that followed. It could well be based on reports of what must have struck witnesses as a cause célèbre, possibly widely disseminated, to which Orderic has added what was known of the disagreement between the two. To this he added his own imaginative reconstruction of the quarrel. Robert is made to demand of William what had been given him in 1066 and William flatly refused to do so. Orderic claims to know why: William regarded the demand as an impossibility, insisting that England was his by conquest and Normandy by hereditary right. He is made to say, 'For as long as I live I will never surrender it!' and to have argued that he had to hold both in order to maintain all those who depended upon him. Robert was told to continue to obey his father, to take part as usual in the government of the realm 'as a son ought to behave towards his father'.

Robert's counter-argument stressed that he was not content to be his father's hireling, a mercenary soldier in his pay. He insisted that he needed his own personal fief so that he could reward those who served him, and demanded again that William hand over the duchy to him, to govern as William himself governed England. The King-Duke repeated that Robert's demands were premature and that he should not seek to snatch recklessly at the power that would be his when the right moment came. He was advised to choose better counsellors and told of the risk that the Normans, a turbulent people prone to disorder, would only take advantage of Robert's 'mad pretensions'. He was rebuked and told in no uncertain manner to cease paying attention to the words of libertines.

Robert, increasingly furious, refused to listen to any lectures: he had heard enough of them from his tutors. He had had enough and was now old enough to know how to behave. Finally he announced that he could no longer live what he called a life of slavery. William simply repeated his decision, saying he would never surrender Normandy to anyone, nor the kingdom; 'Every kingdom divided against itself, as the Gospel says, is doomed to desolation.' Robert then defiantly announced his intention to go into exile and serve some foreign prince and so earn the rewards denied to him in his father's house.

The *Chronicle*[1] sums the affair up more baldly: 'Robert, son of King William, deserted from his father to his maternal uncle Robert in Flanders, because his father would not let him govern his earldom in Normandy which he himself and King Philip with his consent had given him; and the leading men of the country had sworn him oaths and accepted him as lord.' Such a concession had only given Robert an expectation of becoming duke. (Just as an alleged concession by King Edward had given, or created in, William an expectation of inheriting the succession.)

No meeting of minds being possible, Robert and his companions rode off to Rémalard on the frontier and from there to Rouen where he and his men tried to seize control of the castle. From there he was pursued and driven out of Normandy. He paid fruitless visits to his father's rivals and eventually ended up in Paris seeking the help of King Philip, who was only too pleased to seize the opportunity to embarrass William and gave Robert custody of the castle of Gerberoi.

William reproached his overlord for breach of agreements between them and of his obligations under feudal custom. Philip proceeded to betray the son just as he had betrayed the father and ostentatiously joined William at the siege he now laid to Gerberoi (1079). He must have enjoyed the subsequent discomfiting failure of his Norman rival. The castle withstood the siege and, during a skirmish outside the walls, Robert encountered and unhorsed his father in single combat. William received a slight wound to his hand and his horse, pierced by an arrow, collapsed under him. He was saved from capture (which would have been the ultimate disgrace) when Tokig, son of the thegn Wigod of Wallingford, gave William his own horse and enabled him to escape. Tokig himself died, shot by a crossbowman.

The Conqueror was truly mortified. He is said to have complained, 'Which of my ancestors ever had to endure such hostility from a child as I do?' Of course Robert had been designated as Duke in traditional fashion at least twice. A charter given at Mézidon, 29 June 1063, refers to Robert 'whom (the Duke) had chosen for the government of the realm after his death', a *post-obitum* bequest in effect.[2] This had been about the same time as Robert's betrothal to Count Herbert of Maine's sister Margaret, when he ought also to have been presented as Herbert's heir. The other occasion was shortly before the expedition to England in 1066. Various sources do thereafter record Robert as being 'our duke and advocate' and as 'performing his father's office, long may he do so'. One source even says he had been 'entrusted with the dominion of the Norman duchy' and so was 'blossoming in the flower of his youth'. William of Jumièges seems to have thought that William, now a King, had indeed handed the duchy to his son. If so, then he was sadly misinformed.

No other duke ever created a 'co-duke' on the Capetian model and certainly never resigned in favour of a son. William had no intention of doing so either. From youth onwards Robert was only ever referred to as a count (*comes*) or as son of the King (*filius Regis*) and very occasionally as 'comes Normannorum' and twice 'comes Cenomannensis' (of Maine). It could be that these titles stimulated Robert's ambition and sharpened his disappointment when, even after the Conquest, his father failed to give him more power. Instead the King-Duke persisted in calling himself Duke, Prince, Patron or Lord of Normandy, although Robert was allowed in some sense to rule Normandy in association with his father, but never alone. Nor was his position in Maine any better: he did not even hold any lands there.

King William withdrew from Gerberoi and allowed his barons to end a conflict which had severely embarrassed them. Orderic says that when the King was ill (possibly after Gerberoi) he 'made his first-born son his heir and ordered all the magnates to do homage and fealty to him'. They had thus been forced to choose between fighting for their current lord or their future one. A reconciliation was patched up between Robert and his father. At Rouen William grudgingly compromised, agreeing to restore Robert to Court and renewing his promise that Robert would inherit Normandy on his death. This implies that William had been led to accept the possibility of a separation of England from Normandy after his death. But it might mean that William was seeking to downplay the idea that he was a French vassal. William of Poitiers is studiously vague, referring simply to the establishment of a firm peace and serene friendship. The two went together to England, where problems in the North required William's attention.

It is reported that Matilda had quarrelled with her husband over Robert. As her first-born he remained her favourite and she must certainly have pleaded for him with William. She definitely aided him in other ways. One of Robert's great weaknesses was that money flowed through his fingers like water. He was said to be easy prey to usurers and moneylenders. The Duchess tried to ease his financial difficulties by sending him subsidies through a Breton called Samson. William eventually found out and fell into one of his dreadful rages. He chose to blame Samson, saying that if he caught him he would have his eyes put out. Samson fled, seeking asylum at the Abbey of Saint Evroult 'to save at the same time his body and his soul'.

William ordered his wife to stop helping Robert but she refused, allegedly proclaiming, 'By the power of the Most High, if my son Robert were dead and buried, hidden from the eyes of the living, I would if I could, at the cost of my own blood, give him back his life, giving my blood for him!' It is evidence of William's love for her that she never suffered for her defiance.

Before his return to England, William attended the consecration of his Abbey of St Stephen's, Caen (the Abbaye aux Hommes) and presided at a Council at Lillebonne at Pentecost 1080. It dealt mainly with defining the fiscal prerogatives of bishops and the payments they were to receive from clergy and laity and demonstrates how far judicial rights exercised in Normandy were derived from concessions made by the Duke. William was always only too ready to summon for judgement in his own Court cases already decided in episcopal courts, even cases concerning clergy who took wives or concubines. He dealt harshly with such cases, indicating a concern for ritual purity so that priestly prayer would be more effective. It also aligned him with the papal reform agenda.

This was also the year of Pope Gregory VII's notorious letter of 8 May 1080 to King William in which he sought to enforce his claim that William ought to have done homage, saying that 'the Christian religion had disposed that after God the royal power shall be governed by the care and authority of the apostolic see'. That fealty was being demanded is shown by the terms of the refusal of King William, in his letter written in reply. The Pope had already, 4 April 1074, reminded the King of his obligation to send Peter's Pence to Rome. Now, 24 April 1080, Gregory wrote demanding William's obedience to his will, while as usual being very flattering about the justice of William's rule.

Gregory VII's letter is of great interest for its confirmation of the efforts he (then Archdeacon Hildebrand) had made on William's behalf in 1066. However, the papal demand that William render fealty to the apostolic see is not found in any extant papal letter. Judging by William's uncompromising response it must have been made by the legate Hubert. The King denied that he had ever 'consented to pay fealty' (letter to Gregory undated, but in 1080) because 'I have never promised it, nor do I find that my predecessors ever paid it to your predecessors'.

The King went on to forbid the sending of a legate to England, or the publication of any decrees of excommunication or other decrees without his prior approval, even though he always protested his love for the papacy and his readiness to 'hear you most obediently'. Gregory is recognised as 'most excellent Shepherd of Holy Church'. The motive for William's position was political rather than doctrinal. Pope Gregory, in need of support in his dispute with the Emperor, could not afford to turn William against him. His letters repeatedly seek to flatter the King in the most fulsome terms. William could never have agreed to become the vassal of the Pope, since he would have seen that as subjection to him.

Meanwhile, in England in 1079 Walcher, Bishop of Durham since 1076, had been unable to prevent a ravaging raid by King Malcolm, who came down as far as the Tyne. In the following year Walcher, who was both bishop and earl, became embroiled in a local feud in which Leobwin the chaplain and Gilbert (a relative of the Bishop) had killed Ligulf of Bamburgh. In reprisal the Bishop was murdered at Gateshead. William had to act. First he sent his half-brother Odo, as Earl of Kent, to restore order to Northumbria. Then, towards the end of the year, hoping perhaps that extra responsibility would strengthen the reconciliation, he dispatched Robert Curthose at the head of a formidable force to teach King Malcolm a lesson.

It was something of a repeat performance of the invasion of 1072. Robert drove the Scots back and Malcolm again refused to give battle, but was forced to renew the Abernethy agreement of 1072 at Falkirk, and once more having to pay homage and give hostages. Robert then returned to Northumbria, stopping on the Tyne long enough to initiate the construction of the New Castle, from which the city there derives its name. The Tyne was now effectively the frontier between the two kingdoms and Cumbria was in Scottish hands.[3]

King William then made his only recorded visit to Wales. Either in spring after making arrangements at the Christmas Court of 1080, or more likely in the summer (after a Court at Pentecost), he moved into South Wales as far as St Davids. For public consumption it was presented as a military campaign in which many English prisoners were released, though Welsh sources present it as a pilgrimage to the shrine of St David. Caradoc ap Gruffydd, who had been an ally of William fitzOsbern and his son Roger, had helped maintain order, but he had now died, slain by the powerful Welsh prince Rhys ap Tewdwr of Deheubarth.

Some of the Welsh had been punished for participating in the rising of the earls in 1075. A force had been sent on a punitive expedition, William seemingly aiming to demonstrate his power to the Welsh and establish Norman dominance. Rhys ap Tewdwr was forced to agree to pay the traditional Welsh tribute of 40 pounds a year, the same sort of arrangement as had been the custom in King Edward's day. William also established a mint at Cardiff, which encouraged its growth as a town.

In 1082 William was further embarrassed by the behaviour of his half-brother Odo, Bishop of Bayeux and Earl of Kent. He had been growing increasingly discontented with his position within the Anglo-Norman system. He was a proud and ambitious man, disdainful of even the most honourable of subordinate positions. He had quarrelled with Archbishop Lanfranc, back in 1072,[4] over the possession of Canterbury lands seized by the Bishop after the Conquest and incorporated into his earldom. He had lost the case, heard at Penenden Heath by Bishop Geoffrey of Coutances. He doubtless resented Lanfranc's influence with the King and what he saw as his own consequent loss of influence. He had been omitted from commissions of regency during William's absences on the Continent so he now began to foment schemes for his own aggrandisement.

During 1082 he began gathering around him his friends and vassals and recruiting knights for a foreign expedition. Rumour had it that his destination was Rome. It was even hazarded that he hoped to secure the papacy though this seems far-fetched. But he had been distributing money to influential men in Rome and bought himself a palazzo. Both Orderic and William of Malmesbury report his participation in intrigues. The latter thought he 'almost succeeded in buying the See of Rome'. Whatever his plan was, it had attracted some prominent supporters, notably Hugh d'Avranches, Earl of Chester. One possibility is that, knowing of the increasing tension between Pope Gregory VII and Henry IV of Germany, Odo hoped to offer his services to the Pope in hope of spiritual and, more importantly, secular rewards. One idea is that he hoped to reduce the Pope's dependence upon the support of Robert Guiscard.

He chose the wrong time to act. William was still annoyed over Pope Gregory's demands for his fealty. Having learned of Odo's manoeuvre, the King returned swiftly to England, arresting his brother on the Isle of Wight, just as he was about to embark for the Continent. He charged the Bishop with seeking to rob him of the service of his knights and of leading them away from their duty 'into foreign kingdoms across the Alps, with disregard for the interests of his king'. He brought up the matter of his spoliation of Canterbury lands, which he had still not released. One can see here also an echo of William's grievances against his son Robert. Even had the charge only been Odo's misgovernment of his earldom, that could have justified imprisonment.

In the hearing that followed it became clear that the judges did not dare impose a sentence on the bishop. He, for his part, denied the authority of the court, insisting that it had no right to try a bishop who ought to be judged only by the Pope (as Canon Law required). William resorted to casuistry. 'I condemn neither a cleric nor a bishop,' he is alleged to have said, 'but I can arrest my earl.' Odo was sentenced to perpetual imprisonment and sent to Rouen. He lived more under house arrest than as a prisoner. Curiously, his estates were not forfeited and he remained the largest lay landowner in England after the King. He remained a threat to his half-brother and his menace increased when Robert Curthose again chose to rebel.

Robert's personal reputation in Normandy had actually been increased by his first revolt, and King Philip saw to it that he remained a focal point for opposition to William. Before the end of 1083 William's isolation from members of his own family increased with the loss of his undoubtedly beloved wife Matilda. She died on 2 November and was buried in her nunnery at Caen, the Abbaye aux Dames. William's regime now faced a number of serious threats. That he reacted to them is certain but his movements during the next four years are only sketchily recorded. He had ensured the survival of his Anglo-Norman realm for some eight years by unremitting effort expended over wide areas against many enemies. Now the final crisis was upon him.

The year 1084 saw renewed trouble in Maine, where William had been unable to rely on his eldest son. William had been obliged to turn to Hubert of Sainte-Suzanne. Hubert had opposed the Duke in 1063 but, having been reconciled to him, returned to him the fiefs of Beaumont and Fresnay-sur-Sarthe. Hubert had been made Vicomte of Maine. But now, perhaps sensing some weakness in William's position, he recruited men from Burgundy (his wife's native land) and from Poitou, with the possible connivance of the Count of Anjou, and retired to his fortress at Sainte-Suzanne (on the frontier between Maine and Anjou) where he defied the King-Duke.

William entered Maine, where most of the castle garrison remained loyal, but did not yet dare to attack Sainte-Suzanne directly. It was a redoubtable stronghold on a rocky escarpment. He adopted his customary strategy, constructing entrenchments (still visible today), and there was a two-year siege. It is a sign of his complete control over England that his army included many Englishmen. Before the end of the year William left the siege in the capable hands of Count Alan the Red (of Richmond) and returned to England to deal with a new threat. Hubert held out until 1086 and then capitulated.

William was now alarmed by reports of a threat developing from Denmark. There, Cnut II, son and heir of Swein Estrithson, with the support of Robert the Frisian,[5] was preparing a fleet for the invasion of England. The King accordingly made his own preparations. He imported men and horses from Normandy to form an army reported to have been 'so vast ... that it was greater than any that had ever come into this country'.[6] Men were reported to have wondered whether such a vast army could be fed. The Bastard's answer was to billet his men all over England (the south and east) on his vassals 'according to the produce' of their estates.

The coastal districts, presumably those facing the North Sea, especially East Anglia, were laid waste to deprive any enemy of food. The result was a period of great hardship for the affected areas. But then William was informed that the expected invasion had been prevented from starting out so he was able to disband part of his host. As a precaution he held the other part in readiness throughout the winter. William himself held a crown-wearing at Christmas, at

Gloucester, and appointed three new bishops for London, Elmham and Chester. During the remainder of the year he held his Court, and crown-wearings, at Winchester and at Westminster, and at Whitsun he dubbed his son Henry to knighthood. However, the expected invasion never came. First, Cnut II's plans met with domestic opposition, which forced him to delay the attack, then, on 10 July 1086, he was assassinated while at prayer in the church at Odensee and the invasion went into the grave with him.[7]

But before the news of Cnut's death had reached England, and certainly in some way connected with the Danish threat, William had vitally important and serious discussions with his 'witan', as the Chronicler puts it, in Norman terms the 'Curia Regis' or Royal Council. He needed to know all 'about this land, how it was peopled and with what sort of men' and that led directly to the Great Survey known as Domesday. There is no real evidence that the Domesday Survey, as carried out, was William's own idea. More likely it was the work of a cleric who was in a position to know exactly what sort of records already existed to make such a survey feasible. But William must be credited with realising what could be done. His dominant will then drove the process to its completion.

William had initiated a remarkable venture. Commissioners were sent all over (most) of England and into all shires. A note written by Robert Losinga, Bishop of Hereford, says men were sent into areas where they themselves were unknown, no doubt to ensure impartiality.

The Chronicler was appalled. He wrote that the Commissioners were to ascertain how many hides there were in each shire, what land and livestock the King had there and what dues he should receive. King William wanted to know how much land his magnates, both lay and clerical, held and, says the writer, 'though I tell it at too great length, what or how much each man had ... in land or livestock, and how much money it was worth ... [so that] ... there was not one single hide, not one yard of land, not even, it is shameful to tell but it seemed no shame to him to do it, one ox, not one cow, not one pig was left out, that was not set down in his record'.[8] All the records were brought to William afterwards and, as he returned to Normandy that autumn, this description of the country must have been very rapidly completed. There is evidence that the survey caused disturbances in many areas.

Domesday is a multifaceted and fascinating document. It survives to the present day in two enormous volumes. Volume One, known as Great Domesday, comprises the returns, in condensed and abbreviated form, of thirty shires from Kent to Cheshire and from Cornwall to Yorkshire, excluding the far north of England, Durham, Westmoreland, Cumberland and most of Lancashire. Volume Two, or Little Domesday, in a much more comprehensive but less precisely ordered form, covers Norfolk, Suffolk and Essex. Most commentators conclude that the returns for this area were completed last and never reduced to the same format as that used for the other shires. There are also a number of documents containing similar material, which supplement the accounts in Domesday proper and cast light on how it was compiled. It owed a great deal to the strength and efficiency of the Old English administrative machinery of shire and hundred courts and the existence of geld rolls and juries, though a similar if much smaller-scale inquest had been held in Normandy in the 1070s under the direction of Bishop William of St Calais.

The commissioners divided the area surveyed into about seven circuits within which more or less the same layout of information is used but the circuits differ somewhat in the way the information is presented, so the descriptions of the various shires are by no means uniform, presenting great difficulties to those who study this invaluable document. In some ways it resembles a 'feudal book' (or 'feodary') in that it lists landholdings, starting with the King, passing to the higher clergy and abbeys and on to the greater magnates in descending order of rank and power, so allowing an estimate of the total amount of land each possessed. But it is also, especially Volume Two, a description of the country in terms of livestock, acreage, woodland, fisheries and many other things. But, perhaps above all, it records the geld, the land tax, which could be expected from each estate and estimates the annual value of each estate. It also wanted to know whether more could be got from the land than was then being taken.[9] A grant of land[10] in Surrey made in 1086 refers to the inclusion in the grant of 'scot, geld and all customs' and states that this was the 'money tax which is called geld in English'. It is dated 'after the description of all England'.

Domesday was also a great land tribunal which firstly recorded the unquestionable holdings of tenants in chief and their subtenants but then, in sections such as those termed 'clamores' deals with disputes over land, which seem to be reserved for King William to decide. It must have been intended as a solution to the legal and tenurial confusion that had arisen over the previous twenty years caused by the distribution of lands and the many acts of local tyranny and oppression that resulted from it. Ely records, for instance, show that lands lost by the Church since the Conquest, often at the hands of sheriffs like Picot of Cambridgeshire, could be recovered but that whether they were depended on William's decision. The abbey got little protection and struggled to regain its lands from 1075 to 1080.

Domesday stands as a monument to William's power and there is nothing like it anywhere else in eleventh-century Europe. It reflects his keen desire to know more about this land that he had conquered, and demonstrates an unparalleled thirst for knowledge on his part and an iron grip on the Norman lords and their English tenantry. It also reflects the depth of his avarice. As the *Chronicle* remarks in its notice of his death, 'He was fallen into avarice and he loved greediness above all.' It has been observed that 'the stark and grasping mind of the Conqueror is inescapable'.[11] Had he lived long enough, he would quite possibly have used Domesday to extract as much money from his subjects as he possibly could, by a policy of continuous unremitting exactions and extortions. A thegn, Aethelric of Marsh Gibbon (Buckinghamshire) lamented that he held his land 'at rent, heavily and wretchedly' whereas before 1066 he had held it freely.

Lastly, even in 1086, Domesday reflected the King's concern to establish his position as the lawful heir of Edward the Confessor. Harold II's reign is almost totally ignored (there are a few incautious errors) and William is presented as holding the royal estates of his predecessor, Edward, in such a way that one might be tempted to think England was never subjugated at all. All references to estates acquired by Harold, and in 1086 disputed by former clerical holders, are presented as illegal seizures acquired by force. Such phrases are used as 'Harold took it when he usurped the kingdom' or 'after the death of King Edward'. Above all, William is put before the reader as the sole lord of all land from whom all others owe their estates. Domesday reads back into the Old English past a dependency on the King that had never in fact existed. The English are recorded as part of a system of dependency (actually introduced by the Normans) which had already been part of the natural order of things. The Old English Kings were not, like William, the source of all tenure.

While the survey was being carried out, King William completed a review of his forces, travelling around the country, and by 1 August, he was at Salisbury. There he summoned his Council (the Curia Regis) 'and all the landholders who were of any account throughout England no matter whose vassals they might be' and required them to do homage, become his men and swear oaths of allegiance to him 'against all other men'.

It was certainly what would today be regarded as a security measure, to ensure the loyalty of all men of importance in the event of an invasion. It cannot have meant every landholder in the country or even men of the general knightly class. A twelfth-century source expanded the entry and listed 'archbishops, bishops, abbots, earls, barons, sheriffs with their knights'.[12] It almost certainly meant all men of that degree of importance plus what were later termed 'honorial barons', major tenants of the King's tenants-in-chief. That would not have involved an impossible number of men. William also extracted, in his customary manner, as much revenue as he could justifiably claim from his men. It is possible that the preliminary returns to the Domesday Survey were presented to the King, in unbound form. If so, this was the climax of the survey. He then went to Normandy by way of one of his useful staging posts, the Isle of Wight.

Little is recorded as occurring early in 1087 other than the issue of a charter confirming a gift made by Maurice the Chancellor, Bishop of London, to St Amand, Rouen. But William Rufus replaces Robert Curthose in the witness list, a sign of renewed tension between the King-Duke and his eldest son.

Perhaps in relation to the continuing dispute, William made a remarkable intervention in French affairs, by claiming rightful ownership of the whole of the Vexin, on the grounds that it had been granted to his father, Duke Robert, by King Henry I of France, though in fact, if any grant had been made, it was purely temporary and personal and had been rescinded when Robert died. William's claim to the Vexin, therefore, was wholly unjustified. He had never made the slightest attempt during his reign to act as though he had any rights there, so also casting doubt on other 'legitimate enterprises' embarked on by William. In prosecution of this claim to the Vexin, the King carried out an offensive campaign down the valley of the Seine towards Paris. It is just possible that William was reacting to an alleged witticism by King Philip, which had wounded his *amour propre*. Philip was reported to have remarked on the Conqueror's increased corpulence, observing sarcastically, on hearing that William had taken a drug to reduce his obesity, 'The

King of England lies in Rouen, keeping to his bed like a woman who has just had a baby!'

When this remark reached William he roared, 'By the Resurrection and Glory of God! When I go to mass after my lying in, I will offer a hundred thousand candles on his behalf!' Then, towards the end of August (setting out around 15 August), just as the harvest was ready, especially that of the wine, he invaded, ravaging all before him as he went. Entering Mantes, his forces killed many Frenchmen and bombarded the town with incendiary missiles so that it went up in flames and the Church of St Mary burnt to the ground.

According to William of Malmesbury, William, while urging his troops to add fuel to the fire, got too close to the blazing buildings, then was overcome by the heat and injured when his horse, presented with a steep ditch and burnt by flying embers, reared up violently. This threw the Conqueror's stomach against the pommel of his saddle, causing some internal injury. Racked with pain, he ordered his men to retreat and returned to Rouen where he took to his bed.

Doctors were summoned who inspected his urine (perhaps finding it stained with blood) and despaired of his life. William raged against fate, claiming that he had intended to reform his life but then, calming down, summoned priests to hear his confession and give him the Last Rites. The simplest account states that, although reluctant to do so, he gave way to pressure from his magnates and agreed that Robert should have the Duchy of Normandy and that England should be entrusted to William Rufus, while Henry was left the possessions of his mother Matilda.

All those the King had confined to prison were to be released and his treasure distributed to churches with a special sum earmarked for the rebuilding of the church he had destroyed at Mantes. So he set his affairs in order and prepared himself for death. He passed a peaceful night and early next morning, 9 September, hearing bells ringing he asked what they were and was told that the cathedral bell was ringing the hour of Prime. Raising his eyes to Heaven, it is said, he commended his soul to the Blessed Virgin Mary, whom he called his 'Lady', hoping that her prayers would reconcile him to 'our Lord Jesus Christ', and so breathed his last.

Chaos followed. With the death of a prince all rules were suspended until another took power. The great men and clergy who had gathered round the deathbed now scattered to the four winds, each returning to his fief to secure possession of it. The lesser attendants, deserted by the great lords, seized what they could, taking everything, arms, vessels, clothing and curtains, leaving William's body naked on the floor. When they heard the news the townsfolk of Rouen got drunk!

Eventually a semblance of order was restored and the canons and monks of the cathedral came in procession with cross and incense to the Abbey of Saint-Gervais where William's body lay, to perform the last rites. The Archbishop, William Bonne-Âme, announced that in accordance with his previous instructions, William's body was to be buried in St Stephen's, Caen (his Abbaye aux Hommes). But there were no Court officials available to order the embalming of the body for the journey. Instead, a simple knight of the neighbourhood, called Hellouin, took charge of the arrangements. The body was taken and transported from the port of Rouen and sent by sea and land to Caen wrapped in a cow's hide.

There the Abbot, Gilbert, and his monks met the cortège, probably at the port of Caen, but again, the reception of William's body was plunged into confusion. A fire broke out in a nearby house and the secular clergy and bystanders rushed off to put it out. Only the monks were left to carry the body to the abbey. Once there, all the Norman bishops and many of the abbots gathered for the funeral, even Bishop Odo, who had now been released.

A Mass for the dead was said and the sarcophagus which was to receive the body was placed in the grave prepared for it in front of the choir. The Bishop of Évreux, Gilbert, gave a funeral oration, referring to how William had more than any of his predecessors increased the power and prestige of Normandy, maintained justice and peace, chastised robbers and thieves, and protected priests and monks and the whole population. He then asked that anyone who had been injured by the deceased should pardon him and pray for his soul.[13] Yet again there was a disturbance. A man called Asselin, son of Arthur, in a loud voice declared that the abbey had been built on some land belonging to his father for which he had never been paid! Some of those present were able to confirm the truth of his claim. The clergy conferred rapidly among themselves and agreed to pay compensation. Asselin demanded sixty sous, the value of the ground containing the Duke's grave.[14]

One final indignity was reported. When they came to put the body into the sarcophagus, it was found to be too narrow to receive it and it had to be forced into it with the result that the swollen body burst and a terrible stench arose which even the smoke from the incense was unable to conceal. Only Orderic mentions this macabre incident and gives no source for the story. Yet when the tomb was opened four hundred and fifty years later, it was said to have been observed that the body was in a good state of preservation so the embalming had done its work properly. Perhaps Orderic just could not resist the temptation to include a scandalous rumour.

Contemporary sources do not name any laymen as present at the funeral but later sources suggest that the youngest son, Henry, was there (as was William's half-brother Bishop Odo). As for William's other half-brother, Robert, Count of Mortain, and Roger of Montgomery, his old associate, it seems that reasons of State had kept them in England. The other lords were meanwhile taking the opportunity, presented by the eclipse of public authority, to enrich themselves. They drove out the garrisons of the royal castles and took lands they had long envied into their hands. This state of affairs continued until Robert Curthose assumed the dukedom.

William Rufus was not present when his father died. He had been given a letter from William addressed to Archbishop Lanfranc. The King had told his son to take it to the Archbishop. Rufus learned of his father's death just as he was about to embark for England. It had been of the utmost importance that Rufus should get to England and take possession of the kingdom. His first act on arrival was to take control of the royal treasure. Then, with the support of Lanfranc, who had been responsible for his education and knighted him, his coronation was effected and he took peaceful control of the kingdom at least until winter was over.

So ended the reign of William, Bastard Duke of Normandy and Conqueror of England.

18

CHARACTER & ACHIEVEMENTS

One way of evaluating the character and achievements of William the Conqueror is to begin with the assessment provided by Orderic Vitalis. He wrote an account of the Conqueror's last days and in doing so put into William's mouth, in the manner of Roman historians, a great speech, which is in fact the vehicle for Orderic's own opinions. It could be that some of what is said is derived from stories related by those who were there and with whom, like Gilbert, Bishop of Lisieux, Orderic had contact, directly or indirectly. This enabled the writer to create an authentic-seeming atmosphere.

William died surrounded by a group of magnates and higher clergy and the members of his own ducal household. Despite increasing pain he had retained his faculties and was capable of rational discourse. Those present must certainly have passed on their own recollections of what the dying King said but it is not possible to distinguish any such recollections from Orderic's own views.

William, as a pious Christian, would have repented of his sins, particularly of the blood he had shed or caused to be shed. He would have made his last confession and have received absolution and the Last Rites of the Church. Orderic provides a highly coloured account of the wrangling over the succession to the Duchy of Normandy and the Crown of England. His instincts as a historian led him to maintain that William had been conscious of the fact that he owed his crown to victory in battle rather than, as he insistently proclaimed, his hereditary right derived from the bequest of King Edward the Confessor. His conquest of England had cost many lives.

Accordingly, Orderic concludes that he would not have dared to leave the Crown of England to anyone other than God. It could be that Orderic was hinting at English feelings on the matter and so wishes to convey the idea that the succession rested in the hands of God. Orderic would have known of the Vision of Bishop

Britwald.[1] The Bishop was believed to have had a vision of St Peter in conversation with 'a seemly man' (usually taken to signify Edward himself), whom he consecrated as King. When asked who would then be that King's successor, the saint replied, 'The Kingdom of the English is of God and after you he has already provided a King according to His Will.' The statement is ambiguous. It could just as well have been intended to apply to Edith's brother, Earl Harold, as to the Norman Duke. But of course, Hastings was considered by churchmen to have been the judgement of God against the Earl.

Orderic records the designation of William's eldest son as his successor to the dukedom, in accord with both ducal and lordly Norman custom. William fitzOsbern, for example, had left his Norman lordship of Breteuil to his elder son William, and his English estates to his younger son, Roger. Duke Robert had left the dukedom to William, following the custom of his predecessors. Orderic, using hindsight, comments through William that 'the country which is subject to his [Robert Curthose's] dominion will be truly wretched'.

The account correctly states that King William gave his son William Rufus a letter addressed to Archbishop Lanfranc and ordered him to leave immediately for England. Rufus had reached the port of Wissant and was about to cross the Channel when he was told of his father's death. He hurried off to England and, with Lanfranc's support, secured the crown for himself. Orderic reconciles the conflict of ideas by claiming that William had expressed the hope that God would see fit to grant England to Rufus.

Under some pressure from those around him, the dying King recognised Robert as his successor in Normandy and gave to his youngest son, Henry, the sum of 5,000 pounds (one and a quarter million silver pennies). Henry was said to have complained that he was being less well treated than his brothers. Orderic relates that William told him, 'Remain calm my son, trust in God and leave your brothers to enjoy the privileges of seniority. Your hour will come and you will possess all that I have left and surpass them in wealth and power.' By the time Orderic wrote this, that 'prophecy' had certainly come to pass.

That division of the Anglo-Norman realm between Robert and Rufus was to cause great difficulty over the next two generations and beyond. Orderic hints at this by including in his account a reference by William to the warning of Christ in the Gospel that a kingdom divided against itself could not stand.

Orderic's judgement on William begins with the assertion that he 'was bred to arms from childhood' and that as a result he was 'stained with the rivers of blood' he had shed. He reminds the reader that William's own Norman subjects had often conspired against him and concludes from that that the Normans required 'a kind but firm master' because they were 'eager for rebellion, ripe for tumults and ready for every sort of crime'. He then provides a thumbnail sketch of William's reign from Guy of Burgundy's rebellion to the battle of Mortemer, and says that William had 'placed a royal diadem' on his brow, 'acquired by the Grace of God not by hereditary right'. So Orderic, in common with other Anglo-Norman writers, implicitly rejects the claim that William owed his crown to a promise of the succession by King Edward.

William is made to boast how he overcame the city of Exeter and then Chester, Northumbria, the Scots, the Welsh and the Danes. Orderic himself evidently shares Norman pride in these achievements. But he was of the opinion that William had to have been 'a prey to cruel fears and anxieties' because of the barbarities that he had committed. Elsewhere in his history, Orderic, commenting on the harrying of the North, writes, 'I dare not commend him. He levelled both the bad and the good in one common ruin by a consuming famine ... he was ... guilty of wholesale massacre ... and barbarous homicide.'

If William ever intended to create an Anglo-Norman government and aristocracy, then he must have been a very disappointed man by the time he died. His reign saw a continuous atmosphere of recurring crisis, and he never realised where his actions were leading him. In a sense he never 'governed' England at all. His visits were more like tours of inspection than periods of real government. He rested heavily on the prestige gained by a successful career as Duke of Normandy and in his government of England leaned heavily on the support of Bishop Odo, Archbishop Lanfranc and Bishop Geoffrey of Coutances. His overseas wars were financed out of English resources. As the *Chronicle*, 1085, laconically observed, 'He obtained a very great amount of money from his men where he had any pretext for it, either justly or unjustly. Afterwards he went into Normandy.'

Orderic provides the reader with his own judgement on the Conquest. He has William confess, 'I did not attain that high honour by hereditary right but wrested it from the perjured Harold in a desperate battle with much effusion of human blood ... by the slaughter and banishment of his adherents ... I subjugated England to my rule. I have persecuted its native inhabitants beyond all reason ... and ... cruelly oppressed them.' Thus he at once denies William's claim to be King Edward's heir and, by implication, denies that he ever intended to include the English nobility in the government of the kingdom. He also laments the fall of the English aristocracy and says that their conquerors 'grew wealthy on the spoils of England whilst their sons were either shamefully slain or driven as exiles to wander hopelessly through foreign kingdoms'.

William of Malmesbury also makes a similar judgement, albeit less stridently. He asserts that William was 'somewhat too harsh towards the English' because he found them untrustworthy. This 'so exasperated his ferocity that he deprived the more powerful of them first of their revenues and then of their lands'. He tells his readers that William 'established it as a regular practice, by proclamation, that he would allow no one of English nationality, whether monk or cleric, to aspire to any dignity' so he governed the country by 'a mixture of mildness towards the submissive and severity towards rebels'. Like Orderic he speaks of the devastation meted out to northern England, which was 'hamstrung by fire, rapine and bloodshed ... the ground for 60 miles left uncultivated, the soil quite bare even down to today.' The Conquest, he says, was 'a fatal disaster for our dear country as she exchanged new masters for old'. He says this while admitting that 'the Normans ... have my loyalty'. Malmesbury was puzzled by King William's love of money, so unscrupulous was he in the means he used to obtain it. He thought the King feared his enemies and that this drove him to 'squeeze the money from his provinces' in a manner unworthy of so great a monarch.

In the *Roman de Rou*, Robert Wace also condemns the Conqueror. He puts into William's mouth the following confession, 'I conquered England wrongly; many men died wrongly there ... and I took the kingdom wrongly. What I have wrongly taken, to which I have no right at all, I ought not to give to my sons.'

On the credit side Orderic praises William for his generosity towards the Church, and claims that he was never guilty of simony (the buying and selling of holy things, especially bishoprics and abbacies) and 'made a choice of prelates directed by meritorious conduct and wise doctrine', choosing the most worthy. That latter verdict was contested by Eadmer, who says that his choices would have been deemed unworthy had they not been obedient to William's laws and never dared raise their heads against him. They also happened on so many occasions to have been chosen from among those who served him well in his household.

Nonetheless, William, by appointing so well-qualified a man as Lanfranc and introducing Norman bishops and abbots, did move the Church in England into the mainstream of European Christianity. But he did this while allowing the exploitation of Church lands. The 'Old Minsters', such a distinctive feature of the Old English Church, were annexed to the new cathedrals as prebends for their canons. Some were engulfed by the baileys of royal and baronial castles, becoming chapels for the use of the castellan. They had mostly disappeared by 1086. They were replaced by a system of local churches each with its own parish, a process which altered the English landscape. In the long run this would have been beneficial to the religious life of the people.

One thing that did result from William's rule was the introduction of a thorough-going process of rebuilding. Old English cathedrals and monastic buildings disappeared entirely. Their remains are to be found only under the foundations of the vast Norman 'Romanesque' replacements. This can be seen as a deliberate attempt to erase Old English piety from the religious landscape, along with the cults of many English saints. As for the local churches, the majority of those built or rebuilt between the Conquest and the mid-twelfth century cannot be safely classified as either 'Saxon' or 'Norman', instead a hybrid form developed.

This rebuilding has been rightly characterised as due to the 'trauma of the Conquest'² because the momentum of rebuilding continued throughout William's reign and beyond. Some of these churches were the work of the surviving English tenants, who may have felt the need for permanent public monuments as a means of preserving their identity, so the rebuilding marks the permanence of the new parochial system. A high proportion of local tithes were granted away to Norman churches and monasteries. All this was an effect of the reform of the Church under William and his Archbishop, Lanfranc.

Despite the known examples of poorly chosen abbots, such as Turold at Malmesbury and then Peterborough, Thurstan at Glastonbury (who went to war against his own monks), monastic life was improved under William's rule, mainly thanks to the introduction of Norman monks. It is also the case that the Church acquired greater coherence and became more cultured, on the Norman pattern. Synods were held which endeavoured to bring the Church up to the best standards of the age. The real point is, though, that William remained the master, and reform was only possible because, and to the extent that, he supported it.

He showed this in his relations with the papacy. As soon as he could dispense with the support of the Pope he did so, resisting every political claim by Gregory VII. Accordingly, Gregory never dared to raise the question of lay investitures with William. He could not risk William transferring his support to the anti-Pope put up by the Emperor.

Overall, the long struggle, which had occupied most of William's early years as Duke, has to be borne in mind in any estimate of his character and achievements. He had been involved for some years in a defensive war, and there were only twelve years separating Mortemer from Hastings. The strength of Normandy in 1066, which enabled William to effect a successful invasion and conquest, is in strong contrast to its weakness when he became Duke. This can be attributed in no small measure to his strength of character and to the way in which he successfully harnessed the Norman aristocracy and Church hierarchy to his purposes.

He must be credited with a personality hardened not only in the fires of internecine warfare but in the furnace of a disadvantaged childhood. He had been deprived of the love of both his mother, who was married off to another man, and of a father, who had deserted him to go on pilgrimage. That personality later enabled him to persuade the aristocracy to contribute to the strength and unity of the duchy. But that same personality also brooked no opposition, as the English found to their cost.

Despite the harshness of his character and his known propensity for violence and cruelty, he was a faithful husband to Matilda. The marriage is regarded as having been a happy one, despite the twelfth-century slanders to the contrary. It was certainly a fruitful one. William and Matilda had four sons, three of whom survived to manhood. Two became Kings of England after their father. These sons were Robert, later Duke of Normandy, Richard, who was accidentally killed in the New Forest (probably between 1070 and 1080) while still quite young, William Rufus and Henry.

There were also at least six daughters. They are, not necessarily in order of birth, Agatha, Adeliza, Cecily, Adela, Constance and

Matilda. Four of these can be confidently identified. Cecily, born before 1066, became a nun and Abbess of Holy Trinity, Caen. Adela married, in 1080, Stephen I, Count of Blois. She died in 1137. Constance married, in 1086, Alan IV, Count of Brittany. She died in 1090. Matilda is recorded in an entry in Domesday Book,[3] and an entry referring to Geoffrey the Chamberlain also mentions the King's daughter, Matilda.

The others, Agatha and Adeliza, are more difficult to sort out. William of Poitiers asserts that a daughter, whose name is not given, was betrothed to Count Herbert of Maine and that another daughter, whom he does not name, was sought in marriage by two rival brother Kings of Spain, one of whom was probably Alfonso IV of Leon. William of Poitiers also implies that another daughter, who he again fails to name, was betrothed to Earl Harold. Orderic Vitalis claims that a daughter he names as Agatha was betrothed first to Earl Harold and then to Alfonso. She refused to go to Spain and died a virgin. Adeliza, he claims, took religious vows early in life and lived on under the protection of Roger of Beaumont. William of Malmesbury also refers to two unnamed daughters who are betrothed respectively to Harold and Alfonso. Robert of Torigny, a very late source, names Adeliza as the betrothed of Harold.

But William of Malmesbury's account of Harold's betrothal is more precise and asserts that Harold declared himself 'released from his oath because William's daughter, to whom he had been betrothed, died before she was old enough to be married'. Malmesbury adds elsewhere that this daughter 'was not yet of age' (which explained why this was a betrothal not a marriage).[4] He names three of William's daughters: Cecily, Constance and Adela and says there were two more whose 'names I have forgotten', one of whom, who 'died before she was old enough to marry', was betrothed to Harold and the other to Alfonso of Galicia. This would seem to be better founded than Orderic's view since a daughter who died young before 1066 could not also have been betrothed to Alfonso. It looks very much as though Alfonso's betrothed was called Agatha. The other named daughter, Adeliza, identified by Robert of Torigny, might well have been intended for Harold and could, having taken a vow, have been put under the care of Roger of Beaumont only to die before 1066. The 'Aelfgifu' of the Bayeux Tapestry might then have been an Anglicisation of Adeliza. (Note that *aðel* (adel) means noble and that one view of the name Aelfgifu is that it was a noble title given to queens.) But such is the confusion in the sources that complete certainty about all of William's daughters is unattainable.

In Normandy, the new Norman aristocracy was encouraged to take over from the ducal family the task of reviving Norman monasticism. The new Norman episcopate brought about a spectacular revival of the province of Rouen. It was King William who promoted these bishops and abbots. The Normans then proceeded to apply the same policies to the revival of religion in England as they had used in Normandy. William helped bring this about by identifying himself with the aims of the new aristocracy and by enriching them with the spoils of England.

But that the invasion and its success had anything to do with long-standing pre-existing Norman links with England is much more questionable. The link through Emma's marriage to King Aethelred was a tenuous one. She was more or less disowned by her Norman family after she married Cnut. The concept of any intention to invade England and restore Emma's son to its throne is more myth than substance. The Normans who chose to accompany Edward to England had no observable connection with the aristocracy in Normandy and Edward's choice of Robert Champart as Archbishop of Canterbury owed more to personal friendship than a love of Normandy.

From 1052 onwards until 1064 there is no sign of any connection between the Norman Duke and the English King, preoccupied as the latter was with his religious devotions and his project of Westminster. Nor is there any sign of Norman interest in English affairs. The seeds of the Norman Conquest lie in the ambitions of a duke ruling a duchy which sought the independence that attended the status of a monarchy. William wanted the trappings and prestige that came with Kingship and seized upon the opportunity which came his way, when Earl Harold fell into his hands, to handicap fatally the man he no doubt saw as his most serious rival for the crown.

This occurred just after Normandy's position had been rapidly transformed by the deaths of William's most dangerous neighbours, Henry I of France and Geoffrey Martel of Anjou. The acquisition of Maine, by means which eerily foreshadow those employed to justify the invasion of England, also altered the balance of power in northern France to William's advantage. The invasion of Brittany neutralised any threat from that quarter just as the Northumbrian revolt of 1065 weakened Harold's position, depriving him of the support of his brother Earl Tostig.

So the application of political and diplomatic power by a formidable duke made the Conquest possible. Its achievement was materially assisted by the propaganda employed to justify it. Duke William made use of a variety of diverse facts put together in a specious unity and used them to justify the Conquest: the murder of Alfred the Aetheling, the occupation of the See of St Augustine by a schismatic archbishop, the alleged solemn promise of a venerable king, and an equally solemn promise alleged to have been made by his successor, to brand Earl Harold as a perjurer and usurper; all this became a legal brief which won the blessing of a pro-Norman Pope, giving the invasion of England the appearance of a holy war. That has been characterised as a triumph for William's diplomacy, which in itself was probably inspired by contemporary Norman ambitions.

As a result, England was conquered, a great achievement in itself. The Old English aristocracy was replaced by a new foreign nobility. William also achieved domination over the English Church, which enabled him to sponsor reforms acceptable to Rome. He assumed all the sacred prestige of a consecrated monarchy, relating it to the religious sanctions claimed for the Norman enterprise, and both extended and deepened its impact on the people, so disguising to some extent the brute fact that he was a conqueror. For his own purposes he employed the English government and administration, constantly appealing in the great trials, which were such a marked feature of his reign, to Old English Law (when it suited him). This enabled him to effect the complete transfer of property from English into Norman hands without plunging the country into anarchy. Above all he preserved his Anglo-Norman kingdom, which he must have seen as involving a single problem, so that all of his campaigns as king had a common purpose.

Nonetheless, he was a harsh and unlovable man, savage in war and guilty of the horrible devastation of northern England. In forming the New Forest he wasted the countryside for his sport. He was feared but also respected. His will to power was as great as that of any of the powerful rulers, many of them tyrants, the world has seen since. The efficient administration over which he presided must be set against his ruthless demand for money. He was judged by contemporaries to be 'stern beyond measure' though he also provided good order.

Nevertheless, his harsh childhood is thought by some to have bred in him a ruthless cynicism and even caused him to parade his piety as an aid to his quest for power. But that display of piety could well have led to a dependence upon religion. One demonstration of his piety was that he so honoured the memory of his father, Duke Robert, that he tried to have his body brought back to Normandy, though not until near the end of his own life. The result was that the man entrusted with the mission, hearing that William was dead, settled in Apulia and buried Duke Robert's remains there. Another effect of William's religious belief was that ruthlessness and cruelty could breed fear of damnation and that would explain his gifts to churches, lavishly bestowing much English property on churches in Normandy and elsewhere, and the founding of monasteries. It also goes some way to explain his need to secure papal approval for his invasion of England and testifies at the same time to his sincerity.

In religion he was a pious and conventionally 'good Christian', having been taught discipline in childhood and obedience to the requirements of the Church. He attended divine worship morning and evening and regularly attended Mass. The monk of Caen[5] pays tribute in a conventional manner to his wisdom, his magnanimity, his bravery and his perseverance. When one considers his custom of tempering justice with mercy in his treatment of those who rebelled against him, one is reminded of Edmund Burke's aphorism, 'Magnanimity in politics is not seldom the truest wisdom.'

He elicited constant support from the hard-faced men who surrounded him and could always suit his policy to opportunity. His energy was untiring to the end, but while it is perhaps possible to attribute to him a genius for leadership, it remains more doubtful whether this extended to his military abilities. He did, in his mid-twenties, capture Domfront and Alençon, successfully besiege Arques, and repel an invasion by the French King, but in his career he won only one major pitched battle. All the rest of his military campaigns comprised sieges and skirmishes, often against inferior opponents. He never drove another army from the field nor successfully stormed any castle. His enemies grew stronger and the times of Norman expansion came to an end. His most striking achievement was that he survived everything fate threw at him until his horse stumbled at Mantes.

Although credited with constructive statesmanship for the way in which he governed England, this was surely more of a tribute to the strength, resilience and effectiveness of the Old English administration that he inherited. His policy aims were limited to the concerns of his own lifetime. In this he was no better, nor worse, than his rivals Fulk Nerra and Geoffrey Martel.

Some attempt ought perhaps to be made to suggest what sort of physical presence and appearance should be attributed to King William. He is, of course, shown in the Bayeux Tapestry in both civil and military dress, But here one has only an image, not a portrait, and one that is no more realistic than the images to be found on his coinage. In civil dress he wears a long tunic and a cloak and is seen holding a sword, probably a sort of badge of ducal office. His hair is that of a warrior, cut short and combed forward 'en brosse', like a crew cut, and his neck and back of the head are shaven. Leading his men towards Brittany he wears a padded tunic (over which his hauberk or coat of mail would be worn in battle) and carries a baton. Enthroned in the scene where Earl Harold swears the oath, the Duke wears a full-length robe and a large and heavy cloak, not unlike that worn by Harold when enthroned as King. Contemporary accounts suggest a man who was majestic when both seated and standing, and so capable of overawing his audience.

Rather more can be gathered from the account of his death written by the anonymous monk of Caen. He is described as 'great in body and strong, tall in stature but not ungainly'. Orderic Vitalis comments that at the time of the incident which led to his death he was corpulent but that would apply only to his last few years. There are several references to his bodily strength and powers of endurance, indicative of a tough, hardy warrior. On one occasion, while inspecting the terrain around Hastings, he carried back to camp the coat of mail of his companion William fitzOsbern as well as his own. Like his rival, Earl Harold, he was well accustomed to the rigours of a military campaign. His health was remarkably good, with few recorded instances of illness. William of Malmesbury describes him as 'of proper height, immensely stout, with a ferocious expression and a high bald forehead'. His arms were strong and he was able to fire arrows from his bow while riding his horse at the gallop.

He is credited with a harsh, perhaps guttural, voice, which he could soften when being persuasive. In speech he was fluent and expressed his will with clarity. As befitted a soldier, he was temperate in eating and drinking, abhorring drunkenness in others. In his marriage he seems to have been a devoted husband and perhaps deserves to be called chaste (*celebs*) in the sense in which that word was used of

Earl Tostig (who, like William, certainly had children) and of Edward the Confessor. There is no evidence of youthful licentiousness nor of marital infidelity and there is no record of any illegitimate children.

In 1522, at the demand of three clergy from Rome, a cardinal, an archbishop and a bishop (according to the sixteenth-century Caen historian Charles de Bras), the Abbot of the Abbaye aux Hommes, Charles de Martigny, permitted the Conqueror's tomb to be opened so that the body could be viewed. It was found in a state of perfect preservation, which casts some doubt on the story that his corpse burst when placed in its sarcophagus. It was described as the body of a large man with notably long arms and legs. Accordingly a local artist was employed to make a painting of the embalmed corpse and that picture was then exhibited in the abbey's church for many years. Unfortunately the tomb was robbed and despoiled in 1562 during the religious wars and only a femur survives of the King's body. The original of the painting has also vanished.

The femur permits the estimate that William was a man of about five feet ten inches in height, a good height for the eleventh century if somewhat shorter therefore than his rival King Harold. There is an astonishing contrast here with what is known of his wife Matilda, who was remarkably short. The casket containing her bones was opened in 1961, and the body estimated to have been that of a woman about four feet two inches tall. This diminutive lady must have been a most formidable character in her own right.

Although the painting of 1522 no longer exists, it is known that Charles de Bras found it a few years after 1562 in the house of a gaoler called Pierre Hocdé.[6] He kept it in his own possession, hoping to have it restored and put back in the abbey. No more is known of its fate but during the eighteenth century in several of the galleries of the abbey there were paintings made of both William and his wife Matilda. One of those of William, painted in 1708, is preserved to this day. It bears an inscription stating that the monks of the abbey had had a copy made, in homage and recognition of their benefactor, of the 'authentic portrait' of William, Duke of Normandy, which had been painted on an ancient panel (that is, on wood). It says 'An. 1708. Saint-Martin pinxit'. If that old panel had been the wooden plaque or wall panel recovered by Charles de Bras, then the 'authentic likeness' (literally 'genuina effigies') of 1522 might have been copied in 1708.

If Saint-Martin copied the original correctly, then it shows William I dressed in an early-sixteenth-century manner not unlike that of a portrait of King Francis I, of the School of Jean Clouet, *c.* 1525. Its most striking feature is its resemblance to the well-known contemporary portraits of Henry VIII! It is not impossible, though inherently unprovable, that this shows the personal appearance of William himself. The painter might well have been influenced by Holbein's paintings of King Henry. Nonetheless, it is possible that like Henry he could, as the portrait shows, have been a man massive in bulk, with full-fleshed face and red or russet hair.

The resemblance of King William to Henry VIII perhaps extended beyond their physical appearance. Both were capable of great cruelty and brutality, were fond of money and insisted on dominance over the Church in England. Both men could merit the description of King William in the *Peterborough Chronicle* (by one who had 'looked upon him and once lived in his court'): 'A very wise man and very powerful and more worshipful and stronger than any predecessor had been ... stern beyond all measure to those who opposed his will ... so that no one dared do anything against his will.'

NOTES

1. Normandy in the Early Eleventh Century

1. Sister of Count Geoffrey of Rennes, who had himself married Hawisa, sister of Duke Robert II.

2. He was later moved to St Ouen in Rouen where he became abbot, dying in old age in 1092.

3. His parents were married at the latest by 1008 and he had three sisters as well as an elder brother. It is unknown whether the sisters were older or younger, hence the uncertainty.

4. Duke Robert should not be named 'the Devil' as used to be the case. That appellation arose from confusion between the Duke and a mythical character invented in the twelfth century.

5. Interdict; a ban on the conduct of all religious services, especially the Mass and the Sacraments.

6. He had acquired fiefs from the King of France and the Count of Maine as well as those given him by Richard III. 'Talvas' means 'butcher'.

7. This was the fleet that was allegedly intended for an invasion of England on behalf of the exiled Aethelings.

8. *Gesta Normannorum Ducum* (GND).

9. Just like Duke William's fleet in August 1066.

10. GND VI 10 (17).

2. Birth & Upbringing of the Bastard

1. The present keep was built in the time of Henry I, but guides for many years liked to point out to tourists the very window involved as that of the room in which Duke William was born.

2. See *Roman de Rou*, Wace, Part 3 v. 2823–2922, and Benoît de Sainte-Maure, *Chroniques des Ducs de Normandie*, v. 33445–34008.

3. *Gesta Regum* 229.

4. It might even be cited as an early example of 'Droit de Seigneur'.

5. See William of Jumièges.

6. *Gesta Regum* 229.

7. See Orderic Vitalis, William of Malmesbury and Robert Wace.

8. *Chronique*, vol. I, p. 34.

9. William's connection with tanning remained well known for decades. It is said that Bishop Hugh of Lincoln, coming across Henry II sitting in a forest repairing his hunting glove, remarked, 'Still at the family trade I see!'

10. Book V. III. 42.

11. *Gesta Regum* 229.

12. 'Talvas' means 'butcher'.

13. Cited by Barlow; William I and the Norman Conquest.

14. Some date the charter to 1040, which raises doubts, but it could be that completion of the charter came in 1040 after the building of the church was completed. Ducal charters in Normandy were drawn up by the beneficiaries since there was no ducal writing office.

15. He is termed either 'nutricius' or 'pegagogus'. Nutricius bears the meaning 'protector' and pedagogus is obviously teacher or tutor.

16. Charters exist which describe William as Robert's successor; Faroux Nos 60 and 89.

17. Work of Bishop Hugh himself; vol. I, No. xxi covering 1035–37.

18. He was known as the 'Moor Eater' as Spanish Moslems were termed Moors.

19. He was son of a certain Ralph de Tosny, who had acquired or inherited lands held from the Archbishopric of Rouen. Ralph had been castellan of Tillières under Richard II and went off to Italy.

3. Minority

1. GND VI 2, VII 1. Orderic III 86, IV 82. Faroux Charters Nos 220, 259, 262.

2. Some were identified later in the interpolations made by Orderic Vitalis in his edition of the *Gesta Normannorum Ducum* (GND).

3. There were the usual scurrilous suggestions that he had been poisoned.

4. Revived after 1001 by Duke Richard II, who appointed the distinguished monk William of Volpiano as its abbot.

5. Orderic states that there was a pre-existing quarrel between

Gilbert and the sons of Géré. They had been raised by Gilbert in his household along with the young Duke but had been led to believe that Gilbert had somehow deceived them.

6. Orderic interpolating William of Jumièges, pp. 153–54.

7. Charter RADN 100 *c.* 1039.

8. Dukes of Normandy were also Counts of Rouen.

9. RADN No. 100.

10. He was a 'fils du feu' or bastard of Archbishop Robert.

11. Possibly it was not really an accident. The church would have needed to be reconsecrated and perhaps Ivo had plans to build a stone church.

12. Also called 'Malcouronne' or Evil Tonsure as he preferred the military life to that of a monk.

13. Principally William of Jumièges and William of Poitiers.

14. Henry of Huntingdon, p. 189–90, 'fiscus regale'.

4. The Struggle for Survival

1. J. Loth, *La Cathédral de Rouen*, 1879.

2. Tapestry Plates xiii, xvii, xxvii, li.

3. A little way south of Cherbourg.

4. The account of Hubert's actions has all the hallmarks of a 'topos' or conventional anecdote typical of epic poetry and the Chansons de Geste.

5. Not 'God help us'!

6. A saying popular among country people in Wace's time.

5. The Defeat of the Richardides

1. Hugh of Flavigny, biographer of Richard of Saint-Vanne, blames the failure of his initiative in 1042 on 'certain men of ill-will' who preferred the customs of their fathers to Richard's 'novel ideas'.
They opposed the Peace of God initiative and, says Hugh, God visited Normandy with an outbreak of 'Holy Fire' (possibly erysipelas). So the bishops summoned by Mauger gave up.

2. These MSS are found at Rouen, Douai, Laon, Paris, Wolfenbüttel and the Vatican and are copies sent to the various bishops and to Rome.

3. Ordeal; in which a man had to carry a red-hot bar of iron a short distance.

4. That was achieved if the man's hands blistered and festered.

5. *Miracula Sancti Vulfranni.*

6. *Chron. Tours*, p. 107.

7. Betrothals were much more solemn than an engagement and were seen to be almost as binding as marriage itself.

8. It was certainly before 1053. Matilda is labelled 'consort' in a charter of that year for Holy Trinity, No. xxxvii.

9. The purchase of office in the Church.

10. A relationship generated by a marriage.

11. It was once thought possible that Matilda had been married previously to Gerbod, Advocate of St Bertin. But this particular canard has long been exploded. In particular because, as her parents had married after 1031, and Matilda was not their eldest child, she would have been too young.

12. The originator of the offence; see Acts of the Apostles.

13. See Zumthor, *Guillaume le Conquérant.*

14. A ban on all church services and refusal of the sacraments.

15. Abbot John had been set upon by the inhabitants of Radicofani and Acquapendente, during his return journey, and he wrote to complain of this to the Pope, demanding compensation. He mentions the cases of Theobald of Blois and Renaud of Burgundy, who had defied papal decisions concerning their marriages. This implies that the Norman case had been raised at Rome.

16. Compare the exile in 1055 of Earl Aelfgar of East Anglia by King Edward the Confessor.

17. There are many examples recorded in the *Heimskringla* of Snorri Sturlason and several in the *Anglo-Saxon Chronicle.*

6. Foreign Affairs 1047–1061

1. A vast 'motte' and great ditch is still to be seen there.

2. Enguerand of Ponthieu's sister had married William of Arques at about the time that Anjou and France were reconciled.

3. Son of Haimo de Medano.

4. So William of Poitiers reports.

5. Curiously, Geoffrey of Mayenne figures in Geoffrey Gaimar's account of the outlaw Hereward. He claims that Hereward had fought in Maine early in his career where he had 'slain Gauter (Walter) del Bois and kept lord Geoffrey del Maine in prison a week'.

6. It lay on the frontier with Blois and Chartres.

7. Orderic Vitalis ii 73.

8. Ibid. ii 80–91.

9. That is, they paid an agreed sum equal to the amount of tax they were expected to collect and then collected the money from those who owed it, setting the rate high enough to make a profit for themselves.

10. Offences reserved for judgement by the King.

7. The Duke in Church ... & State

1. D. C. Douglas.

2. Though it might not have been imposed when the grant of land was first made prior to 1050.

3. Called 'Norman' in England.

4. 'Doctor Goebbels with two heads' (i.e. William of Poitiers and William of Jumièges) and 'nauseating sycophant' are but two critical comments.

5. It was a debate over whether the 'substance' (the unseen substrate imperceptible to the senses which underlies all matter in Aristotelian philosophy) of the Bread and Wine could be changed while the 'appearances' (colour, taste, etc.) remained after Consecration, or was replaced by the 'substance' of the Body, Blood and Divinity of Christ. Berengar's view was close to Martin Luther's doctrine of 'Consubstantiation' in which both substances are present in the Eucharist.

6. David Bates, *William the Conqueror*.

7. Bourg; a town or more specifically a market town.

8. Zumthor, *Guillaume le Conquérant*.

8. The Matter of England

1. S 998 I, Edward, king, bearing the royal dignity.

2. Now attributed to John of Worcester, previously known only as the Continuator.

3. Worcester version 1051.

4. Chronicle versions C, D and E from Abingdon, Worcester and Peterborough.

5. See *Regesta Regum Anglo-Normannorum*, Bates, No. 11, in the names of Willelm Cing and Willem eorl.

6. Edward that is. E. van Houts dates this, if true, to between mid-

Lent 1051 and 8 June.

7. GND VII 31.

8. Some think he last wrote about England in about 1060.

9. Faroux Charters Nos 69, 70, 73, 76 and 85.

10. See *Encomium Emmae*.

11. *Vita Edwardi Regis*, p. 8.

12. The outward sign of his recognition as archbishop by the Pope.

13. Robert fitz Wymarc, Clavering.

14. Peterborough 'E' 1052 based here on a text, now lost, from St Augustine's, Canterbury.

15. They were probably among the hostages exchanged between the King by Earl Godwin during the negotiations in 1051.

16. Ewias Harold, Herefordshire.

17. That is, 'Florence' of Worcester.

18. Peterborough 'E' based here on a text from St Augustine's, Canterbury.

9. William Consolidates his Hold on Normandy: Harold Becomes his Prisoner

1. My italics.

2. *England before the Norman Conquest*, p. 630.

3. Bayeux Tapestry Plate 15.

4. *Historia Novella*, pp. 6–8.

5. *Heimskringla* 76.

6. *Gesta Regum* 228, 2.

7. *History of the English* II 25.

8. In his interpolations into the text of William of Jumièges.

9. Plate numbers are those used in *English Historical Documents* vol. II.

10. Plate 25.

11. Plates 36, 37.

12. Eadmer, *Historia Novella*.

13. The argument is that of Sir Frank Merry Stenton.

14. GR ii 228. He also says that Harold was given the hand of the Duke's daughter.

15. This argument is that of Garnett, *Conquered England*.

16. These points have all been most cogently argued by Garnett, *Conquered England. Kingship, Succession and Tenure*.

17. DB I 2b.

18. E. van Houts. EHR cx 1995. *The Norman Conquest seen through European Eyes.*

10. The Duke Versus the King

1. *Vita Edwardi*, p. 50.

2. GG, 'the unbroken custom of the English [is] to treat death-bed bequests as inviolable'.

3. Note how translators differ.

4. Herman of Bury St Edmunds, *Miracula Sancti Eadmundi.*

5. Or perhaps 'gave security'.

6. Jolliffe, *Constitutional History*, pp. 79–80.

7. He became Pope Gregory VII in 1073.

8. So William of Poitiers says.

9. Eadmer HN 7–8; Malmesbury GR i 452.

10. Trinity College MS B 16.44.

11. When Stigand was deposed all reference to his time as Bishop of Winchester was erased and his Norman replacement, Walkelin, was made bishop with all the rights of Bishop Aelfwine, Stigand's predecessor.

12. Banners were sent to the Normans who invaded Sicily and to Roger de Hauteville.

13. Writ in *Regesta*, Bates, No. 141.

14. *Rector Navis Regis Edwardi.*

15. See the account from William of Jumièges.

16. He is in Domesday Book, holding two houses in Southampton.

17. The upper chamber.

18. Another version has William fitzOsbern say, 'You have England in your grasp! You shall be king!'

19. The number 60,000 seems to have been used in medieval sources simply to imply a vast number.

20. Supposedly 700 ships, which is totally impossible, though seventy or less is possible.

21. The locale is called 'Sandlake'.

11. The Battle of Hastings

1. It resembles, in miniature, the Field of Waterloo.

2. Shield wall or 'scyldburh', also called war-hedge or 'wighaga'.

3. *Regesta*, Bates, No. 213, for Mont-Saint-Michel, dated about 1070.

4. If the fleet was about 700 vessels, then 14,000 represents, an average of twenty men per ship. A by no means unreasonable number.

5. Not, of course, 'God help us!'

6. 'Oops! Who said charge?' Andrew Roberts, *Sunday Times*, 30 January 2005.

7. Plate 73.

8. See edition of the *Carmen* by Morton & Muntz.

9. His name might have dropped out because Hugh de Montfort was also mentioned.

10. William of Malmesbury GR ii 243.

11. William of Poitiers is here echoing the *Iliad*.

12. This may be derived from the death of Hector in the *Iliad*.

13. Just like Pompey after the battle of Pharsalia in Lucan.

14. *Waltham Chronicle* and William of Malmesbury GR 247.

15. *Regesta*, Bates, No. 15.

16. *Worcester Chronicle* D 1066.

12. Collaboration & Continuity

1. Turris Fracta; unidentified.

2. That is perhaps the earliest reference to William as 'Conqueror'.

3. Writ S 1163 from the *Liber Albus*.

4. See Garnett *op. cit.*

5. The phrase is that of Orderic Vitalis.

6. Peterborough E 1066 and Worcester D 1067.

7. DB Fol. 142 Herts.

8. Garnett, *Conquered England*.

9. The present monarch's heritage bypasses the Conqueror because Henry I married Matilda, niece of Edgar the Aetheling.

10. Garnett *op. cit.*

11. They could have been used during the installation of a duke but there is no direct evidence.

12. Romano-German Pontifical.

13. Orderic's own judgement as a historian.

14. The entry in Domesday Book for Berkshire, 1. 56 v. records a much lower levy under King Edward; Berkshire paid only 7 pence on the hide for a common geld.

15. DB Beds. 216v.
16. *Regesta* No. 216.
17. Domesday II Fol. 59.
18. A History of New Things or possibly Novelties.

13. Conflict & Contradiction

1. Garnett, *Conquered England*.
2. Hemming's cartulary 1. p. 269–71.
3. See Barlow, *The Feudal Kingdom of England*.
4. He held land in 1086 in nine shires.
5. Garnett, *Conquered England*.
6. James Campbell cited in Garnett *op. cit.*
7. Possibly a 'happy accident', as it allowed Lanfranc to rebuild it in Romanesque style.
8. He still possessed his episcopal powers but officially lacked canonical authority to exercise them.
9. Aethelfleda, Lady of the Mercians, built the original walled 'burh' at Warwick.
10. Geoffrey Gaimar, *L'Estoire des Engles*.
11. Notably D. C. Douglas.

14. Revolt, Rebellion & Repression

1. A major thegn.
2. There are more details about all this in my *1066: A New History of the Norman Conquest*.
3. If the twelfth-century lawbook *Leges Edwardi Confessoris* can be relied on.
4. An obvious guess.
5. For a full account of this see my *Hereward: the Last Englishman*.
6. It rings true, since 'By the splendour of God!' was said to be William's favourite oath.
7. *Regesta*, Bates, No. 232.
8. See *op. cit. Hereward* above.

15. Lordship in Church & State

1. Fol. 62 Berkshire.
2. Robin Fleming, *Kings and Lords in Conquest England*.

3. Abbot Baldwin's Feudal Book.

4. They are found in Lanfranc's own collection.

5. *Historia Novorum in Anglia.*

6. Harold had abbots with him; Leofric of Peterborough and Aelfwig of New Minster, Winchester.

7. Perhaps 1072.

8. Barlow, *Feudal Kingdom*, p. 131.

9. Printed in Lanfranc, *Opera*, p. 32 .

10. Letter of 24 April 1080.

11. A land grant in Surrey (*Regesta*, Bates, No. 326) says 'the money tax which is called geld in English'.

12. Dialogue of the Exchequer by Richard fitz Nigel, the Treasurer.

13. *Regesta*, Bates, No. 130.

14. Peterborough E 1067.

16. The Norman Settlement

1. *Regesta*, Bates, No. 67.

2. History of the Church of York.

3. Eight and one quarter hides in Huntingdonshire at Upton and Coppingford.

4. This was new in England. Pre-Conquest England had not used imprisonment as a punishment.

5. So Orderic; location unknown.

6. Charter for Le Mans Abbey, *Regesta*, Bates, No. 174. Names the place of the treaty as 'Castellum Valleum'. Dated 1077–78.

17. Dynastic Quarrels and Foreign Perils & the Death of William

1. *Anglo-Saxon Chronicle* D Worcester 1079.

2. Faroux Charters No. 158.

3. William Rufus was to reclaim it for England.

4. *Regesta*, Bates, No. 69.

5. Robert's daughter was Cnut's wife.

6. *Peterborough Chron.* E 1085. With the possible exception of 1066?

7. Buried hastily in 1086, he was disinterred in 1096 and reburied under the High Altar. In 1101 he was canonised as a saint.

8. This account most closely describes the text of Little Domesday, covering Essex, Norfolk and Suffolk.

9. *Inquisitio Eliensis*.
10. *Regesta*, Bates, No. 326.
11. Michael Wood, *In Search of the Dark Ages*, p. 250.
12. Florence (a.k.a. John) of Worcester II 19.
13. So Orderic Vitalis.
14. Documents belonging to Lanfranc about the contruction of the abbey confirm this story.

18. Character & Achievements

1. See *Vita Edwardi*.
2. Blair, *The Church in Anglo-Saxon Society*.
3. Vol. I fol. 49.
4. *Gesta Regum* 238. 2–4 & 228, 3–5.
5. Author of *De Obitu Willelmi*.
6. De Boüard, *Guillaume le Conquérant*.

BIBLIOGRAPHY

Anglo-Norman England, M. Chibnall, Blackwell, 1986.

Anglo-Saxon Chronicle, G. N. Garmonsway, Dent, 1955.

Anglo-Saxon Chronicle, J. Stevenson, Church Historians of England, 1853.

Anglo-Saxon Chronicles, M. Swanton, Phoenix, 1996.

Anglo-Saxon England, Sir Frank Stenton, OUP, 3rd ed., 1971.

ANS 6 *William the Conqueror and the Church of Rome*, P. A. Maccarini, 1983.

ANS 8 *The Military Administration of the Norman Conquest*, B. S. Bacharach, 1985.

ANS 9 *The Participation of Aquitanians in the Conquest of England, 1066-1100*, 1986.

'Towards an Interpretation of the Bayeux Tapestry', H. E. J. Cowley, 1986.

'The Ship List of William the Conqueror', E. van Houts, 1986.

ANS 12 *The Bayeux Tapestry; Why Eustace, Odo and William?* 1989.

Art of War in the Middle Ages, vol. I. Sir Charles Oman, Greenhill Books, 1991.

Battle of Hastings, Harriet Harvey Wood, Atlantic Books, 2008.

Battle of Hastings, M. K. Lawson, Tempus, 2002.

Bayeux Tapestry, Lucien Musset, trans. Richard Rex, Boydell, 2005.

Campaigns of the Norman Conquest, Matthew Bennett, Osprey, 2001.

La Conquête de L'Angleterre par les Normands, André Maurois, Editions Albin Michel, 1968.

Constitutional History of England to 1485, J. E. A. Jolliffe, A & C Black, 1967.

Chronicle of Florence of Worcester, J. Stevenson, Church Historians of England, 1853.

Chronique de Saint Maixent 751-1140, ed. Jan Verdon, Paris, 1979.

Conquered England. Kingship, Succession and Tenure 1066–1166, George Garnett, OUP, 2007.

Domesday, Michael Wood, BBC Books, 1999.

Domesday Book, Hallam and Bates, Tempus, 2001.

Domesday Book and Beyond, F. W. Maitland, Fontana Ed., 1965.

Domesday Book, Alecto Historical Editions, Penguin, 1992.

Dukes of Normandy and their Origin, Rt. Hon. Earl of Onslow, Hutchinson, 1945.

Edward the Confessor, Frank Barlow, Eyre Methuen, 1970.

England before the Norman Conquest, Sir Charles Oman, Methuen, 1921.

England Under the Normans and Angevins, H. W. C. Davis, Methuen, 1949 ed.

English Historical Documents, vol. II, ed. Douglas and Greenaway, Eyre & Spottiswoode, 1953.

EHR 110.1995. *The Norman Conquest through European Eyes*, E. van Houts.

EHR 94.1979. *Edward the Confessor and the Norman Succession*, Eric John.

EHR 93.1978 *The Carmen de Hastingae Proelio*, R. H. C. Davis.

EHR 80.1965. *Edward the Confessor's Early Life, Character and Attitudes*, Frank Barlow.

EHR 51.1936. *A Visit of Earl Harold to Flanders in 1056*, P. Grierson.

EHR 20.1905. *The Battlefield of Hastings*, F. Baring.

English Resistance, Peter Rex, The History Press, 2009.

Feudal Kingdom of England, 1042-1216, Frank Barlow, Longmans, 1966.

Gesta Guillelmi of William of Poitiers, R. H. C. Davis and M. Chibnall, Clarendon Press, 1998.

Gesta Pontificum Anglorum, William of Malmesbury, David Priest, Boydell, 2002.

Gesta Regum Anglorum, William of Malmesbury, Mynors, Thomson and Winterbottom, OUP, 2006.

Guillaume le Conquérant, Michel de Boüard, Fayard, 1984.

Guillaume Le Conquérant, Paul Zumthor, Tollandier, 2003.

'Guillaume le Conquérant et son temps', F. Neveux and P. Bouet. *Art de Basse Normandie*, No. 92.

Harold, The Last Anglo-Saxon King, Ian W. Walker, Wrens Park, 1997.

Harold & William; the Battle for England, Benton Raine Patterson, Tempus, 2001.

Heimskringla, Snorre Sturlason, Erling Monsen, Dover Publications, 1990.

Henry of Huntingdon History of the English People, Diana Greenway, OUP, 2009.

Hereward. The Last Englishman, Peter Rex, Tempus, 2007.

House of Godwine, Emma Mason, London, 2004.

In Search of the Dark Ages, Michael Wood, BBC Books, 1981.

King Harald's Saga, Magnusson and Pálsson, Penguin, 1966.

Kings and Lords in Conquest England, Robin Fleming, CUP, 1991.

Last English King, Peter Rex, The History Press, 2008.

Laws of the Kings of England, A. J. Robinson, CUP, 1925.

Liber Eliensis, Janet Fairweather, Boydell, 2005.

Making of English Law, Patrick Wormald, Blackwell, 2001.

Medieval Foundations of England, G. O. Sayles, Methuen, 1948.

New Cambridge Medieval History, vol. IV, parts 1 and 2, CUP, 2006.

Norman Conquest, Hugh M. Thomas, Rowman Littlefield, 2008.

Norman Conquest, R. Allen Brown, Edward Arnold, 1984.

Norman Conquest, D. J. A. Matthew, Batsford, 1966.

Norman Conquest of the North, W. E. Kapelle, Croom Helm, 1979.

Norman Heritage, Trevor Rowley, Paladin, 1984.

Ordericus Vitalis; Historia Ecclesiatica, M. Chibnall, Clarendon, 1980.

Origins of English Feudalism, R. Allen Brown, George Allen & Unwin, 1973.

Queen Emma and the Vikings, Harriet O'Brien, Bloomsbury, 2006.

Reassessing Anglo-Saxon England, Eric John, Manchester University Press, 1996.

Regesta Regum Anglo-Normannorum, David Bates, Clarendon Press, 1998.

The Church in Anglo-Saxon Society, John Blair, OUP, 2005.

The English and the Norman Conquest, Ann Williams, Boydell, 1995.

1066. A New History of the Norman Conquest, Peter Rex, Amberley, 2009.

1066 The Year of Three Battles, Frank McLynn, Pimlico, 1999.

1066 The Year of the Conquest, David Howarth, Collins, 1977.

TRHS 5th Series xxxvi 1986, *Coronation and Propaganda*, George Garnett.

The Normans; a Brief History, Francois Neveux, Constable & Robinson, 2006.

The Normans and their World, Jack Lindsay, Book Club, 1976.

The Road to Hastings, Paul Hill, Tempus, 2005.

Time and the Hour, Collected Papers of D. C. Douglas, Methuen, 1977.

William the Conqueror, David Bates, Tempus, 2004.

William the Conqueror, D. C. Douglas, Eyre Methuen, 1969.

LIST OF ILLUSTRATIONS

19. Count Guy I of Ponthieu arrests Earl Harold. With special permission from the city of Bayeux.

20. At Beaurain, Guy admonishes the Earl who surrenders his sword. With special permission from the city of Bayeux.

21. The Duke returns to Bayeux after his campaign in Brittany. With special permission from the city of Bayeux.

22. The Duke confers arms and armour on Earl Harold. With special permission from the city of Bayeux.

23. Earl Harold swears an oath on two reliquaries containing saints' bones. With special permission from the city of Bayeux.

24. King Edward scolds an embarrassed Earl Harold after his return. With special permission from the city of Bayeux.

25. The funeral procession for King Edward's burial. With special permission from the city of Bayeux.

26. Above, the dying king stretches his hand out to Earl Harold. According to the *Vita Edwardi* he confided the kingdom to Harold's protection. Below, Edward lies dead. With special permission from the city of Bayeux.

27. Harold is enthroned as King. With special permission from the city of Bayeux.

28. A messenger informs the new King that a Comet shines in the sky and an amazed crowd views it. With special permission from the city of Bayeux.

29. A Motte and Bailey castle is constructed at Hastings. With special permission from the city of Bayeux.

30. Norman knights, using their lances as spears, charge into battle. With special permission from the city of Bayeux.

31. The charge continues, supported by others. With special permission from the city of Bayeux.

32. The charge reaches the English shield wall. With special permission from the city of Bayeux.

33. Horses and men fall as they are repelled from the shield wall. With special permission from the city of Bayeux.

INDEX